7/23/02

This copy is for my WWII,
22d Marines, Comrade,

— William A. Mack —
in honor of our mutual friend,
"Heavy" Pfuhl.
Semper Fi, Bill!
Tom Jones
Col. USMCR (Ret)
WWII, 2d Bn., 22d Marines

THE VIEW FROM MY FOXHOLE

by

Lieutenant Tom Jones, USMCR

"The View From My Foxhole." by Lt Tom Jones, USMCR.
Copyright © 2001 by Col. Thomas S. Jones, USMCR (Ret.)

Published by: Jones, Maher, Roberts, Inc.
916 Silver Spur Rd., Rolling Hills Estates, CA 90274
email: jmradv@earthlink.net

Library of Congress Cataloging-in-Publication Data
ISBN 0-9707862-0-4
Printed in the United States of America

Book and cover design by David Haberer
Cover painting by author (from memory)

DEDICATION

This book is dedicated to the raggedy-assed
Marines of the Twenty-Second Marine Regiment
of World War II. No regiment ever looked worse
in repose nor performed better in battle.
Semper Fidelis.

ACKNOWLEDGEMENTS

For reinforcing my memories, a special thanks is owed to my former comrades: Colonels Ed Pesely, "Jack" Fitzgerald, and Al Kirtz. And, of course, without my wife, Peggy, and her computer word processing skills, none of my writing would ever have gone beyond the yellow copy paper of my Smith-Corona manual typewriter into useable format for publishing.

CONTENTS

THE VIEW FROM MY FOXHOLE
by
Lieutenant Tom Jones, USMCR

PREFACE

I t has been said that for any infantryman, the war is what's happening 200 yards around him. And that's the perspective of this book. Larger, grander literary tomes have been written about World War II and the war in the Pacific, and every Marine battle from Guadalcanal, Tarawa, and Iwo Jima through Okinawa has been reported, analyzed, and faithfully recorded as significant chapters in the glorious history of the U.S. Marine Corps since its inception in 1775.

This book makes no pretense to be part of that extensive library of classic military histories. Nor does it seek to rival those popular books glorifying war by dramatizing the super heroes and their most gory deeds in battle. Not that you won't find those super heroes here – for you surely will – but they will be so plentiful and so unlike their Hollywood prototypes that you may not recognize them. They will be the unnamed privates and PFC's who fight unnoticed side-by-side with the heroic medal winners, just quietly doing their jobs and accomplishing their missions.

I wrote this book 54 years after the fact, trying to build each chapter around a remembrance so persistent that it was still there in vivid detail a half century later. But this is more than a story about me and my remembrances. It is the story of a group of Marines in one battalion in one regiment who suffered through three years of training and fighting in the jungles and on the sand spits of the equatorial Pacific. We not only fought the enemy but also suffered in common with him every indigenous disabling agent such as filariasis in Polynesia, dengue fever in Micronesia, malaria in Melanesia, and dysentery everywhere.

I am hopeful that this book finally fulfills a sacred promise I made to myself and my closest comrades at the end of the final battle of the war. I vowed that someday I would write a book not to glorify war but to deglorify it. I would write a book extolling the virtues of just warriors like those Marines who could be invincible in battle – sacrificing everything for comrades and a just cause – and still be modest and compassionate in victory.

This book is dedicated to those WWII Marines of all ranks, living and dead, who simply did their jobs as best they could – which was splendid enough to make the gods cry.

Chapter 1

Shipping Out

They came together from the farthest reaches of America — from the ivory tower universities of New England and from the sea shores of the East and the West. They were America's children, the finest in the land and our promise for the future. They were the World War II generation. They came together to fight in a war against a tyranny that threatened the future of our civilization. And one small group of them became United States Marines. This is one man's story as a member of that one small group

With my Bachelor of Arts degree safely in hand, I reported with a group of other fresh Marine Corps recruits to a tough semiliterate Drill Instructor who would introduce us to the special boot camp for officer candidates at Quantico, Virginia. It was September 15, 1942, and the Marine Corps needed brave young second lieutenants as willing canon fodder to lead brave young privates in amphibious landings against deadly hostile beaches in the Pacific. Strangely enough, even then I knew that, but I had chosen the Marine Corps anyhow.

In six months, I was a second lieutenant and ready to go to war. A captain at the Replacement Training Center in New River, North Carolina, spoke to our small contingent of new second lieutenants. "Gentlemen," he said, "I know you're eager to get out of here and see some action. Well, most of you are going to get your wish this week; but I need three of you to ship out with a contingent of enlisted replacements in the morning. Who's ready now?"

Immediately, all hands were up, and the captain pointed to me and two lieutenants by my side. The captain dismissed everyone except the three of us and then continued: "I'm assigning a company of replacements to you You'll take them by troop train to your port of debarkation and overseas to your new designated command."

He asked us for our serial numbers and then went on: "Okay, it looks like Lieutenant Atkins has the senior serial number, so he will be company commander. Jones and Barrett, will assist him as platoon leaders."

I knew that Atkins was from Massachusetts and was a recent Harvard graduate. He was young, naïve, and enthusiastic. Barrett was also from New England. He was a Dartmouth man, football and crew, who had recently married. He was intelligent, very laid back, with a droll sense of humor.

"One other thing," the captain added, "forty of these replacements are brig rats. They've been conditionally released from confinement for the sole purpose of engaging in combat. So you'll be keeping that contingent under armed guard from this camp as you cross country by troop train, and you'll keep them under armed guard until they are safely aboard ship and the ship has departed the stateside dock."

"Now if there are no questions, see the sergeant major for your orders." "Yes Sir," we responded, and we left the room with strong mixed feelings. We were eager to leave this replacement center and join a real Marine Corps unit. We had joined to fight the war, and we were primed to do it, but we had serious misgivings about our detachment of brig rats. However, orders were orders, so we picked up our orders from the sergeant major, packed our bags and went looking for the farewell party in a nearby officer's tent.

It was now getting late, and sky was very cloudy and turning black and ominous. Obviously, it was about to break into a thunderstorm. Amid the darkness there was a bright leakage of light seeping out of the flaps of the officers' party tent.

Inside there was a small gathering celebrating the farewell of those who were shoving off in the next few days. Some had been in a holding pattern for several weeks and were well acquainted with each other. As a relative newcomer, I really didn't know anyone well enough to enjoy the party, so I slipped away early and headed down the dark company streets back to my own quarters.

The wind was blowing, and the storm was imminent. I hurried

Honolulu Star-Bulletin 1ˢᵗ EXTRA

HONOLULU, TERRITORY OF HAWAII, U. S. A., SUNDAY, DECEMBER 7, 1941   ✸ PRICE FIVE CENTS

WAR!

(Associated Press by Transpacific Telephone)

SAN FRANCISCO, Dec. 7.—President Roosevelt announced this morning that Japanese planes had attacked Manila and Pearl Harbor.

OAHU BOMBED BY JAPANESE PLANES

Washington D.C., December 7, 1942: one year after Pearl Harbor, the author as a newly commissioned second lieutenant, reads that Lieutenant Colonel Evans Carlson has just won his third Navy Cross on Guadalcanal.

along and had just gone inside my quarters when a private entered and asked for Lieutenant Jones. He showed me a piece of paper on which was scribbled part of a message – "Gramma passed away…" He explained the message had come by telegram but had been delivered by phone to the Sergeant of the Guard.

Outside the rain had started, and I could hear it striking the windows of our BOQ Quonset hut like tiny hard pellets. I asked the private if there was an on-post telegraph office. I knew my mother would expect me to get emergency leave to be present for the funeral, but I also knew that I had just volunteered for duty that would not make any leave possible. The private led me out into the rain to show me the way to the on-base telegraph office.

It was only a moderate rain, but the wind blew it hard against my clothes and made them stick to my body as I moved. I didn't mind the rain. It was a welcome annoyance – a tangible thing that I could struggle against. The on-base telegraph office was not open. I had to go to town, to wire a reply and send money for flowers.

I double-timed through the camp streets, my feet splashing in the puddles on the ashphalt. Just trying to run away from my feeling, just running to run – for no practical purpose. When I got to town my feelings stuck in my throat when I found the office was closed. All right, so everything was closed. So they closed the damn town when it rained. I walked around just getting wetter; hoping that the rain would mask my tears, but the tears never came. It was six months before I could cry. I went solemnly back to camp.

The rain had died down, but the wind continued to blow. As I passed the party tent, I ignored the officers still living it up, reveling in their good-byes, and I went directly to my quarters. I climbed out of my wet clothes and into a warm, dry bed. Something secure, something soothing about crawling into bed. Outside the wind continued to blow and the streets were wet and cold, but I was thinking only of my dead grandmother, the one who had raised me as her own child.

I was thinking that my grandmother was probably the most honest woman who had ever lived, a woman who had lived through epochal periods. She had been born at the time of

Lincoln's death, from the womb of her mother who had been born in Napoleon's time. She was a woman who, in her youth, had crossed the Atlantic by a "sailing/steamer", spending a month below in the depths of steerage, suffering the rough and sickening Atlantic seas. Yet, just 50 years later, she had cruised on a modern steamer across the calm Pacific to Catalina Island to enjoy a luncheon at a modern hotel. A hard worker, she was also a party queen. I had flashes of her now, standing at a laundry tub, digging in the yard, cooking on a hot wood stove. But I also remembered her with white hair freshly curled, new false teeth — all brushed and clean, as she readied herself for her Tuesday night card party.

Remembering all that I grew very tired, and involuntarily I began uttering the prayer she had taught me as a child "Now I lay me to down to sleep…" The rain was starting again… the lights were fading… and I was wrapped safely in the arms of my grandmother as I fell into a deep, deep sleep.

Shortly after dawn, with the first two platoons of Marine replacements securely aboard, Atkins, Barrett and I stood by the troop train waiting for our contingent of brig rats to arrive. Soon a platoon of Marines under guard was marched up to us by a first lieutenant. We had already received our orders and the orders for this group, including the two-armed guards, from the sergeant major. Now Atkins simply receipted for their delivery, and the first lieutenant was on his way.

For the most part, the platoon of brig rats looked no different than any other platoon of Marines. Still there was a sense of defiance about them that was different. We knew that they had been in the brig for various offenses, some much more serious than others, including physical assault, AWOL, and general disobedience to orders. So now it was questionable whether they would accept orders from these three green second lieutenants.

With the first lieutenant gone, they were already becoming restless and unruly. There was snickering and "grab assing" in the ranks. Second Lieutenant Atkins, the Harvard graduate in command, looked at Barrett and me for support.

"What should I do?" he quietly asked us. Atkins was young, naïve, and enthusiastic. He was very intelligent but indecisive.

"Call them to attention," I told him; and we'll march them

aboard the train."

The boyish-looking second lieutenant turned and faced the platoon. "Attention," he said weakly; but his voice obviously lacked authority, and the group remained at ease with continued snickering and talking.

Atkins turned to us again and whispered, "What do I do now?"

Although Atkins was small and unintimidating, Barrett had played football and rowed at Dartmouth, and I was over six feet tall, about 180, and with an athletic build. As a former intramural gymnast and boxer in college, I could be physically intimidating, so I said: "Call attention again, and we'll make sure they snap to!"

This time, when Atkins called attention, Barrett and I immediately confronted the trouble makers, nose-to-nose, telling each snickering face in a firm loud voice: "The lieutenant said 'Attention!'" The wayward brig rats quickly got the message and straightened up. Now they knew we meant business.

Once aboard the transcontinental train, the trip was routine and uneventful. However, the sight of two armed guards marching a company of Marines through small towns to the nearest local restaurant for meals was probably eventful enough for the small-town residents.

During the trip, I noticed that two of the guarded Marines had stripped themselves to the waist and were hugging each other in one of the Pullman berths in the obvious expectation that as officers we would report them. It was obvious they were bucking for a discharge for homosexuality at a time when even sitting on a bunk with another Marine was forbidden. But I ignored the ploy and decided to allow them – homosexual or not – the privilege of combat.

After a brief stopover at Camp Elliott, San Diego, and the mandatory course of medical shots against all known diseases, this latest contingent of Marine replacements was securely berthed aboard one of the converted Cunard cruise liners. We were soon all safely underway to some unnamed tropical island. Well, maybe not so safely underway, since our ship was running free in waters still controlled by the Imperial Japanese Navy that had recently wreaked such havoc at Pearl Harbor. We were running free without benefit of an armed convoy because the U.S. Navy could not afford to convoy every troop ship plying both oceans. It was calculated that any ship that could do 16 knots could out-run the Japanese submarines and would just have to risk a possible encounter with a Japanese surface warship.

Still, at this time none of us felt any special fear of enemy subs or hostile planes. And it occurred to me how strange it was that our troops, sitting through the action movies shown aboard ship every night, were often frightened by Hollywood submarines lurking in the celluloid depths; but they refused to be apprehensive about the very real possibility of submarines lurking under our ship. As feckless teenagers they weren't going to worry until the actual danger struck.

So as our troop ship proceeded without incident through the first several nights, I began to enjoy my after-dinner time on deck, hanging over the rail mesmerized by the white phosphorescence of the ship's wake. It was during one of those moments as I stood on deck watching the last glow of day dissolve into night when I suddenly realized that here I was a lieutenant in the United States Marine Corps. Here I, Tom Jones, was no longer just a liberal arts college major struggling to become a professional writer, hoping to become a great poet. A flush of euphoria come over me as I savored my new status as a Marine Corps officer, a leader of those enlisted men bunked below. Men I was now on my way to lead into combat. It was, of course, a momentary feeling of arrogance overriding the reality of my gross ignorance and inexperience at the time.

In the middle of my conceited reverie, there suddenly came a brilliant flash of light from a ship silhouetted on the horizon. From across the black expanse of the open sea, from a mile or two away, came this flash that could only be from the firing of one of the big guns of an enemy warship. I froze waiting for the shot to strike. But no sound followed, and no shot struck.

Barrett had just walked up and said: "Jones did you see that?" "Yeah, I did," I answered. "What do you think it was?" "Well there it goes again," Barrett noted as another flash bore through the night. Then we both realized it was just the signal light from a passing ship. Hopefully, a friendly ship. It was later identified as a Dutch merchant vessel, going about its business despite the war.

For most of the two-week passage there was little for us and
the troops to do. Of course, none of us had ever been at sea before
so we spent much of our time watching the sea and bird life like
any tourists on their first cruise. I was often able to stake out a
deck chair in officer's country and sit comfortably, staring
spellbound at the wake of the ship, with the occasional
interruption of the slender winged sheerwater sea birds, as they
soared tirelessly over the ink-blue Pacific water. At other times, I
would stand on the fo'c'sle, facing into the wind, watching the
porpoise cavorting off the ship's bow. And I can never forget the
first flight of an entire school of flying fish leaving the water and
taking to the air like a flock of startled birds. Those small,
streamlined, speedy creatures flew low and flashed silver in the
sun, flapping and soaring with their fins, traveling close the water
but covering a hundred-yards or more at a flight.

The sunsets too became more beautiful with every day of our
voyage. More than fifty years later I can still see the sun setting in
a field of cloud formations, painting the sky with brilliant amber
and fiery red patches, then magically transforming those clouds
into fantastic mounds and hills that to my eye slowly became a
tropical island set against an opalescent background. It was
Shangra-la, but like all dreams, without substance, and it quickly
faded. Yet, for the two-weeks of our voyage, it was very easy to
forget that we were heading into the serious business of war.

Of course, as officers in charge we couldn't totally neglect our
responsibilities. We knew we had to maintain troop fitness,
discipline, and morale. So the three of us had a short staff
meeting, and we agreed upon a daily on-deck exercise and
workout schedule for the troops that consisted of the usual
military stretching and in-place running and jumping exercises.
Aside from that there was none of the famous Marine Corps unit
bonding – nor any need for it – with this temporary company of
replacements.

Since troops aboard ship are literally packed like sardines in a
can with four or five bunks stacked one on top of the other, they
often resort to an activity they would never do when ashore – they
read books. When the only private space you have aboard ship is
the 12-inches of space between your bunk and the one above you,

there are few things you can do other than read. So it was not unusual that I was reading Somerset Maugham's famous short story "Rain", which is set in Samoa, just as our troop ship pulled into Pago Pago, one of the world's most beautiful natural harbors.

As a would-be writer, I was exhilarated by Maugham's crisp accurate description of the Pago Pago harbor. *There was a thin strip of silver beach rising quickly to hills covered to the top with luxuriant vegetation. The coconut trees, thick and green, came nearly to the water's edge, and among them you saw the grass house of the Samoans and here and there, gleaming white, a little church.*

It was indeed the most beautiful tropical island harbor that I could imagine. There before me in three-dimensional reality was this picture postcard scene: a breathtaking, lush-green mosaic of tropical trees and plants overlaying the green-carpeted volcanic cliffs that rose sharply out of an indigo blue sea.

That was the scenic background, with a foreground of a dozen native canoes full of beautiful island girls paddling out to meet this new shipload of Marines. And the beautiful young ladies in each of the boats, with flowers adorning their long black hair, were all singing what seemed to me like some romantic love song. They were singing a charming melody, and the only recognizable words were" *Ai Ki Malini.* That is so beautiful, I thought, not what I expected to find in a combat zone. Not what I was prepared for at all.

Once ashore, an old Navy chief petty officer set me straight: "What they were singing, Lieutenant," the chief told me is "Eat shit, Marines," which I was sure the U.S .Navy had taught them. Well, so much for the romance of the island paradise.

Still, Samoa was very romantic, once you got away from Pago Pago and traveled twenty miles back to the little village of Leone, to the Jungle Warfare School at the Marine Corps Replacement Training Center. But if the Leone village and villagers were romantic – the Jungle Warfare School set in their midst was not. We soon learned that its primary goal was to train replacements under conditions that simulated the worst possible combat situations – conditions far too severe to be practiced in the civilized environment of the United States.

Chapter 2

Jungle Warfare School

Marine Boot Camp is always tough, but during a war when lack of proper training and discipline means unnecessary deaths in combat, Boot Camp gets tougher. In the States, however, under the watchful eyes of Washington Brass, answerable to Congress and the mothers of the Boots, some limits must be observed. But 6000 miles away on an isolated island in the Pacific called Samoa, things were different. At the U.S. Marine Corps Jungle Warfare School in this remote village of Leone, a lieutenant colonel in the United States Marines ran an independent fiefdom pretty much as he saw fit. And what he saw fit to do was wait out his time to retirement by hanging out in his own colonial cottage headquarters while he totally delegated all his authority and the activities of his training battalion to three Marine captains. The three captains were then in total charge of the three companies of replacement troops that constituted the training battalion. With such independent authority, each of the captains was free to run his company as he saw fit.

Atkins, Barrett and I along with the company of replacement troops that we brought to the island, were assigned to Captain Oppenheimer, who was a wiry little guy who had to stand on his toes during his enlistment to meet the Marine Corps minimum height requirements. But whatever the captain lacked in size and bulk was more than made up by his first sergeant Matkovich, a six-foot-two, two-hundred and fifteen-pound poster Marine. Matkovich had quickly taken charge of our replacement company by dividing the group into rifle platoons, leaving the assignment of the three second lieutenants up to the captain.

Atkins, Barrett and I had reported to the captain while Matkovich was organizing the company. As the four of us walked out to the assembly area where Matkovich stood at ease with the troops, he called the company to attention. All the newly formed platoons immediately came to attention except one, which was composed primarily of the brig rat contingent that we had brought to the island. While the tiny captain stood facing the company waiting for the snickering platoon to come to order, Matkovich immediately strode over to the defiant group and, much to the shock of everyone present, he struck their leader with a blow so hard that it knocked the man off his feet and back through the rank behind him.

The first sergeant then asked: "Is there anyone else who doesn't want to come to attention?" There were no takers – not then nor during the rest of their time at the Jungle Warfare School.

On the morning following the incident with the first sergeant and the brig rats Atkins, Barrett and I reported to the captains' *fale* for platoon training assignments. *Fale* is the native word for a Samoan house, which are traditionally constructed as simply a huge palm frond umbrella roof supported on log poles. However, the U.S. Navy CB's had built the officers' fales at the Training Center of lumber to stateside standards with screens in place of windows.

The captains' fale housed the three captains who were part of the permanent Jungle Warfare School staff, as opposed to the other officers and troops who simply passed through training here before being deployed to combat units throughout the Pacific Theatre.

The inside of the fale was very much like the living quarters of the doctors in the Korean War Mash Unit depicted many years later in the popular TV series. The captains had done the best they could to make themselves comfortable, and they had been there long enough to have accomplished a good deal in turning a raw hut into a domestic domicile.

The lieutenants later discovered that after training their platoons hard in the island mud and jungles from dawn to dusk, if their captains were satisfied with their work they would be invited into the captain's hut for happy-hour drinks at the close of the day.

Drinks offered were usually whiskey or rum in coke or water, but Captain Oppenheimer offered a civilized martini made with a proper measure of vermouth and an olive.

Captain Oppenheimer was a highly educated Marine. He wore his hair cropped close to the scalp, and he sported a British-officer-style mustache. He had been schooled at Harvard, and it was rumored that he had graduated with a PhD in Anthropology at the age of nineteen. I was now twenty-two and I learned that the captain was only a year older, but that year of seniority in the Marine Corps made for a two-rank difference. However, the captain soon proved to be an extremely well read military historian and tactician and a worthy CO.

When the three of us had first entered the captains' fale, Captain Oppenheimer had taken charge and presented us to the other two captains, who were introduced as commanding officers of training Companies B and C. He had explained that he was commanding officer of Company A, and that we and our replacement contingent were being assigned to his company.

He further explained that the Marines were in Samoa for two reasons. First, they had been sent there originally to help set up a defense of the island against expected Japanese invasion. Early in 1942 when Oppenheimer had arrived in Samoa, Guam had fallen, Singapore had surrendered, and the Japanese had invaded New Guinea. Samoa had looked very vulnerable. So the captain's first assignment had been to help organize a native defense force of Samoan Marines. He was selected in part because of his background in anthropology. He soon taught the eager young Samoans how to be Marines, and they taught him how to understand their culture and speak their language. And although by March of 1943, the threat of invasion was less likely than it had been a year before, it was still considered a real threat. However, by now the Marine Corps had deployed the Twenty-Second Marines to the islands, which took the primary responsibility away from the native defense force.

In March of 1943, the second reason the Marines were in Samoa was to train under realistic jungle conditions and prepare for their first combat. The regular regiments like the Twenty-Second Marines trained their own units in company and battalion-size operations. But with the casualties of Guadalcanal and Tarawa, it was evident that the Marine Corps needed a replacement pipeline to keep regular units at strength. The need for replacements became even more evident in Samoa as scores of troops became infected with filariasis and were so badly stricken that hundreds were sent home without ever seeing combat action. To ignore the early warning symptoms of filiariasis could eventually result in full-blown elephantiasis, which the natives called *mumu*. The victims of elephantiasis usually developed monstrous limbs like an elephant's leg, hence the name. In 1943 at least one in every adult group of Samoans displayed the shocking signs of elephantiasis —usually a huge swollen arm or leg or a scrotum the size of a punching bag — and to us the cause was still a mystery.

If the brig rat who defied the first sergeant wanted his revenge, the opportunity to take on Matkovich came quickly, if he was fool enough to try. Within a few days A Company was ordered to report to Matkovich for instruction in judo and knife fighting. As leader of the first platoon, I marched my group to the training field where the first sergeant was waiting.

"Now who wants to volunteer to help me demonstrate some basic judo and knife fighting moves?" Matkovich asked. The response was total silence, of course. No volunteers, and the wise-guy brig rat proved himself wise enough to silently decline.

Then without asking me, Matkovich told the platoon: "Ok, then the lieutenant and I will demonstrate some judo and knife fighting techniques for you, and then you'll pair off and you can try it with a buddy."I was not happy with the first sergeant who seemed to be testing my authority. Without my consent, he was using me literally as his "fall guy" in his demonstration, riding roughshod over a superior officer. Sure, I was just a 22-year-old second lieutenant with six months in the corps, whereas Matkovich was a 28-year-old Marine veteran with a couple of enlistment's behind him. And, of course, the first sergeant knew that I was not likely to know much more than the green replacements about judo or knife fighting. But what the first sergeant didn't know was that, although at 180 pounds I weighed 35 pounds less than he did, I was a boxer, a gymnast, a rugged athlete, and a quick learner.

First, Matkovich demonstrated how to disarm a man coming at you with a knife. As I came at him with a knife, he easily flipped me to the ground. Then he went through a whole series of maneuvers – totally incapacitating me with each move. As I was picking myself up from the first sergeant's last slam-dunk, I heard him telling the men: "Okay, now that you've seen how it's done, I'm going to have you try it."

I knew that Matkovich was from a poor immigrant Yugoslavian family and that he had dropped out of high school long before the war to join the Marines. And I admired his natural intelligence and the physical and mental toughness that had allowed him to climb up the enlisted ladder to become a first sergeant. But having watched him disregard our little captain on several occasions, I sensed that his main fault was a smoldering resentment of officers, especially those who seemed to rely on their rank rather than their capabilities in the exercise of their authority. I was determined to illustrate to him and the troops that I didn't fit into that category, so I stopped him and said: "Okay, First Sergeant, that was a good demonstration, but I think they need to see it one more time. Only this time, why don't you play the aggressor, and I'll just defend myself."

Matkovich had not expected this and didn't welcome it because now he would be the "fall guy" on the receiving end of all those embarrassing moves he had just taught me. But the men in the platoon fully enjoyed it. They liked watching this young second lieutenant flip the first sergeant and stand his ground with one of the toughest Marines in the Corps.

Matkovich proved that he was a disciplined Marine when he got up from the ground after the last throw down, brushed himself off, and said: "All right, now let's see if you men can do what the lieutenant has just taught you." The first sergeant had now deferred to the second lieutenant who had just physically proved himself and demonstrated his leadership. I instinctively knew what every enlisted man learns soon enough – it takes more than a commission to make a leader.

To serve the physical conditioning program at the Jungle Warfare School, the command had built a professional boxing ring, and the platoon leaders were to pair off men of equal size and have them box in two and three-round matches. Since I had boxed in college, I voluntarily participated in these matches and felt I could go two or three rounds with anyone of any size in my platoon. So that's what I did, and I usually had to pull my punches to avoid hurting even some of the most rugged looking Marines who were inexperienced boxers.

The exception came one day when a very healthy looking two hundred pound nineteen-year-old from Pittsburgh took to the ring with me. It was soon clear that I wouldn't have to pull any punches with this Marine who obviously knew exactly what he was doing. Round one was a bloody nose for me. In round two, I managed to strike back and cut the kid's lip. In round three, the fight was getting rough, and the captain came along and stopped it. We settled for a draw. But the platoon laughed and cheered their enlisted man. And while I was wiping the blood off my face, one of the squad leaders came up to me and confessed:

"Lieutenant," he said, "we set you up. Wysocky was Golden Gloves Champion of Pennsylvania last year."

But the Jungle Warfare School wasn't all fun and games. There were rugged field exercises that required traversing *Oletele's* 1800-foot summit to the lea side of the island, with everyone carting rifles, machine guns, mortars, and ammunition on their backs. There was living in the wet, mosquito-infested jungle, where it rained three times a day in the wet season and once a day in the dry season, and where two weeks without rain meant serious drought and no drinking water.

There were the live-fire exercises when the instruction from the captain was "Give the men one hour to dig in and then start shooting at them. We don't want you to kill anybody, but if you 'pink' a few, that's all right. We're training for combat."

And sure enough, we pinked a few. Our first casualty caught a 30-caliber slug in his butt. It was not a serious wound, but he was bleeding. We were still a mile across the jungle from our camp with no transportation for our casualty, when I saw a jeep on a muddy road a few hundred yards away. As I approached the jeep at full run, hoping to beg a ride for my wounded man, I saw that the passenger was a lieutenant colonel. Then before I realized that the jeep was hopelessly stuck in the mud I heard myself say: "Oh Colonel…" and then quickly added "are you stuck in the mud?"

Came the swift reply: "No Lieutenant, I'm speeding down a dusty road at 60 miles-per-hour." With my 40-man platoon, we soon extricated the colonel's jeep from the mud and got my casualty back to our camp sick bay.

Then a few days later, after I managed to get two of our large 6x6 trucks stuck in the mud, the captain said: "Jones, I think you've been training too hard. Why don't you borrow my jeep and take a day off?"

"Thanks, Captain", I said. "But where am I going to go in this jungle?" Except for a few sandy beaches in the flatland coconut groves, the island was basically a volcanic ridge covered with jungle growth.

"Why don't you visit the girls' school," he suggested.

Chapter 3

Romance, Heroics and Heroism

Since we were in a transition period between replacement contingents, Lt. Atkins and I decided to explore the civilian countryside as visiting tourists. As the captain had suggested, we borrowed his jeep and drove a few miles to the girl's high school that had been established by the London Missionary Society some years previously. It was said to be the only high school on the island at that time.

Although in American Samoa during World War II, the natives of the island were required to be schooled until the age of 16, schooling was by native teachers and native standards. This meant that young children from the age of 6 to 16 were gathered together and seated on straw mats on the ground in a simple native fale in each village. A local teacher did the best she could to teach them basic subjects like the English language, often by singing songs. An island favorite at that time was "You Are My Sunshine," which could be heard from a great distance as sung in the high-pitched childish voices.

However, at the Leone High School for Girls, things were a little more formal. First, the school was actually housed in one of the few European style structures on the island. It had been built by the British missionaries as a British colonial style villa, two stories with screens but no windows and a second-floor veranda surrounding the building. Arriving at the school, we parked our jeep, entered the building and were immediately greeted by a handsome middle-aged Samoan woman with gray wavy hair and glasses. She wore a flowered mumu dress but no shoes, walking barefoot Samoan style, which seemed strangely incongruous for this otherwise sophisticated older woman.

"*Talofa*," she greeted us.

"*Talofa*," we both replied.

She led us into her small office and seated us in two comfortable wicker chairs. Then she sat down and clapped her hands. Almost immediately, as if they had been standing in the wings waiting for that signal, two beautiful young Samoan girls appeared, each wearing a simple flowered *lava lava* wrapped snugly around her shapely torso and each bearing a tray of fresh tropical fruits.

While the youngest of the two served Atkins, the eldest, who appeared to be about eighteen, approached me and said: "May I serve you, Sir?" as she offered me a choice of fresh bananas, pineapples, and canned pear slices. I was struck by her natural beauty, enhanced by a flower in her hair. The camp, the Corps, and the war simply vanished for that moment and I was swept up in this unlikely new reality.

Even though the island produced wonderful fresh fruit, I sensed that we were being honored by an offering of "imported" canned pears along with the domestic products, so I took a few pear slices on a saucer and thanked the girl in the Samoan language that I had studied in an old Missionary text book.

The girl responded by saying, "I'm sorry, Sir, I didn't understand you because my English is not so good."

The principal smiled and told the girl. "He was speaking to you in old Samoan."

I flushed as I realized the "old Samoan" I had studied sounded to the contemporary Samoans like Chaucer sounds to us. Be that as it may, I wanted to know this young lady better, so I forged ahead, using my ancient Samoan to ask her if I could "take a walk in the moonlight" with her, using the expression *eva-eva* that meant "promenade" instead of the simple verb for "walk", *savali*. Again, she looked at me dumbfounded and then turned to the principal for a modern translation, which was quickly forthcoming. And the girl smiled and said "yes,"

Whatever plans that I might have had for an escapade with Faalua never materialized beyond one walk in the sunset, without even progressing to the moonlight phase. I met her once more, and we talked. I learned that she was ninetten years old and a very bright young lady. Bright enough to be the hygiene teacher at the Missionary High School, with plans to go to school some day in Hawaii and become a nurse. More importantly at that time – she wanted to see me again. But wars have a way of interfering with people's lives, so it turned out that I saw her just one more time

From a passing jeep, I saw her with a flock of native girls from the school, all dressed like antebellum ladies in white lace dresses and wide brimmed straw hats, with their strong brown legs and large bare feet carrying them to the village church for Sunday services. It was an image that put a giant gulf between us. I preferred the image of her in simple native garb as she had so innocently appeared when we had first met.

After a short respite between replacement contingents at the training center, I learned that a new officer had been assigned to share the fale with Barrett, Atkins, and me. Atkins had learned the news the hard way. Returning from the mess hall one afternoon, Atkins had just opened the screen door to the fale when a combat fighting knife zoomed from somewhere and nicked a finger of his hand that was still holding the door. There across the room in combat dungarees and a green T-shirt stood the culprit – a small brown man with a shaved head and a sardonic grin on his face.

"Lieutenant," he said, "never let anyone surprise you. In combat you've got to be ready at all times. Your first surprise could be your last one. Then he held out his hand and said: "I'm your new roommate; I'm Captain Lammock."

He could call himself Captain Lammock, but his reputation had already preceded him. Among those in the Corps who had encountered him, he was known as "The Green Hornet."

This quick, wiry, ape-like man had been an enlisted Marine before the war and had achieved a commission in the field, but he was best known for his most recent exploits aboard the troop ship that brought him to Samoa.

Since the Marine Corps was slow to adopt camouflage field uniforms and safe non-reflecting helmet covers, the good captain had decided to modify his general-issue dungarees, boots, and helmet to his own camouflage standards. To Captain Lammock that meant "jungle green" – everything had to be jungle green. So he soon painted all his uniforms, shoes, and field gear green.

Hence, he was known as the Green Hornet.

But color wasn't enough for the captain. He had to behave like the Green Hornet as well. Perhaps his bizarre behavior would not have come to anyone's attention aboard a troop ship carrying thousands of men except for one peculiarity of his. It seems that the shipboard sickbay was being inundated with wounded Marines. Since the troops were all safely aboard a ship that was still many miles from the war zone – the puzzle was to find who was inflicting all those knife wounds on these Marines?

Each wounded Marine had the same story to tell. It seems that while they were on deck, usually at night in some quiet and isolated section of the ship, a solitary figure would sneak up on them and shout "Marine", and the Marine would turn just in time to see a shadowy figure thrusting a knife at him.

Eventually, the troop commander located the culprit. It was, of course, Captain Lammock. The captain unabashedly admitted that he was the responsible culprit. But he explained his action as simply a realistic training exercise, pointing out that any Marine should know how to immediately disarm anyone coming at him with a knife. And if he didn't know how, the captain felt it was the responsibility of any Marine officer to teach him here and now where the only danger was a superficial cut or nick, not a deep deadly stab as in combat.

The troop commander accepted the captain's explanation that his actions were well-intended, but he ordered him to cease and desist with any more such irregular training exercises. So now, here was this loose cannon two ranks above us sharing our fale. However, the Green Hornet was not responsible for our greatest tragedy and most heroic action at the Training Center

The Battle of Midway was over, the Marines had taken Guadalcanal by the end of 1942, and no other enemy action seemed imminent to us. Still the command in Samoa was insecure enough that Observation and Listening Posts were manned twenty-four hours a day on the lookout for a possible Japanese invasion.

Posts were manned in open areas where paratroopers might land, as well as at vulnerable spots along the volcanic cliffs and sand beaches where a seaborne enemy might attack. Night sentry duty at these listening posts was more dangerous because of local hazards than it was because of the unlikely event of a Japanese invasion at this time. And so it came to pass that one morning at the end of his 24-hour tour of duty as Officer of the Day, a new second lieutenant replacement learned from his Sergeant of the Guard that two of his sentries were missing. It turned out to be an avoidable tragedy.

The two-man listening post that the sentries were to patrol was along the rocky volcanic ledge that was elevated about forty feet above the sea. And as all the natives and experienced Marines knew, there was a large blowhole about dozen yards back from the ocean. Those with island experience all knew how dangerous such blowholes were. They had seen how the ocean waves would rush in with each breaker so hard that compressed air and water spray was spouted up more than thirty feet into the air like Old Faithful at Yellowstone Park. Needless to say, anyone who falls into such a blowhole is not likely to survive.

Since I knew the area well, when I heard that the sentries were missing, I feared the worst. I told this green new lieutenant to follow me, and the two of us rushed out to the blowhole and looked in. There were the tragic remains of the two Marines forty feet below, submerged a few feet under water, bodies being bashed with each swell against the rocks.

As mute testimony to what had happened, there laid out neatly along side the blowhole was a helmet, cartridge belt, bayonet, and M1 rifle. The tragic circumstances were obvious: when one Marine accidentally fell into the hole, his buddy immediately laid down his personal gear and – as it turned out – his life to enter the blowhole and try to save his friend.

The lieutenant was chagrined that this had happened on his watch, but he didn't seem to accept his responsibility in the tragedy. Why hadn't he walked that patrol first to learn of the hazards out there and then warned his men before sending them to that area?

The problem now was how to get those Marine bodies out of there for a decent burial. Since the lieutenant was too unnerved to take charge and was still a stranger to the island, I reported the situation to our captain. He and I hurried to the nearest Samoan village, and spoke to the *Matai* and told him what had happened. We then asked for his help in recovering the bodies.

The *Matai* was a handsome man about fifty years old with a full head of straight gray hair combed back in a pompadour. He wore only a lava lava wrapped around his portly tattooed frame. "We come right away," he said. And then he turned to a young man and spoke to him in Samoan. "*E te sau*". Soon a half a dozen other young men joined him and he shouted – "*Matou O!*" – and the entire group followed us back to the tragic scene.

Once there, the *Matai* took command completely, speaking only to his young men in Samoan. He sent one small boy out to the farthest reach of the volcanic ledge where he could be the first to see the oncoming swells and yell warnings to the rest of his crew in the water. This was essential since it was obvious that the only way the bodies could be recovered was by swimmers actually entering the water and putting themselves in the same danger that had crushed the Marines against the rocks.

Soon two sturdy young Samoan men leaped into the ocean, just outside of the danger area, treading water while taking orders from the *Matai*. Then the *Matai* shouted something to the young boy lookout, who waited a few moments and then responded with hurried shouts of "*vave! vave!*" Immediately, the two young swimmers entered the danger area, and they could be seen underwater grappling for the bodies. But there was not enough time between the crushing onrush of new sweeps of water to get the job done, so they exited the danger area and clung to some rocks on the side of the cave that led to the blowhole.

Then the entire process was tried again. Again with no luck. Finally, it was decided that despite the onrushing waters one swimmer would have to stay in the danger area long enough to tie lines around the bodies so they could be lifted up through the blowhole. And that's what the young Samoan did. Although the oncoming waters did catch him and crash him against the jagged volcanic rocks, he managed to twist himself around and ride in a crouched position, hitting the rocks with his heavily-callused feet forward. That left him, as the waters receded, clinging like a crab to the rocks he had hit.

Meanwhile, up on the ledge, the tragedy was brought home to

me and other Marines who had now gathered to watch the procedure. Looking at the bashed bodies of these two young Marines, I sought some meaning to this sad event. Then looking at the bravery of the Marine who had died trying to save his buddy, I felt I had learned an important truth that day. Although we were still far from combat, in or out of war, Marines are a very special breed, and there is no stronger bond than that between two close comrades.

Chapter 4

Tofa to the Jungle Warfare School

There was very little about the Jungle Warfare School that resembled the chain of command and the organizational structure of the established regiments and battalions of the Marine Corps. The purpose of the Jungle Warfare School was simply to practice company and platoon level tactics in the closest possible simulation to combat conditions. The niceties of regimental, battalion, and company organizational structure would be learned soon enough once these replacement officers and troops were assigned to established units. As Corporal Turner, one of my more seasoned squad leaders, soon told me "This ain't the Marine Corps, Lieutenant. It's entirely different when you join a regular unit. Then you'll have to go by the book."

Corporal Turner was a career Marine and my only squad leader with the proper NCO rank. He had earned his rating during stateside duty by keeping his uniforms crisp and clean and by staying out of trouble. But since I wasn't too impressed with the performance of this corporal squad leader, I ignored his counsel and trained the platoon my way. Unfortunately, my way was more Hollywood than Marine Corps. Not that I neglected to provide my men with the basic Marine Corps combat training required – but I went far beyond that into John Wayne never-never land. I was determined that my platoon was to be the most physically fit platoon in the United States Marine Corps.

Like Errol Flynn and his merry men of Sherwood Forest, I was determined that I and my merry Marines would be able to march farther and faster — in any conditions over any terrain — than any other military unit, friend or foe, in the entire world.

To prove it, I took the platoon on forced marches through the jungle, over the volcanic peaks, across the coconut groves and beaches of the island. Often in the blackness of the rain-swept nights. Always ending with a thorough cleaning of individual weapons before anyone hit his bunk. And when I considered platoon performance to be under par by my standards, there was an immediate repeat of the exercise with no time-out for rest.

The only thing that kept my men from hating me with a passion was the fact that no matter how excruciating the exercise, I was always in front of my troops, and I often helped carry an exhausted Marine's personal load. And on one occasion, when I had forced marched them all day long, through nearly impenetrable jungles, over volcanic mountain trails, and finally in salt water up to their necks across a narrow bay – they voluntarily began singing robust obscene songs extolling how tough they were. So I was sure that my extreme training methods were working.

With a training philosophy honed by Hollywood movies, I insisted that each of my three squad leaders must be the best physical performer in his squad. However, since squad leaders are normally selected by seniority, experience, and disciplined behavior – each of the squad leaders selected by me had to meet one other criterion. He also had to do whatever it took to become the physical leader of his squad.

It was therefore a shock to Corporal Turner when I ordered him to step aside and turn the squad over to PFC Bloom, who was one of the best physical performers in any of the three squads, whereas Corporal Turner was physically inept and by my standards a poor leader. It was not the sort of thing that could happen in a regular unit, but at the Jungle Warfare School every training officer had full command over his unit, subject only to a rare veto by his own immediate superior officer.

As it turned out, Corporal Turner never had to relinquish his squad, because soon after my talk with him I received the shocking news that my platoon was being released for assignment to a regular organized unit, but I wasn't being released to go with it.

I had trained the best platoon in the Corps because I had wanted to go into combat with the best platoon in the Corps. Now my men, with their combat skills honed to a razor's ledge, were to go into combat under the leadership of some other lieutenant, and I was to stay behind.

"Captain, how come I'm not going with them?" I asked Oppenheimer. Atkins, whose platoon was also being shipped out while he was remaining, stood with me in front of the captain but said nothing. "Because I need you and Atkins here," the captain replied. "We always keep several of the best officer replacements at the training center to train the new replacements coming in. Besides, there's no guarantee that your platoons will be assigned as a unit. They could be scattered and sent anywhere, just as we could. So we just follow orders, lieutenant, that's all we can do." "Yes, Sir," I answered, and Atkins and I returned to our fale.

There were six officers assigned to our fale, which had three double-deck bunk beds, one against each of the three walls away from the screen door entranceway. Now, as we entered, we saw that only Barrett was there. He stood at his bunk packing his gear to move out with the replacement troops who had just completed their jungle warfare training.

It was an awkward moment. Barrett, our Dartmouth graduate friend and companion since Camp Lejeune, had received his orders to depart the training center, whereas Atkins and I had been selected to stay on as training instructors.

Barrett looked at us and said: "You two are staying on , aren't you?"

"Yeah, we've been ordered to stay on as instructors," I answered.

It seemed ironic to me, but typical of indifferent fate, that of the three of us Barrett was the only married man – and a newlywed at that – to be the first of us committed to a combat unit. But we knew that he was a Marine ready to go and get the job done. As he finished packing and turned to leave all he said was: "Well, I'm going to miss you guys. See you in the mud," And he was gone.

Shortly after Lieutenant Barrett had left, the Green Hornet buzzed into the room with his exciting news. "I just came from the colonel's fale," he said. "I told him I didn't join the Marine Corps to hang around in a training camp. I asked him to cut me some orders for combat as soon as he could."

"And what did he say," Atkins asked.

"He said that he had received his orders returning him to the States, and he thought that we might all be getting orders to regular units soon."

We didn't know whether to believe the Hornet, with his fanciful imagination, or not. So I said: "That isn't likely, Captain, because Captain Oppenheimer just told Atkins and me that we are being kept here as training instructors, which doesn't sound like they're closing everything down."

"Who are you going to believe, the captain or the colonel?" the Hornet replied. "All I know is I'm getting out of here, and I'm going to kill me some Japs!" he added.

Of course, we couldn't tell him it wasn't a choice between believing a captain or a colonel – but a choice of which captain to believe.

As it turned out, The Hornet was right. Within a few days Captain Oppenheimer called us in again and said: "Gentlemen, I've got news for you. The colonel's been shipped back to the States for personal reasons, and because I've been here since early '42, I also have my Stateside orders. The school is being disbanded, and you'll be getting your orders to an organized regiment soon."

Within a few weeks, I was assigned to my first regular unit in the United States Marine Corps. My orders assigned me to the Second Battalion, Twenty-Second Marines. Atkins and the Green Hornet were assigned to other units, and I never saw either of them again. But the Green Hornet's reputation preceded him wherever he went, and no senior officer ever dared to give Captain Lammock command of a unit. However, that did not deter him from becoming a one-man fighting machine. I was told that he later distinguished himself in combat in the jungles of Bougainville by going deep into enemy territory on scouting missions and setting up one-man ambushes. It was said that he was badly shot-up on one of those escapades, but like any other good Marine, he fought bravely – if foolishly – as long as he could hold enough of his body parts together to continue to do what he saw as his mission.

Chapter 5

Talofa to the 22d Marines

F inally, I was to discover the real Marine Corps. I was no longer assigned to an artificial boot camp or Officers' Training Class at Quantico, nor an advanced version of it at a specialized Jungle Warfare School in a Samoan village. No, Second Lieutenant Tom Jones was now reporting to the Second Battalion of the Twenty-Second Marines.

The regiment's campsite was closer in miles to the village of Leone, where I had spent the past few months, than it was in culture. As I entered the camp area, I could see that I was joining a formally structured organization.

The campsite was set in one of the many coconut groves that covered most of the beachfront. The camp fales, constructed by the CB's, were the same as those at the Training Center. They were arranged neatly into company streets, with unit identification on each structure. So here I was reporting to my first regular unit in the "real" Marine Corps that Corporal Turner had described. It was *tofa* to John Wayne and Hollywood fantasy, and *talofa* to the 22d Marines.

I knew that the 22d Marines had already been in Samoa for about a year before I joined them. I also knew that they were an independent "orphan" regiment that had been formed in Linda Vista, California only a few weeks before they were sent to garrison British Samoa, and I knew that they belonged to no Marine Corps division. Now they had been sent across 60 miles of water from British Samoa to Tutuila, American Samoa, to await the arrival of additional equipment and personnel to fill out their TO&E before going into combat.

I reported to the commanding officer of the Second Battalion,

Lieutenant Colonel Tommy Marks, who was like a father to many of his young troops with whom he had served since the formation of the Twenty-Second at Linda Vista, California, in the spring of 1942.

"Glad to have you aboard, Lieutenant," the colonel said. "I see you have been on Tutuila longer than we have, so you probably know your way around. No need to warn you about the mosquitoes and the *mumu* or the danger of the blowholes."

"No Sir," I responded; "at the Training Center in Leone we did our time in the jungle foxholes, and we worked a lot of night exercises around some of the worst blowholes on the island. I'm sure you heard about our tragedy there, Sir," I added.

"Yes, I know about it," the colonel replied, "but wasn't it also a marvelous example of Semper Fidelis – one Marine laying down his life to try and save his comrade? That's why the Marine Corps has been my life, Lieutenant," he said, "that's why it's been my life."

"Yes Sir," I responded to this World War I career officer, a dedicated Marine who I sensed no longer had the youth and vitality to lead an infantry battalion into combat. The colonel then directed me to report to Captain Goldberg in Company F.

Captain Leon Goldberg was an amiable leader with a perennial grin on his face who spoke like a New Yorker. I also thought, without any evidence to support my theory, that the captain was no career Marine like the colonel. I felt that he would never have been in the Marine Corps had there not been this particular compelling war.

In his informal matter, the captain greeted me casually. "Okay, Jones," he said, "I can always use another officer, but I can't give you a platoon. All my guys have been with me for awhile, so a platoon billet isn't open. You'll just hang out with me at company headquarters. See the first sergeant about bunking arrangements," the captain continued, "and he'll tell you which fale you're in."

When I entered my fale a second lieutenant got up from his bunk and came over to introduce himself. He was a tall lean Marine with light brown hair and a fair complexion. "Hi, I'm Clint Wilmsen," he said, extending his hand.

"And I'm Tom Jones," I replied, as we shook hands. I took

Author reports to F Company CO, Captain Goldberg (seated second from left) and stands on the left with lieutenants Harris, Wilmsen, and Green.

note of his firm friendly handshake, not overly strong, not too weak.

"Are you new to the island?" he asked.

"No, just new to the Twenty-Second. I've been a platoon instructor at the Jungle Warfare School since March," I told him.

"That's great," he said; 'we can use your experience in F Company."

"Well, all my experience is in training. I've never been in combat."

"Who has," he replied. "I think the only one in the entire regiment who has ever been in combat is the regimental commander, Colonel Walker. He was in World War I."

"How about Colonel Marks?" I asked.

"Well, he's a regular officer, and he's been in the Corps a long time, but I don't think he's ever seen combat."

"Do you think he'll be taking us in on our first landing?"

"I don't think so," Wilmsen replied. "He's a great guy, and we all love Uncle Tommy. Some of us from the 6th Marines in Iceland have been with him since we formed the Twenty-Second at Linda Vista. But he's not that young anymore, and I don't think he could ever order any of "his boys" to charge a machine gun nest. Uncle Tommy would charge it himself, but I don't think he could give us the order."

"That's because we're not really professionals," I told Wilmsen. "Since we're all amateurs going against combat-experienced Japs, I think we've got to train like hell under tough combat conditions. At the Jungle School I put my guys through as much hell as my captain would allow because I don't think you can be too ready for the real thing. What do you think?"

"Well, I kind of like the Samoan expression – *fi fi lemu* – 'take it easy', and that's become the motto for the 22d Marines. Of course, we want our guys to be in A-1 shape, but don't you think there's more to it than being in good shape?" Wilmsen responded.

"There's always more to it than the physical," I said, "but it has to start there, doesn't it? And I think superior fitness builds morale."

"I'm sure you're right," he replied; then, changing the subject, he said; "When you get your gear squared away, I'll introduce you to some of the other guys in the battalion."

Stepping out of the fale, one of the first guys we ran into was Second Lieutenant Bob Carey, the Bn-4 supply officer. He was looking for me, but he spoke to Wilmsen first. "Hi, Clint," he said; "I guess this is Lieutenant Jones," he added turning to me and putting his hand out.

As we shook hands, he continued: "I just heard that you've been assigned to F Company. If you'll drop by the battalion supply office later, I'll issue you your company gear."

Lieutenant Carey was a large, round-faced, farm boy from the agricultural center of California. He had a casual easy-going manner, and I was later to learn that he was also very efficient. To any task he was assigned, he always seemed to be able to apply just enough horsepower or brainpower to accomplish it. Without a lot of fuss and fury, he always got the job done.

It was only a few days after I had picked up my gear from

Carey and settled down in the F Company when the colonel discovered that Captain Goldberg had not given me a platoon.

The colonel told Goldberg that he couldn't afford to waste a good officer and immediately transferred me to battalion headquarters. He assigned me to assist Bob Carey in the Bn-4 supply section, which normally only rated one officer. However, since the entire regiment was being reinforced for independent combat duty, even the unflappable Second Lieutenant Carey was beginning to flap a little under pressure from Regimental Headquarters. Although I was slightly senior to Carey, we were both second lieutenants, so it didn't matter much which one assisted the other. The saying in the Corps at that time was: "Seniority among second lieutenants is like virtue among whores." I don't know if that's a good metaphor now, but it seemed to make sense there and then.

Second Lieutenant Wilmsen, the mild-manner Scandinavian from the Midwest with the *fi fi lemu* philosophy, seemed to be operating on the same wavelength as Second Lieutenant Carey. They were both men of high virtue, impeccable moral standards, and indifference to their officer status. Both were very private individuals, but whereas Carey was more outgoing and at ease with a group, Wilmsen was more of a loner to whom I could relate. He seemed to me like a real-life Gary Cooper.

At this state of the war neither Wilmsen, Carey, nor I drank or smoked, although for Carey and me that would change soon enough. It was a change that came easy for us as we learned that after each smothering exercise in the hot muggy Samoan jungle we had the choice of drinking hot chlorinated water from a canvas Lister bag or drinking a cold beer chilled by ice from the Navy CBs.

The cigar habit came about with insidious ease as well. Following the evening mess, as we sat on coconut logs waiting for darkness in order to see the outdoor movies, we passed the time watching the giant fruit bats flit about while we puffed on fat cigars from somebody's birthday box received from home.

But the beer and cigars never tempted Wilmsen. He seemed to remain quietly in control of his appetites. He was like someone living on a higher plane, as though the war was simply a temporary trial and tribulation for his soul and not something he had to get deeply involved in. And that feeling of isolation, of being a third-party observer, was something that I shared with Wilmsen.

Operating with the Bn-4 out of battalion headquarters soon brought me into each of the company camp areas and in contact with all forty five officers assigned to the battalion at that time. Of course, they were from every part of the country and from every walk of life. There were the football players and other jocks from the major and minor universities. There were teachers and principals from the high schools. There were even a few lawyers, as well as a couple of doctors who had joined the Navy and were now assigned to us. But mostly there were just the ordinary American boys who had either finished some college before they went for a commission, or were outstanding enlisted men who had received their commissions the hard way at an ad hoc officer's school in Samoa.

I was soon introduced to Second Lieutenant Richard M. Pfuhl, one of the ordinary American boys who proved to be an extraordinary Marine. He had been one of those selected out of the ranks to attend officers' school and was a newly commissioned second lieutenant when I met him. Even among our many football players, he stood out as a large impressive figure.

"I hear you're from the University of Illinois," he said as we shook hands. Did you play any ball there? I'm from St. Louis" he added modestly, not noting that he was an outstanding football player.

"No, I did track, gym, and boxing, but no ball," I told him.

"Well track figures," he said; "I had you pegged for a quarterback."

I immediately like this amiable hulk that everyone called "Tiny" in contrast to his huge size, or "Heavy" in acknowledgement of his bulk.

Next I met Second Lieutenant Ed Pesely, who also had been selected out of the ranks to be commissioned in Samoa. I first got acquainted with him because of my laundry problem. The way we got our laundry done Samoan-style was to make an arrangement with a local native woman – or with her husband or child intermediary – to pound out our skivies, utilities, and khakis on lava rocks. It was up to each Marine to find his own laundry woman, and since I left mine when I left Leone, I was looking for a new one. Because the influx of naive replacement troops had been responsible for a 300% increase in laundry prices, I was advised to see veteran Marine Ed Pesely before making any new deals.

I found Pesely standing in front of a native fale, casually smoking a cigarette and consummating a laundry deal with two teenage girls, dressed in colorful *lava lavas_*wrapped tightly around their shapely figures. Pesely was a handsome young man with fair complexion, brown hair, and a light brown Errol-Flynn-type moustache popular at the time. He and I had met a couple of times in the company mess hall, so he knew who I was. But before we could speak, one of the young girls who was giggling from the conversation that had been going on as I arrived reached over and grabbed Pesely's private part, exclaiming to me – "Oh look, Lieutenant Pesely has *mumu!*" Certainly, if he had not had that gigantic swelling symptomatic of *mumu* before she grabbed him in that vulnerable spot – it was clearly evident that he did have it now.

I noted that Pesely, a pre-Pearl Harbor Marine, seemed to be enjoying his laundry deal making. But for the girls of Samoa it was all innocent fun. Natural body parts were not taboo subjects on an island where the women never bothered to cover their breasts when swimming or bathing in public view – unless, of course, there was a missionary around.

Later, back in our officers' area, there were no missionaries around when Pesely spun some sizzling sea stories about his Honolulu duty before Pearl Harbor. Pesely was five years older and much more experienced than I was, so I listened in naïve amazement. He had joined the Marine Corps in 1936 after two-and-a-half years in a Catholic seminary, studying to be a Franciscan priest. When I asked him why he hadn't stayed with that goal, his honest reply was – "I knew I could never live up to that vow of celibacy." Judging from his sea stories, he had made the right decision. One of his stories, which related more to the serious business of war than to the frivolity of sex, illustrated clearly the negligence and incompetence of a lazy U.S. Pearl Harbor command prior to the December 7,1941 attack.

Pesely told us that as a private stationed at the Navy Pier, Honolulu, in 1937, his pay was $21 a month, which he received in two biweekly payments of about $10 each. Obviously, after paying for his laundry and basic necessities, there was little left for a beer or recreation. That's when the Japanese came to the rescue of the low-paid U.S. enlisted men. He recalled that there were always several Japanese Naval vessels docked at the Pier, and every weekend the red carpet was out for enlisted Marines to come aboard and enjoy a beer and sake party.

Of course, this was an offer the Marines could not refuse, so they partied, they drank, they talked. While they were drinking and talking, a Japanese sailor would point to various harbor installations and U.S. warships and with casual innocence ask such questions as: "What is that over there? How long has that ship been at dock? How many battleships and carriers have you seen here?" But if a Marine asked any questions about the Japanese warship hosting them, he was met with silence or a shake of the head that meant it was a forbidden subject. And this was four years before the "surprise" attack on December 7, 1941, with our high command sleeping through all these preliminary indicators.

Fortunately for Private Pesely, he was not still stationed in Hawaii when the infamous Japanese attack was launched from six aircraft carriers, with support from submarines and battleships. For two unrelenting hours Japanese bombers, fighters, and torpedo planes swarmed all over Pearl Harbor sinking or seriously damaging eight U.S. battleships and fourteen smaller vessels, destroying 200 aircraft, killing more than 2000 seamen, 400 others, and wounding 1300 Americans. Because the American command was caught totally off guard, the Japanese suffered fewer than 100 casualties and lost only 29 planes and five midget submarines.

Despite the obvious dereliction at some level of the U.S. command, a special commission appointed by the President was unable to pinpoint the blame, and no court martials were ever held. Meanwhile, the day went down in Japanese history as a tremendous tactical success for their famous Admiral Yamamoto and his task force commander Vice Admiral Chuichi Nagumo.

Question: why had Private Pesely and his enlisted friends been the only ones to notice the obvious ominous signs long before the attack?

Chapter 6

Let the Games Begin

Human nature puts a limit on how long you can tolerate getting ready for something that never happens. Unfortunately, in the summer and fall of 1943 many of the men of the Twenty-Second Marines had already exceeded their limits. This pernicious situation was brought to the attention of the command by a number of suicides.

Weeks had long ago run into months, and months were running into years. So the monotonous daily grind of repeating the same combat maneuvers, soaked in the perpetual rain, fighting the ubiquitous mosquitoes, and living with the pervasive jungle rot had gradually pushed many of our young men to the brink. All of that pressure was bearing down on this regiment of teenage troops who never expected to see home again because they knew that the Marine Corps was the only military service without a rotation policy. Whereas the other services rotated their servicemen home after 12 to 18 months of combat duty. Marines were thought to be voluntary professional warriors whose job it was to stay out in the jungle and fight until they were killed, seriously maimed, or until the war was over.

So the men were depressed, and many of those not lucky enough to be among the 400 Marines infected with *mumu* that were being shipped back to the States found another way out. They looked to a Marine's best friend, his rifle, for help. Too many were simply putting the muzzles of their rifles into their mouths and pulling the trigger. It was the surest, fastest way out of their hell. And yet, for them combat hadn't even started. However, it would come soon enough.

We'll never know whether Lieutenant Colonel Marks initiated

his own removal from command of the battalion, but he would have had sufficient reason to do that. Already deeply distressed by the suicides in his battalion, he knew he was too emotionally involved with his troops to lead them effectively in combat. And he was physically tired.

So in November of 1943 Uncle Tommy Marks relinquished his command of the 2d Battalion, 22d Marines, and I remember marching by him as he stood in review. Tears were welling in his eyes as he said his last farewell to "his boys" who were on their way to war without him.

However, the path to war for the 22d Marines involved a one-month stopover on the side of a mountain in Hawaii. Before Thanksgiving 1943, the Battalion – now under the command of Lieutenant Colonel Donn C. Hart — was camped about half way up the 10,000-foot Haleakala, a volcanic mountain on Maui. Word was soon coming back to us that our comrades from Samoa in the Third Marines were already engaged in bitter hand-to-hand fighting in the jungles of Bougainville. That news was shortly followed by worse news of a tragic costly amphibious landing by the Second Marine Division on a tiny atoll called Tarawa. We took this news as a foreboding forecast of what lay ahead of us.

To compound the apprehension of the green officers and troops of the Twenty-Second, Lieutenant Colonel Evans Carlson of Marine Raider fame, spoke to a gathering of our junior officers and senior NCOs. Our group was seated outside on a grassy knoll near our campgrounds. With the colonel's casual informal manner, the meeting was like a football coach briefing his team on what to expect when they come up against that tough opposing team.

Carlson described the action he had witnessed on Tarawa, not as a line officer on the landing team, but as an official observer. "I went in with Colonel Shoup and his Second Marines headquarters group. The first three waves had gone in amtracs and were able to crawl over the coral reef, but we, in the later waves, were in LCVPs. So we were stopped by barbed wire and dumped in the water. We had to wade in the last 150 yards, taking heavy casualties all the way.

"Still in the water, Colonel Shoup and our small headquarters group found cover at the side of a pier. Despite withering small arms fire, Colonel Shoup continued to direct the battle while waist-deep in the water, even though he was wounded in the leg. It was noon before we managed to get ashore and set up a command post. That's when the colonel ordered me back to the command ship to expedite his request for more men, water, ammunition, and weapons. And that's where it ended for me.

"Although it's not official and its off the record, you may already know that at Tarawa we lost over a thousand Marines killed and two thousand wounded. But we also learned a lot, so that's what I'm here to talk about. Why don't we start with your questions."

First Lieutenant Phil Laden, the Bn-2 intelligence officer was the first to speak up: "Sir, we all know that we're going to have more atoll fighting to do. Can we expect them all to be like Tarawa?"

Phil Laden was a little older then most of us. He had a slight wiry build, and I thought he looked and acted like a New York lawyer — which he proved to be. He also proved to be a very bright and a good staff officer.

"No, Lieutenant, I hope not," Carlson responded. "You see, Tarawa was the first time anyone had ever made a landing on a heavily defended atoll. Atoll fighting is new to us and different from the jungle warfare of Guadalcanal and Bougainville. So there were some hard lessons we had to learn, and we had to learn them the hard way.

"Now we know that all the assault waves must be sent ashore in tracked vehicles. To reach the beach on a heavily defended atoll, we can't rely on Higgins boats or any kind of floating vehicles that we have used on other kinds of beaches. On the atolls, we've got to be ready to climb over coral reefs, concrete obstacles, and chop through barbed wire. We don't ever want to dump our troops into neck-deep water again. And once ashore on Tarawa, we quickly learned the value of flamethrowers against an enemy fighting from underground positions."

Captain Goldberg from F Company raised his hand, and Carlson nodded for him to speak. "I'm sure there's a lot more that you can tell us that we need to hear, Sir, but are you going to tell your story to the top brass so we get the equipment you didn't have on Tarawa."

"That's right, Captain. It's a top priority in my report that I intend to hand- carry to Washington."

Then the colonel continued: "But now there's something just as important as the equipment that I want to mention. Some of you might know that some years ago I traveled as an observer with the Chinese 5th Red Army of Mao Tse Tung. As I studied their tactics, there were two things that impressed me. One was a spirit of comradeship that they called *Gung Ho*. I was told that it means 'Work Together' in their Chinese dialect. I decided that it was their Chinese version of our Marine 'Esprit de Corps.' Now I don't think U.S. Marines need to take lessons in Esprit de Corps from anyone else. It's the one thing that money can't buy and nobody can take away from us. The world can learn that from us. But the Chinese did have a unique small-unit military organizational structure that I learned to admire. I noted that while we organize our infantry platoons around a squad structure, they went one step further and broke their squads down into small groups of three or four soldiers who worked as a team. And each man in that group was responsible for the lives of the other three. So you may have heard that I have already introduced that idea into our Raider Battalion. It's a four-man group that I call a fireteam – three men with rifles and one with an automatic weapon. You might want to talk to your battalion commander about trying out the concept."

"We already got that word, Colonel," Second Lieutenant Pfuhl responded, "and we've already organized our squads into fireteams. We're training that way here on Maui now."

"Good," the colonel replied; 'never be afraid to borrow good ideas."

Lieutenant Colonel Carlson was a tall, thin, distinguished looking fellow with a deeply furrowed face and an aquiline nose. He had the kind of celebrity presence that made you well aware when he entered a scene or when he left it. When he was in the meeting, officers and NCOs took strength from him and his narrative, but when he left, that strength went with him. Then each man realized that soon, when face to face with the enemy, he could not look for strength from an icon. He could only rely on his own personal resources.

At this time, I was the adjutant of the Second Battalion, which is among other things a military version of a personnel manager. The adjutant is the battalion "One" officer, designation as the Bn-1. When not in combat, he and the battalion sergeant major and a couple of corporal clerks take care of the administrative business of the unit. In the field, the Bn-1 takes his orders from the battalion CO and the XO executive officer. As adjutant, I was privy to news before the line company officers received it, so I was first to know that the Twenty-Second Marines would soon be going into combat. Although I didn't know where, I guessed it would be in the Marshall Islands to continue the atoll leapfrogging started at Tarawa. With that reality looming over us, the Marines of the Twenty-Second began to prepare seriously for war.

Our regiment was being reinforced with heavier armaments, including both artillery and tanks, and training took on a risky demeanor. In the middle of December 1943 the Second Battalion was ordered to participate in a full-scale amphibious assault exercise. The entire battalion, complete with equipment and munitions, was to be transported across the island to an embarkation point and loaded aboard ship for a week-long exercise that culminated in a simulated assault landing that was to include close-in air support with powerful live munitions.

However, to avoid unnecessary danger to our troops, the close-in air support was changed to an air-strike demonstration to be held after the completion of the ground assault operations. For the demonstration, our troops were to be positioned as observers on a hill approximately a thousand yards from the target hill. On the morning of the demonstration I looked up from my field desk and saw a tall skinny private standing there.

"What can I do you for, Private?" I asked.

"Sir, can I speak to you?" came the reply.

"Yes, what's your name, Private?"

"I'm Private McCoy," he stated. "I'm in the First Platoon, Fox Company."

"What can I do for you, McCoy?"

"Sir, I don't want to go on the field exercise today."

"Why not, McCoy? Are you sick?"

"No Sir, I'm fine, but I had a bad dream that something bad will happen to me if I go."

"What will happen to you?"

"I'm not sure. I just know that it's something bad."

"Well, Private, did you talk with Captain Goldberg?"

"Yes Sir, but he said he couldn't excuse me. Only the colonel could do that. That's why I came here to battalion headquarters."

"Well, McCoy, you've got to have a better reason than a bad dream. This is a serious exercise demonstrating close-in air support – aerial strafing and bombardment — so everyone has to participate. I can't tell the colonel that I let some guy off because he had a bad dream. I'm sorry, Private. You have to go."

"Yes Sir," he responded, squaring up his narrow shoulders and trying to stand tall like a Marine. But all I could see was a scared rabbit of a kid probably not over seventeen years old. The private did a quiet "About Face" and walked away dejectedly.

It was about this time on Maui when I was becoming better acquainted with Tiny Pfuhl, our legendary Marine who best personified the Twenty-Second Marines. At 6-foot-one and 240 pounds, Tiny was very casual- mannered for a former college football star. Because he was no spit-and-polish Marine, everybody from the colonel to his bunk mates felt comfortable calling him "Tiny" or "Heavy". And like "Tiny", the Twenty-Second Marines, was no spit-and-polish regiment. It had been hastily formed at Linda Vista, California in 1942 and unceremoniously shipped to the jungles of Samoa. Somehow the mustang lieutenant, who got his commission in the field on Samoa, and the hapless orphan regiment were a natural fit. There was no sense of Quantico or Annapolis about either one of them, but for guts and spirit they were all-Marine all the way.

Since I was the battalion adjutant at this time, Tiny took the opportunity to drop by once in a while to see if I had any scoop that hadn't got down to the companies as yet. The scared rabbit private had just left me when Tiny walked up to ask about the air demonstration scheduled for the afternoon. For a laugh, I told him about the private's bizarre reason for wanting to be excused, and Tiny surprised me by not laughing it off.

"Well, maybe the kid knows something," he said.

"Come on, Tiny," I said, 'you don't really think I can go to Colonel Hart with that dream story?"

"Not unless you want to watch the Old Man throw a fit," he replied. "Anyhow," Tiny continued, "Goldberg told me we're just going to go out there and sit on a hill and watch them dive-bomb another hill about a thousand yards in front of us. Is that the scoop up here at Battalion."

"That's all there is to it, Tiny. An easy finish to a hard week," I replied. "We sit on a hill and let the Naval aviators entertain us."

Tragically, it didn't turn out that way. We sat on our hill okay, and we patiently watched the hill a thousand yards in front of us, waiting for the Navy dive bombers. Finally, the planes show up and do their run, but something horrible happens, and the bombs are exploding in the middle of our F Company area, instantly killing twenty-one and maiming twenty-eight Marines.

By the time I rush to the scene a few yards away, the ground is covered with bleeding bodies, torsos, arms and legs. Our battalion surgeons and our medical corpsmen are there instantly. Doctors Wiley, Rogers and Hedgecock have already instituted triage. They're moving down the line of bodies pointing at each and declaring them as number one's, two's, or three's. One's get first priority, two's come next, and forget three's – they're too far gone.

It was a scene more shocking than I expected to see in combat, but the shock didn't stop there. Once the wounded were jeeped away to the hospital and the dead were removed to a makeshift morgue, as battalion adjutant I was one of those who had to go the morgue to identify the bodies and body parts as best I could.

The scene in the morgue was even more shocking than that on the outdoor hill. Here on the floor of this cramped room, were the bodies and human remains of twenty-one Marines, some of whom I knew very well. Among the bodies, there were two sights I will never forget. One was a body completely intact, except for the head. Where the head should have been was an esophagus coming out of the neck with only a mouth and a full set of white teeth hanging on the end of it. The other sight I was shocked to see was that of the scared-rabbit private who had begged to be excused from this exercise because he knew something bad was going to happen. I carefully inspected his body to see what had killed him. All I could find was a very minor wound from a small piece of shrapnel high in the left shoulder. Our doctors told me that it was not a physically lethal wound. But if that didn't kill him, what did?

I decided that the boy died of fright. Convinced that something terrible was going to happen to him that day, when he felt the tiny piece of shrapnel hit him in his shoulder, his heart just stopped. Not even our doctors had a better explanation. And no one ever had an explanation of how this private was the only one who seemed to know in advance that a tragedy was about to happen.

Chapter 7

Facing Reality

It was Christmas Eve 1943, and we were still camped at the 5000-foot level of Haleakala. Our isolation did not deter the ex-college football stars and former BMOCs like Tiny Pfuhl from seeking out and finding recreational activity, near or far. And, of course, there was nothing like spirits for lifting their spirits.

At this phase in my life, I didn't drink hard booze, and I was pretty much of a loner. And there's nothing more depressing than being a loner on Christmas Eve when you are one year and 3500 miles away from home. So another lonesome lieutenant and I accepted the invitation from the Maui Red Cross Chapter to spend Christmas Eve with a family in Wailuku.

It was a typical American family home, and we spent the evening decorating the Christmas tree in traditional fashion. The family tried so hard to make us feel comfortable, it was awkward for them and for us. Having lived in a jungle and on a mountaintop for the last year completely isolated from civilization, it was not easy for us to shift gears into a civilian mode. We felt like we were a clumsy intrusion into this soft social scene, and we were actually relieved at the end of the evening to get back to our tents on the mountainside.

In the first weeks of 1944, we knew that our time in combat was soon to come. With a full year of advanced combat training behind us, with briefings by Colonel Carlson and others who had returned from the combat zones recently – we were ready. We were as ready as any green troops could be who have yet to learn the difference between war stories and reality.

We were soon combat-loaded and steaming to our first

objective somewhere in the Central Pacific. We thought it would be in the Marshalls, but there are a lot of atolls in the group. Our Tactical Group I consisted of our orphan regiment, the Twenty-Second Marines, and two Army battalions under command of Marine Brigadier General Watson. We were traveling in a huge convoy of troop transports escorted by more than a hundred warships including battleships, cruisers, destroyers, destroyer escorts, submarines, and smaller vessels.

We knew we were part of something big when we learned that the 4th Marine Division and the Army's 7th Division were also in our party. And then we soon heard that those two divisions were to attack Kwajalein Atoll, the world's largest atoll, with 93 islands and a lagoon 60 by 30 miles.

We were told that the Marshall Islands had been held by the Japanese for a quarter of a century and that Kwajalein was their administration and communications center, so we expected the battle to be worse than Tarawa. But we were relieved to know that as reserve units we would be in a position to observe the Army's 7th Division attack against Kwajalein, the main island of the atoll, before we would be committed to our first combat.

 Upon arrival at Kawajalein Atoll on D-Day minus one, our powerful armada had immediately entered the lagoon, with the troop ships taking their invasion positions a few thousand yards off shore, while our destroyers, cruisers, and battleships methodically worked over the beaches from point-blank range.

It was a strangely surrealistic scene as we stood in the pre-dawn dark of D-Day at the rail of our transport during the final naval bombardment observing rather than fighting our first battle. It is hard to believe that scene today. Here was one of Admiral "Close-in" Connolly's huge battleships cruising a thousand yards off shore on a course parallel with the hostile beach. The ship had one 16-inch gun leveled broadside for action. Moving deliberately, it would direct a brilliant searchlight on each enemy pillbox, which was quickly followed by the impact of a one-ton projectile from the battleship which pulverized the pillbox and its occupants.

I couldn't help wondering what those doomed enemy soldiers were thinking when they realized what was about to come their way and how they felt with the brief glimpse of the searchlight as their last experience on earth. It was a few days before I would pick up a clue that could contain the answer for one enemy soldier.

By 0900, the warships had moved out of the way, the dive bombers had finished their job, and the 7th Army Division troops were attacking the beaches under the cover of overhead naval gunfire. Meanwhile, as reserve troops we had no mission unless committed to support the Army, so most of us hung over the rail watching the action on shore. And in one of those inexplicable and incongruous incidents of war, somehow the ship's exchange store opened up and for a short time was offering soft ice-cream sundaes.

Lieutenant Pesely, who had been named battalion transport loading officer for this operation, came alongside me also eating his chocolate sundae. "Pese," I said, "you never warned me that combat would be like this – we just stand around eating ice cream while the Army and the Navy blasts the enemy to hell."

"I don't think the troops ashore are eating sundaes," Pese answered. You can bet that those guys in the platoons are taking their licks now. But maybe we'll get a break this time. Maybe they won't have to call in the reserves."

Of course, he was right about the assault platoons and fortunately for us they didn't call in the reserve. But without committing us in the reserve, it took the Army 32d and 184th Regiments four days of hard fighting to secure the crescent-shaped Kwajalein Island – twice as long as it took the 23rd and 24th Marines to secure the more lightly-defended Roi and Namur Islands in the north.

On the seventh day, when I went ashore with a party of observers, it became obvious to me that additional reserve troops would have served no useful purpose. The scene was shocking. There on that tiny island – which was simply a coral sand spit about two miles long, 800 yards wide, and 10 feet above sea level – we encountered the rotting bodies of four thousand Japanese soldiers. It was almost impossible to walk among those black, swollen, smelly bodies that had been lying in the tropical sun without stepping on them. And it was unnerving when one of the huge, bloated, green flies feasting on a corpse would flit up on to your face and try to crawl into your nose and mouth.

This was grim reality. Forget the John Wayne movies. Forget Errol Flynn and his merry men of Sherwood Forest. Our military bodies had already been carefully removed, but it didn't take much imagination to put yourself into the place of any one of those dead Japanese soldiers.

And so it was that I reached down and picked up a letter from one of the bodies. It was written in Japanese characters, of course, so I couldn't read it. But it was obviously a last letter that had been written in such desperate haste that what had started out as neat carefully scripted *Kanji* ended up in an unreadable scrawl. I wondered whether this young Japanese soldier was writing this final letter as he watched that searchlight of our battleship preceding our amphibious attack? I decided to keep the letter until I could have someone translate it for me, and it remained untranslated for the next fifty-five years.

For me and Lieutenant Carey it was a quiet solemn ride back to our troop transport, but some of the platoon leaders in our boat like Tiny Pfuhl were stimulated to the point of controlled agitation. Tiny, like all of us greenhorns, had been preparing himself to fight a Hollywood war. It was the only kind of war we had experienced. In the Hollywood war of those days, there were heroes and villains. And the heroes always won, or they died fighting in a noble, dramatic last scene. The actors were also carefully costumed and made-up nicely to look like heroes. It was during this ride in the boat that I first paid attention to the new red growth on Tiny's solid round face.

It was clear that like the Viking, Eric the Red, Tiny was growing a red beard, which I presumed he thought would scare hell out of those little bastards on the beach. I wondered if that beard still seemed important to him now that he had just seen the true face of what would be waiting for us on our first beach.

We didn't have long to wait before hitting our first beach. Once back aboard ship, we briefed the troops on what we had seen on the beach, insofar as it was possible to describe. Then we told them that we had just received word that we were headed for a place called Eniwetok. We would hit there within two weeks.

Eniwetok, we learned was another large atoll of about 40 islets and a lagoon that is 20 miles by 17 miles. Our intelligence units told us that the Japanese had concentrated their troops on three of the islands, Engebi, Parry, and Eniwetok. Our "Secret" combat maps made from aerial photographs showed what appeared to be an impregnable perimeter defense of pillboxes, coastal gun emplacements, and machine guns dotting every linear foot around Engebi, the target island of our first assault. Engebi had been picked because of its one-mile long airstrip. On the map, we saw that the island was a one-mile equilateral triangle, with the airstrip running abreast of the northern coast, from the lagoonside to seaward.

Once our objective was declared, every echelon of the battalion went to work studying the battle plan. The field grade officers held planning meetings with the captains; the captains with the lieutenants; and the lieutenants with the NCOs and the

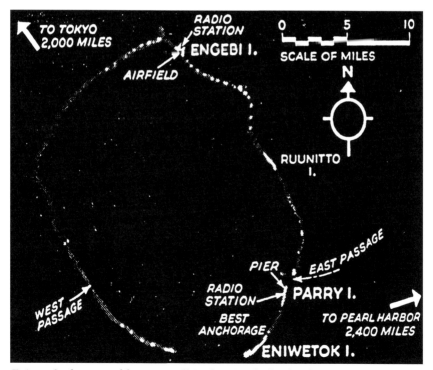

Eniwetok, the second largest atoll in the Marshall Islands, consists of about 40 islets around a lagoon that is about 20 miles by 17 miles.

troops. Next, every Marine unit from battalion headquarters, through the companies, platoons, and squads – even down to the 4-man fire teams – studied the combat maps and isolated their specific mission within the attack plan, memorizing every foot of enemy terrain and every gun emplacement in their sector. Each man in each unit knew what his personal responsibility was during each phase of the battle. Every action was totally preplanned, and once the Marines were ashore there would be rare opportunity for anyone above a platoon leader to exercise command and control.

Despite the fact that every Marine in our battalion, from colonel to private, knew the minute details of the amphibious battle plan better than anyone in the U.S. Navy, the transport ship's captain saw fit to call a briefing of the ship and troop officers, and his Navy chiefs and our senior NCO's on the day before the invasion.

The ship's captain was a man in his mid-fifties who had graduated Annapolis around the time of WWI, but who had never achieved an important command in his twenty-eight year Navy career. World War II was his last chance to command a battleship, the dream of every black-shoe naval officer. Instead, here he was the skipper of a converted cruise ship, but at least his ship was as committed to action as much as any transport could be.

So his briefing began: "Gentlemen, I have assembled you here to discuss the operation we have embarked upon. First, I suppose you know we are now positioned in the lagoon of Eniwetok Atoll but we don't call it that. We are using code names for the atoll and its islands. They are all named after flowers."

At this point the Captain put up some charts and showed the three main islands with their code names – Sunflower, Violet, Zinnia … "Fragile." Realizing that "Fragile" was not a flower, the poor man quickly corrected himself and then said, "Well, maybe they're not all named after flowers."

The briefing went on far too long to the extreme embarrassment of the captain's own ship's officers who were acutely aware that the troops knew far more about this operation than the befuddled captain. Finally, hoping to end his briefing with an inspirational message, the captain concluded with: "I want you to remember this as you go into combat tomorrow. This ship may not be a battleship with 16-inch guns, but our small boats are our 16-inch guns and you troops are our projectiles." Apparently the captain wasn't aware that we weren't' making the invasion from his ship in his small boats, but we were to transfer immediately to LSTs from which we would invade in the morning in amtracs.

I stood next to the red-bearded Tiny Pfuhl who I knew was scheduled to land in the first wave in the morning, and I whispered: "Hey, Projectile, that was some inspiration, wasn't it?"

"Well, he's right Jonesie. Projectiles break things and kill people, and that's what we'll be doing in the morning."

I looked at this hulking Marine that many of us called "Tiny", and somehow that nickname didn't fit anymore. He had already let his beard grow, and it had come out a much brighter shade of red than his sandy hair. Now I visualized him as he would look to the scrawny little enemy soldiers waiting for him on the beach. Not satisfied with normal officer armament of a lightweight carbine and a utility knife, he had sent home for a mean-looking hatchet which he intended to carry in his right hand as he charged the beach. And to top that image, he would have a green Red Cross ditty bag pulled over his helmet with a small peanut can inserted in the bag. The purpose of the can was to break the round outline of the helmet, but the can managed to push one corner of the bag up and back like the hat on one of the elves in a Disney cartoon.

So here would be a six-foot-two, 240-pound elf with a flaming red beard, swinging a lethal hatchet, coming at some poor little enemy soldier in the morning. It was with that image in mind that I then decided to switch over from calling him "Tiny" even in jest to his other nickname, "Heavy". And "Heavy" was not only physically heavy; he was a heavyweight by any standards by which a Marine or a man is measured. He was soon to become one of the legends of the Twenty-Second Marines.

Chapter 8

Engebi, The First Landing

After the Naval captain's ill-conceived briefing, with his "inspirational message" still resonating in our heads, we transferred all the assault waves of our battalion to LSTs to prepare for our morning attack in amtracs. If troops are always crowded aboard transports – which they are – you can imagine how much worse it is aboard an LSTs, the small, square-nosed, shoe-box ships of the Navy.

But as bad as the LSTs were for healthy young teenagers, it was much worse for our 30-year-old Captain Goldberg, CO of Fox Company, who became deathly ill with sea sickness the minute he went aboard one of those gyrating shoe-boxes. He was perhaps the only man among the assault troops who was eager to go ashore with the first wave. I think he would have invaded the beach alone on D-minus-one had the colonel let him go.

It was getting dark, and I had found some standing space topside along the deck railing. We couldn't have been more than 1500 yards off shore. And there sat this once-beautiful little tropical island, just a sand spit fading into the dusk of night. But there was still enough light to see the shattered remains of the coconut groves that had been demolished by the Navy's big guns and dive bombers in preparation for our attack.

Ravaged as the island appeared, we knew that the enemy fortifications had not all been destroyed. I had in my pocket a combat map of the landing beaches that detailed the most formidable defenses imaginable. Every possible type of gun emplacement was there: pillboxes, coconut log barricades, machine gun emplacements, antiaircraft and antiship coastal batteries were all there, stretched side-by-side across the full mile of the lagoon-side of the tiny triangular island. I questioned whether the Navy's big guns and dive bombers had been able to neutralize such an overwhelming mass of enemy fortifications and armament.

We would find the answer to that in the morning, but I was somewhat relieved to know that as adjutant I wouldn't be in the first wave. I was ordered to go in the same third wave as the colonel to help establish a battalion command post ashore. But I also knew that as part of the third wave, we would be hitting the beach a mere six minutes after the first wave – not a big safety margin.

Now on the deck and all around me I could overhear the company commanders and the platoon leaders reviewing their missions and giving their final orders to their troops.

"Easy-Two, you've heard this before." It was Heavy Pfuhl laying it out for his platoon. "I repeat so there can be no question on the mission. We're first-wavers. You know your amtracs. You know how to get to them. There should be no doubt. You will chow at 0400. We'll talk a little more. Then we go.

"Sirota, you will anchor at Enervate trail in the assault. Roy, you'll be abreast to the left. Don't forget to contact Columbo. I'll be in the center with Joe and Johnny. Timko, you're in reserve, and you move in behind Sirota after we land…"

Heavy then went on to lay out once again the entire operation for his platoon. "After landing, we'll meet here at Whiskey Road," pointing to the map. "Then we'll reorganize and attack. We'll attack by fire and movement the way we've been training. Keep you eye on me for tempo. If you're pinned down, the other guys will bail you out. If you see a juicy target, we can call air and naval gunfire. Don't forget, they started this bullshit. Now we're going to kick the hell out of them. See you on tank deck after breakfast. Sleep well, good friends. Sleep tight!" It could have been a half-time talk at a football game, but this was no football game – and they all knew it.

Not everyone's style was as breezy as Heavy's. Most of the platoon leaders were a lot more solemn bunch, and they had good reason to be serious. Casualties among Marine infantry platoon leaders were known to be the highest for any officer assignment –

percentage-wise even higher than for the troops that served with them. So while Heavy was making his short enthusiastic pep talk, some of the other platoon leaders like Second Lieutenant Al Kirtz were very methodically going through a verbal rehearsal of every phase objective of their combat mission.

Kirtz, a "mustang" officer who had been commissioned in Samoa like Heavy and Pesely, showed his troops the secret combat map that he carried in his breast pocket, and he instructed his platoon sergeant to make a tissue overlay of the map to carry in his own pocket, with the expectation that one of them might be hit and the other could go on to complete the mission.

Of course, no one slept well. No one slept tight, and I wrote a rambling poem that seemed to make sense that night:

> *Thoughts Before H-hour*
> *—By a Lieutenant—*
> *Out of the hour…into time –*
> *A moment…or a world of years;*
> *Out of the lull and the lapse, into tears,*
> *Out of the dull-and-die, into fears –*
> *The fact, the evidence and the crime.*
>
> *Out of space and journey, into fear, —*
> *A pause, just a pause for the thought…*
> *The fathers died, they also fought –*
> *Out of love and of life – these are bought –*
> *The giant effort and the sought, still unclear.*
>
> *Into the world of worlds, the interim,*
> *a look, just a glance with the eye –*
> *Naught seen, naught sought, espy, decry –*
> *Weird world for the weary to try –*
> *Yet I! Yet I! – Oh for the interim!*
>
> *When you leave the moment… it is gone.*
> *Why reason then with the head?*
> *Is the moment there? or dead?*
> *Out of the moment – the soul instead…*
> *Now enough with the soul – it is dawn.*

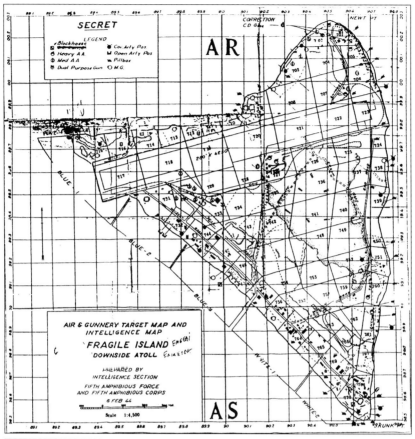

Note the airstrip and beach fortifications on this map of Engebi. (Courtesy of Lt. Kirtz)

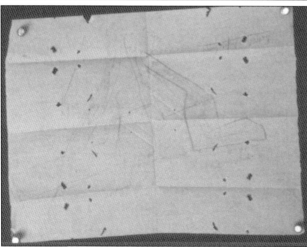

Notice the fatal shrapnel holes in this overlay carried in the breast pocket of Lt. Kirtz' platoon sergeant. (Courtesy of Lt. Kirtz)

But everyone was up in time to watch night change to day on that quiet atoll lagoon. Then all hell breaks loose as the prelanding barrage begins. Here come the planes from our aircraft carriers, repeatedly strafing and dive bombing the beach. Next followed by the Navy's big guns from the battleships, cruisers, and destroyers. Suddenly, the show is over for me. Now it's time for me to go down to the tank deck and find my amtrac.

As I open the hatch to climb down the ladder onto the tank deck, I am almost overcome with the noise and the fumes. The ear-splitting noise of the powerful amtrac engines and the choking carbon monoxide gas turns the tank deck into a literal hell. For a moment we forget our invasion fears and are eager to have the bow ramp lowered so we can see daylight and breathe air again.

I find my amtrac and climb in. I'm packing only a light knapsack containing a small shovel, a poncho, an extra pair of socks, and a K ration. That pack plus my carbine, fighting knife and a canteen of water are all the baggage I need or want. Once on the beach – if I make the beach – I intend to use speed and maneuver for survival.

The bow ramp is lowered, and the amtracs begin filing out. After the darkness in the hull of the ship, the daylight is blinding. But the eyes soon adjust and take in the dramatic scene. Here are other LSTs on our left and our right; all disgorging dozens of other amtracs with their precious cargoes of American teenagers headed for hell.

I look into the faces of the men in my boat. Although I'm only 23, I'm appalled at how young they are. Many appear to be 15 or 16 years old with nothing more than peach fuzz growing on their faces. It occurs to me that these are high school kids. What are they doing in this war so far away from their mothers? Do their mothers know the danger they're in? How will their mothers take the news of their deaths?

The time for contemplation passes swiftly. I come back to my senses. We're all in the same boat – quite literally. If they don't make it to shore, neither do I. Now, I concentrate on the beach. It seems to be on fire with thick black smoke from the naval air bombardment swirling about. And then I hear the rustle of the large Naval projectiles passing over our heads as our amtracs move relentlessly toward the beach at an excruciatingly slow speed of three or four knots, giving the beach defenders plenty of time to zero-in their guns and knock out our boats.

Finally, the first wave reaches the beach. I can already hear the chatter of the enemy machine guns mixed in with the explosions from our heavy gun fire and theirs. I peek over the gunwales to see Heavy's troops jumping down from their amtracs, hesitating on their bellies a few moments, and then charging inland behind their leader. Then, in another quick look, I see the second wave doing the same thing. Three minutes later, my amtrac crunches ashore, and I quickly leap down from the eight foot high gunwales of the amtrac and land with a jarring jolt onto the hard coral sand of the beach.

I bury my face into the coarse sand to stay under the trajectory of the small-arms fire that is coming from all directions. I look to my right and to my left, and I see scores of Marines just lying there at the water line, hugging the ground for dear life. Then a hundred yards to my left I notice intermittent black puffs of smoke moving slowly in my direction over the backs of prone Marines.

Suddenly I realize that those black puffs of smoke are Japanese "knee" mortar shells exploding on the backs of Marines – not blowing them apart like some Hollywood movie – just killing them with thrifty efficiency, sending deadly shrapnel splinters through their bodies.

Immediately I yell out: "Get up! Let's move in! Those are "knee" mortars coming our way."

Then I jump up and lead the men in my area off the beach, racing for cover in the shellholes left by our pre-invasion bombardments. Two enlisted men and I leap into the same huge shellhole. It's occupied by two unconscious Japanese soldiers, who may or may not already be dead from the bombardment. We'll never know because we immediately bayonet them as we enter their hole.

The hole is about eight feet deep and ten feet across, with two feet of water in the bottom. We declare it our battalion command post, and that's where the colonel and his staff will spend the next two days, along with the two dead Japanese bodies floating in the bottom of our CP. It is only much later that we learn that this battalion command post is just a few yards away from an underground Japanese 75mm gun emplacement that continues to fire sporadically on our beach craft for two more days after our landing.

Once the colonel, his staff, and our command communications are firmly established in the shellhole, I am ordered to move on with the battalion executive officer to establish a forward command post. Although the forward CP is useful whenever there is a substantial linear distance between the forward and rear elements of a battalion, on this tiny island there is only a few hundred yards between those elements, so the need for a forward CP is questionable.

Nevertheless, Major Felker and I move forward through the shattered remains of a coconut grove that fringes the one-mile long airstrip. Heavy Pfuhl, Al Kirtz and the other assault platoons have already moved swiftly through this area and have secured the lagoon end of the airstrip, but their mission is to take such territorial objectives as the airstrip, without stopping to eliminate all the enemy troops as they go along. Therefore, we receive the same kind of heavy sniper fire and hand grenade attacks from the broken palm tree debris and the unique one-man spider holes as our forward elements have received. Fortunately, our hand-carried flamethrowers are an effective weapon against this kind of chaotic warfare with no front lines.

There was nothing strategically classic about this fight. Although the photographic mapping of the enemy beach defense was thorough and accurate, detailing every gun emplacement and pillbox, the intelligence passed on to us about the strength of the enemy forces was badly underestimated.

We had been told to expect about three or four hundred enemy soldiers defending this island so it was assumed that one or two Marine battalions would give us that classical 5-to-1 numerical advantage needed in an amphibious assault. As we were finding out, our six companies of about 900 Marines were actually facing an enemy with superior manpower, later determined to be 1200 well-entrenched island defenders. In short, it was a cat-and-dog fight, with the outcome in the hands of each individual Marine.

Passing quickly by the charred remains of enemy soldiers who had been caught by our flamethrowers, Major Felker and I come to the end of the broken coconut grove at the edge of the airstrip. There we encounter our first dead Marines since leaving the landing beaches. The two bodies are lying prone on their faces, a corporal a few yards in front of a private. Both with their rifles in hand stretched out in front of them, obviously used to break their fall when they had been shot, falling just as they had been taught in boot camp.

The scene moved me to tears of admiration, not because they had died, but because of the way they had died. Their squad mission was to take out an enemy machine gun emplaced 800 yards across the airstrip so that the remainder of their squad would not be exposed to withering fire as they crossed the open area.

It was clear that the corporal squad leader and the private died right on course to their objective, raked down by the Jap machine gun, which their squad then managed to go on and destroy. Those two men gave their lives doing their job without on-the-spot orders from any superior, simply because they were self-motivated Marines and this was their mission.

By 1500 hours, approximately six hours after our first wave hits the beach, the 22d Marines occupy the entire island of Engebi, and the command declares the island "secured". Well, if it was secured for the command, possibly toasting each other somewhere aboard ship, it was not secured for us in the foxholes. So far, all we had done was take some Japanese acreage and kill some of their soldiers who had stood in our way. We knew we had not destroyed enough of their forces to consider the island "secure."

The major and I learned that the advance platoons had done their work well. They didn't need any help from Battalion. They didn't even need any help from their company headquarters. Even though it was their first day in combat, these kids knew their missions going in, and they carried them out superbly. So after a brief discussion with the company commanders on night defense strategy, the major and I headed back to the battalion CP in the shellhole near the beach.

With no shade on this bombed-out barren island, the tropical sun had been merciless, and the backs of my hands and my neck were badly sunburned. Also, I had long ago used up the last of the water in my aluminum canteen, so I couldn't wait to get back to the beach for a drink of water.

Lieutenant Bob Carey, our Bn-4 supply officer, had taken charge of our 2d Battalion beach logistics. I find him standing among scores of 5-gallon multicolored cans. Some are painted green, some blue, some red. I'm not sure which ones are water; but I know I need some water fast. "Bob," I ask him, "which are the water?"

"Over there", and he points to some cans by a jeep.

Now that I am so close to a drink of water, I am even thirstier than before, so I rush to the nearest can, unscrew its cap, and quickly fill my canteen cup with the precious, colorless liquid. Then I take in a great mouthful. With a choking gasp, I spit it out. It's white gasoline!

Marine Corps standard operating procedure in combat is for the troops to dig in for the night, usually practicing a buddy system. Since it's already late and will soon be getting dark, I ask Carey if he has a foxhole buddy. He says "no", so I tell him I'll find a spot and start digging while he posts a couple of privates on the beach to watch over our battalion supplies.

I select a foxhole position not far from the battalion shellhole CP. The place I select is at the root of the only intact coconut tree in our area. Like all the other trees, it has taken a beating from our bombardments. Still it has withstood the beating better than most of the others, which have been literally broken in half and stripped of their fronds. There are also a couple of fallen coconut logs lying next to the tree that I figure we can use for cover against a night attack or infiltrators.

I plan an "L" shaped foxhole, so that our heads will meet at the apex, with our bodies and legs going off at right angles. This will allow us to incorporate the tree trunk and the fallen logs into our shallow foxhole fortification. I immediately start digging with my tiny "Mickey Mouse" entrenching shovel. It's getting dark fast, and I don't' want to be in the dark without a foxhole, so I don't' wait for Carey to come and do his share. He apologizes when he gets there later, but he happily accepts the shallow grave I have dug for him.

As we crawl into our foxholes, a soft drizzle starts to fall, and clouds move intermittently across the face of a full moon. It's an eerie, desolate scene with the intermittent moon silhouetting the torn fronds of our lone coconut tree. It looks like a graveyard scene out of one of those Hollywood horror films.

We certainly have enough dead bodies lying around. One of them is a Japanese soldier sticking half-way out of a spider hole where he was incinerated by our flamethrowers while in the act of flinging a grenade, a grotesque scene that was later featured in the April 13, 1944 issue of Life magazine. And there are still two Japanese bodies floating at the bottom of our nearby battalion CP shellhole.

Then some relief comes in the form of star shells being fired from our supporting naval vessels, as requested by our forward platoons. Each starburst lights up our entire area, turning night into day for enough time to allow us to spot infiltrating enemy. The trouble with star shells is they are like dope – you get hooked on them. If a little light once in a while is good, a lot of light all the time would be better. But, of course, there has to be a limit, and we soon have to settle for our intermittent moon to light our area.

There's something about frightened troops in combat foxholes that brings out little white dogs and little white chickens. I certainly saw my share of them that night, running across my field of vision. I couldn't explain those visions then, and I can't now. But they were there, and many of us saw them.

Strange as that may seem, I have a far stranger experience that night. During the passing of one of the clouds across the face of the moon, I feel a gentle tropical breeze blow across my face. I look up and see that the wind is blowing gently through the three remaining palm fronts on our coconut tree, moving them slowly like the nodding head and two outstretched wings of a giant vulture. And then I hear the music. Ever so softly I hear the death song being played on a lyre, as though this mysterious winged maestro is conducting a solemn requiem for the hundreds of dead and dying on this desolate island on this fateful day.

But, of course, the night isn't over. It has just started – the longest night of our lives – our first night in combat. As Carey and

I try to rest in our shallow graves, we agree to stand alternate watches, with one of us awake while the other sleeps to avoid a sneak knife or bayonet attack by an infiltrating enemy.

I take the first watch, which I hope will remain uneventful except, of course, for those imaginary white chickens and dogs scooting across the ground a few dozen yards away. But within an hour, as the visions of the chickens have waned, a new object comes dimly into focus. It appears to be the real threat, an infiltrator crawling silently toward us on his belly, maybe ten yards away. I can't see the face. I see only the customary Japanese *Hachi-Maki* wrapped around his head. And although I see no weapons, I am sure he carries a knife and grenades, as we all do. Our orders are to avoid shooting at night except in dire self-defense. But as this creeping creature creeps closer and closer to our foxhole, it begins to look more and more like dire self-defense to me. So I want to put a bead on this crawling creep and blow him away at the first threatening move, but I find that it is physically impossible.

I dug my first foxhole in combat under this mysterious winged maestro.

*On 18 February 1944, we make our first landing against a heavily entrenched
enemy on Engebi and then repeat it within four days on Parry Island
(USMC Photo)*

As a combat greenhorn, I now find myself resting comfortably
on my back with my carbine cradled between my legs and the
muzzle aimed at my own chin. There is no way I can get into a
firing position without alerting the infiltrator, who can then finish
us off with a grenade before continuing what now looks like his
attempt to escape to the beach.

Since I can't move, I quietly wake Carey up and whisper,
"Bob, do you see anything out there."

Without hesitation, he whispers back. "It's a Jap."

"Yeah, I tell him, but I can't move. Can you get a bead on him
from behind the tree trunk next to you?" I ask.

"Yeah," he says, "but we can't shoot. We're too close to our
CP. We might draw fire on them."

"Okay," I whisper back. "Let's just keep him covered and
hope he goes away."

So we hold our fire and hold our breath while watching him
disappear toward the beach, where Bob has left several riflemen
guarding our supplies. The next day we find that Bob's men on

We eliminate sniper fire and hand grenade attacks from the broken palm tree
debris and one-man spider holes. (USMC Photo)

the beach have quietly nailed our infiltrator. And for me, I've
learned a valuable lesson. I promise myself I will never get caught
in such a vulnerable position in a foxhole again.

By the second day in combat we are gradually becoming
disillusioned veterans. First, we're winning the game and killing a
lot more Japs than they are killing Marines. But as our assault
platoons with Heavy Pfuhl, Clint Wilmsen, and Rusty Green
continue with their mopping up operations, burning and blasting
the Japs out of the caves and spider holes, reality is slowly coming
into focus. Winning isn't without a price. Our dead and wounded
are coming back on stretchers, and all those who die on our
second day on Engebi make a mockery of the Command's
contention that the battle has been won in five hours of the first
day.

By the end of Day Two, the serious Lieutenant Al Kirtz is
more somber than ever. Even though his platoon has lost only four
men killed and five wounded, the dead includes his platoon

We advanced through the shattered remains of the coconut groves that had been demolished by the Navy's big guns and dive bombers. (USMC Photo)

Three exhausted teenage survivors of our first combat mission—two days before they were ordered to do it again on the next island.
(U.S. Coast Guard Photo)

sergeant, who has caught a burst of enemy fire through the map overlay that he carried in his breast pocket. This time Lieutenant Kirtz has been the one spared to finish their mission.

Heavy, our great hulking Marine, the hard charger who has led his platoon on a blitz through the enemy on Day One, throwing grenades like football passes, by Day Two is beginning to show some respect for the hazards of battle. He is still up front and charging, but as he watches some of his best men get cut down by hidden snipers he begins to realize that even a little 25 caliber Jap bullet fired by a 5-foot solder can take out a huge football player with a red beard and hatchet just as easily as it can a skinny farm kid from Kansas. And unlike football, in war the score is a serious and final tally. So what if we're killing ten to one – when it involves your comrades, any trade-off is too great a price to pay.

In any recounting of the great battles of World War II you are not likely to find the battle of Engebi because officially our casualties do not seem great, with only 64 killed, 81 missing, and 158 wounded. But in that fierce 48-hour battle, we destroyed more than a thousand enemy troops and captured only nineteen – which says something for the determination of the enemy. Still, the agony of that battle is not told by numbers. It can only be told in terms of the human equation.

Here were the 900 raw teenage Marines in our assault infantry companies going into combat for the first time against 1200 older more experienced enemy defenders who were entrenched in an underground network of interspersed spider holes. Picture those two forces of more than 2000 desperate fighters pitted against each other in a fight to the finish on a tiny sand spit covering less than a square mile. Picture that scene and you will know that even those young Marines who weren't physical casualties this time had already suffered wounds too deep to measure.

Chapter 9

Parry, A Second Chance to Die

By Day Three, after two days of close combat and two sleepless nights, those of us who had survived the ordeal felt like we had earned a period of rest and recovery. But war makes no allowance for such feelings. We no sooner climb aboard our troop transport when we're hit with a lot of bad news.

First we hear that the Army has faltered in the battle for Eniwetok Island and so our regiment has now been assigned the Army's job of taking Parry Island, which translates into another assault landing for our combat-shocked troops within three days. So much for rest and recovery.

Next we see that, for reasons known only to the Navy, the ship's executive officer (a former merchant marine sailor with a lieutenant commander's commission in the Navy Reserve) has decided to paint much of the ship's deck while we are ashore. So now, with the still-wet paint, there's very limited space on deck for our men to flop down and rest while cleaning their weapons for the next assault. Worse yet, the exec doesn't even want us to use what space there is, and so he comes to me, the troop battalion adjutant, with his complaints and demands.

"Lieutenant," he orders, "get your men off the deck and down below. Also", he goes on, "I want you to give me forty of these men for a working party to shift cargo in the hold."

I was shocked that this civilian sailor, who for the last two days has been sitting on his fat ass in the officers' mess eating hot meals off the ship's fine china and silverware while my men are fighting for their lives on the beach, could now presume to give us, the combatants, outrageous orders. I knew I wasn't going to accept them, and I sure wasn't going to pass them on to my troops.

My response to the lieutenant commander was very direct and insubordinate. "Commander," I said, "these men have just come back from hell. They're dead-tired from two days without sleep; they're thirsty, and they're in shock from their first combat. So I'm not asking them to get up off this deck and go below to their sweltering bunks. They're just going to sit here in the fresh air while cleaning their weapons and rest up for our next landing on Parry. And for sure, I can't give you a working party from this group. Use some of the men who didn't hit the beach with us."

The lieutenant commander, with his gold oak leaves, was not used to that kind of response from a junior officer wearing single silver bars. You are insubordinate, Lieutenant," he responded seething with anger. "I order you to get these men off this deck and to provide me with that working party."

"I take my orders from my troop commander," I told him; "so if you have any orders for me, go through the proper chain of command."

I knew I could be setting myself up for a reprimand and maybe even a court martial, but I wasn't going to be this merchant sailor's instrument of idiocy. Besides, what's the worst that could happen – would they kick me out of the war?

Fortunately for me, our executive officer, Major Felker, had some brains and had just been through combat with the rest of us. Before joining the Marines, Felker had been a high school principal in Minnesota. He was about thirty years old and totally level-headed. When I was called before him, he calmly inquired: "What happened between you and the Exec?"

After I told him the whole story and the motivation for my insubordination, he simply said, "You did the right thing. Don't worry, I'll take care of it. Just make sure that the men are ready for Parry."

"Yes Sir," I replied: "that's all I wanted to do."

The war didn't pause to take up the petty business of the ship's XO's complaint against me for insubordination. And as it turned out we had only one fitful night of sleep aboard this hostile troop transport before we were all transferred to LST's, preparatory for our attack in amtracs the following day.

On February 22, 1944, our landing on Parry was Engebi all

over again, coming just three days after our withdrawal from that hellish ordeal. Still in shock from that first combat experience, we were now like a force of sleepwalkers going through the motions of launching another attack against another hostile beach. We had used up all of our emotional resources of fear, hope, and prayer on that first mission. Now there was nothing left but numbness as we proceeded in our amtracs against this new beach at the funeral pace of three knots. We were each hoping that we had a deep pocket of luck, but none of us ever knew at any time just how close we were coming to the bottom of our well.

As usual, I'm to go in with a battalion headquarters group in the third wave; again just six minutes after the first assault platoon hits the beach. This time I'm not in the colonel's amtrac, but I've been assigned to Major Copeland's boat. The major is the Bn-3, the battalion operations officer and number three in command. He's a well-built Marine with a plain face and a straight prominent nose. He's a very practical, down-to-earth, no-nonsense guy who probably saw fewer of those imaginary white dogs and chickens running around on Engebi than anyone else, and I figure that's good. I don't see him as a great tactician, but I like Copeland's common-sense approach to things.

As we move toward the beach in our numbed déjà vu state, it's the second chorus of Engebi. It's a repetition of the same chaos – the big guns firing over our heads, the planes strafing and bombing the beach, and us heading into a wall of black smoke and fire. Then something goes wrong with the naval gunfire/dive-bombing coordination, and one of the pilots blasting the beach dives into our own naval gunfire and his plane explodes in midair. For that brief moment, it looks to us like a Hollywood war. And then we hit the beach.

Copeland and I leap out of our amtrac and, together with the men in our boat, we take refuge behind an eight-foot-high sand embankment that parallels the waterline. This extensive sand berm provides cover against flat-trajectory fire from enemy rifles and machines guns, but it is useless against the high-trajectory Japanese "knee" mortars and hand grenades, so we know we can't stay here long.

As I edge my way up the sand embankment to peer over the

top to locate the source of the enemy machine gun and rifle fire that is so clearly audible – but invisible – I hear the major say: "Move in, Jones!"

It's an order I didn't want to hear, but I jump up over the berm and I move in faster than any man has ever moved in the history of the world. I run and I zig-zag like a fiend from hell, trying to outrun or outsmart the machine gun and rifle bullets whistling past my ears, then diving head-first into the nearest bomb crater I can find. Seeing me safely in the crater and noting the intense mortar fire on the beach, the major yells "Move in!" to the troops, and he duplicates my "run-for-your-life" maneuver, landing squarely on top of me in the bomb crater.

"Okay Jones," he says; "we made it. This is going to be our battalion CP. Go back to the beach and find the colonel and bring him here."

Yes Sir," I say, stalling as long as I can to give our forward platoon leaders like Heavy Pfuhl, Clint Wilmsen and Rusty Green a chance to locate those machine guns and snipers before I jump out of the hole and make that death-dash back to the beach again.

Aware that I haven't moved, the major turns to me and says, "Jones, are you still here?"

"No Sir," I answer, I'm gone." But as I pop my head up out of the shellhole, I see that the colonel and Lieutenant Laden, our Bn-2 officer, are already dashing in our direction, and they quickly fling themselves into our hole, along with a radioman and a couple of riflemen. Now we have an official battalion command post.

As soon as the colonel establishes communications with our forward companies, Easy and Fox, we learn that the going is tough. Heavy Pfuhl has managed to survive a grenade or mortar blast on the beach, taking the full force of the concussion while magically eluding the shrapnel. And he and his platoon have charged ahead, still throwing grenades and satchel charges like football passes, knocking out a covey of machine guns and squad of Imperial Japanese Marines along the way. Having inflicted maximum damage to the enemy in their sector, they reach their Easy-Company objective by 1630, although the official record puts it at 1400. Anyhow, they now rest on the line and wait for

Clint Wilmsen's and Rusty Green's platoons in F Company to catch up with them. They don't know that Wilmsen and F Company have run into heavy resistance.

Earlier in the action, while the colonel is establishing a forward CP behind the two advancing companies, Capt Goldberg of Fox Company, who had been a hard-charging Marine leader on Engebi, later featured in Life Magazine, suddenly appears at our rear CP shellhole.

Major Felker and Major Copeland are astonished to see this company commander away from his command in the middle of a battle. "What are you doing back here, Goldie?" they both ask.

"I need more men," came the reply, as he wanders around aimlessly and recklessly, taking no heed of the danger of presenting an upright target to the enemy. "Come on, Jones," the captain yells at me. "Get out of that damn shellhole."

Automatically, I jump up to follow the captain, when Felker tells me, "Stay put, Jones; he doesn't need more lieutenants, and your job is here." Then addressing the captain, Felker goes on: "Goldie, if you need more men, give us a casualty report. Tell us how many men have you lost and how many you need? Now, get back to your company, send us a report, and we'll give you whatever support we can."

The captain doesn't react to the major's words. He continues in his careless, aimless walk, but he does change direction and soon disappears back toward his company. If there was any purpose to the captain's visit, it was not his need for more men, even though his company had hit stiff resistance and was suffering casualties. He just seemed resentful of the fact that he and his troops had been put in far greater danger than those of us with less treacherous assignments. His complaint seemed to be that he had been given the wrong end of the stick, and like any good New Yorker he didn't like it.

When the colonel returned to our CP and learned of Captain Goldberg's visit, he tried unsuccessfully to reach him by field phone. Then he decided to send Lieutenant Carey and me to follow our wires to Fox company to get a full report on the captain's needs.

As we made our way under sporadic sniper fire along a dirt

pathway through the bombed-out coconut groves, we passed the usual mix of dead bodies – ten Japs to every Marine. Even with the count so outrageously in our favor, the sight of every dead Marine sent a jarring jolt through us. The shock was as great as though we had gone hunting and lost a hunter for every ten quarry bagged.

It is bad enough when the dead Marine is unknown to you, but when it is one of your best friends, one of the finest people you have ever met, and now you encounter him lying cold and dead like road-kill on a dirt pathway – the shock numbs you to your bones. There before Carey and me lay Lieutenant Clint Wilmsen.Big amiable Bob Carey fights to hold back the tears, trying not to weep for the loss of his very best friend; and I fight to hold back my tears, trying not to weep for big amiable Bob Carey.

By the time we return with our report to the colonel, both Easy and Fox Companies have achieved their objectives and the firefights are over. Some pockets of resistance have been stiff, but our platoons have done their jobs and entirely eliminated all organized resistance. At dusk, Easy Company is pulled back near the beaches, and Heavy Pfuhl proclaims that their withdrawal to this reserve area feels like a vacation in San Diego.

Well, as the night comes on, it isn't quite San Diego. In combat, eliminating all organized resistance is no life insurance policy. The enemy may be reduced in numbers, but he's still out there. And now you no longer know where he is because his frontlines have been obliterated. Now he's everywhere.

With night coming on fast, I realize I haven't had time to dig a foxhole, and we never spend the night in the large shellholes which offer poor protection against shrapnel from aerial bursts and mortar and grenade attacks. So I start digging in the sandy beach near our battalion CP. I plunge my little entrenching tool into the sand and shovel like a fiend, knowing I have only a few minutes to finish or risk getting shot in the dark by our own troops. As I dig, the loose beach sand keeps filling back in, so I dig harder and faster than it can fill back. I am a digging dervish. Finally, as I lay down in my shallow trench on the beach, our Bn-2 officer, Phil Laden, approaches me with a complaint that he didn't have time to dig his hole and begs me to share mine. I feel a moment of resentment since I have worked my butt off to create this life-saving hole, knowing that he has not bothered to dig his own hole and has not contributed to digging mine, but of course, I invite him in. Later, as I begin to shiver from fear and cold, I welcome the warm presence of his shivering body against my back.

With the morning comes the sobering reality of the battle. Now our graves registration detail begins the process of bringing our dead to the beach to be identified and disposed of in some acceptable manner. As battalion adjutant, it is my task again to help identify the bodies and to secure any personal valuables such as rings and watches. This gruesome unwelcome task is topped off by a grim assignment. The major appoints me as the officer in charge of transporting our dead Marines to a nearby island in the atoll for temporary burial. He gives me an LCD with a Navy coxswain and a couple of Marine privates. We load about eighteen bodies on stretchers aboard the LCT for each trip. The bodies are already swelling and turning black from the hot sun. Many, of course, are gashed and badly mutilated. The smell is almost unendurable. It is the pungent acrid smell of meat-eating Marines, not like the sweeter cheesy smell of the vegetarian Japs. It is a slow laborious trip in the LCT as we stand among the corpses, watching the big green flies chew on the bodies. The nearby island is perhaps a mile away, and we have to make several trips before we can close the books on Eniwetok.

We have conquered Eniwetok Atoll three months ahead of schedule at a cost of 254 Marines killed and 555 wounded; but we have destroyed many times that number of the enemy and have significantly accelerated Admiral Nimitz's. Central Pacific Campaign.

Chapter 10

Repose, Reflection, and Booze

How you feel and what you do after an experience like Eniwetok depends on who or what you are. If you are a senior commander in a fledgling Marine Corps regiment that has just achieved fighting fitness in its first victorious battle, you are eager to do battle again. And even if you are only a lowly second lieutenant but a member of that minority group of Regular Officers who intend to make the Corps their career, you may still be eager to do battle again because just one single campaign that you have survived unscathed may not be sobering enough to bring you to your senses. And of course as a Regular, you know you'll need battle stars and campaign ribbons to further your career.

But major wars are not fought by career soldiers. They are fought by ordinary people brought into the military by extraordinary circumstances. The enlisted men are usually drafted, or pressured to volunteer by threat of the draft. And most of the officers have commissions in the Reserve and are eager to revert back to civilian status as soon as circumstances permit. And so it was after our first ordeal at Eniwetok that we each responded according to our individual natures.

After Eniwetok, as our regiment was enroute to the northern islands of Roi and Namur on Kwajalein Atoll, the junior officers had a chance to trade their combat experiences with each other, which led to trading some of our hopes and fears as well.

We tried to recall the funny or bizarre incidents, which even in the gravest circumstances seem to crop up. There were jokes about Heavy Pfuhl's blast on the beach. It was decided that he was too damn big to be taken out by a crummy little Japanese "knee" mortar. If they wanted to get him, they would have to bring out their big artillery.

And I told how the New York goldbrick, Phil Laden, was too damn lazy to dig his own foxhole and had jumped into mine. Then he told how he had watched me dig the biggest, deepest foxhole in soft sand in the history of warfare, and how he didn't want to see all that hard work wasted just to protect one Marine.

So first there are the usual diversionary jokes and funny stories, but gradually we face the reality of the campaign as we recount the individual tragedies of each of our dead and badly wounded, one case at a time.

As the mood turned serious, Heavy Pfuhl was quick to speak up: "Look, guys, I lost five good men," he said, "and I had eleven more wounded, and some were pure gold Marines like Corporal Tony Damato. You got to score him with a winning Rose Bowl block, the way he put his fine body between a Japanese grenade and his buddies in that foxhole. He's KIA on the record, but he lives forever in my book."

"No argument, Tiny," Phil Laden said; "but you also reported one of your guys from New York as MIA. Did he ever show up?"

"No, and we looked everywhere for him. I sent patrols through our area, but there was no sign of him. He could still be wandering around dazed. I hope he found his way into the First Battalion. Anyhow, he's a damn good Marine wherever he is."

An alternative possibility occurred to me, so I said: "Heavy, you know I had to identify the dead and transport them to that little island south of us for temporary burial. I have to tell you we couldn't identify all the bodies. Some were too badly blasted with their tags blown away. Maybe your guy is lucky and will find his way back to New York some day, or maybe he's just one of those that I put at rest back there with a lot of his good buddies. Anyway, if that's it, he doesn't have to worry about hitting any more beaches."

I could see that big amiable Bob Carey was choking up now that the conversation had turned serious. No one mentioned the death of his best friend, Clint Wilmsen. I knew that Carey couldn't' bring himself to talk about it, but I also sensed that he felt it should be talked about. That's when Rusty Green spoke up. He and Clint were both in F Company.

"Well you guys know we lost Clint Wilmsen on Parry. His platoon was on the left flank of mine when he ran into machine gun and sniper fire coming from some thick tangled underbrush. His platoon was in an open area, totally pinned down. They couldn't move without taking casualties. Clint yelled for a corpsman, and the corpsman got hit. Then he tried to help the corpsman, and he got hit. Finally, his first squad worked around the enemy's right flank, and my first squad worked around the enemy's left flank. We won the firefight, but we lost Clint and about a dozen other good Marines."

"Clint was the best friend I ever had," Carey said, swallowing a sob. That brought this bull session to an end; no one was in the mood for more talk about hitting beaches. And yet our very next beach came as a pleasant surprise for most of us.

The pleasant surprise was our return to the islands of Roi and Namur on the northern tip of Kwajalein Atoll for brief garrison duty and a little rest and recreation before our next combat mission. Within the few weeks since the 23rd and 24th Marines had captured these two islands from the Japanese, the Navy CB's had cleared tons of debris and leveled a reasonable site for us to pitch a campsite of comfortable pyramidal tents on Namur. That allowed most of us time to kick back and enjoy the white sand beaches and swim in the shallows of the coral reefs with the brilliantly colored tropical fish. It seemed like a paid vacation in the Caribbean.It seemed like a good time to lighten up the war and laugh at ourselves. It would have been a good time for a USO visit. But our islands were not Australia, New Zealand, or any other civilized location where world-famous celebrities like Bob Hope or Betty Grable would be allowed to visit. Certainly, we in the 22d Marines were never based anywhere that could qualify as a reasonable setting for such high-powered entertainment. Consequently, we had to provide our own.

One very creative production stands out in my memory. It was a typical "Mickey Rooney" kind of production. You know – "Come on, guys: we've got the talent, we've got the time,' we've the place. Why don't we put on a show?" Anyhow, here we were back from our first very traumatic combat operation when some clever young enlisted men sketched out a full "Off Broadway" production starring someone called "Hook Orum." So one night instead of the usual outdoor movie, the battalion was treated to a gallows-humor stage review.

The bizarre plot line centered on our Graves Registration Section – those Marines assigned the dismal task of recovering from the battlefield the dead bodies of their fallen buddies. The production featured very little dialogue. It was mostly just the pantomime of the players reenacting their field procedures – putting on their face masks and rubber gloves; picking up their body hooks and body bags; smelling out the location of the bodies ripened from the equatorial heat; and then desperately holding their breaths while they hooked the smelly remains and stuffed them into plastic body bags.

Not very humorous now, but our circumstances were so desperate and our future so bleak at that time, this sick production was our version of a Broadway musical comedy so hilarious that our stomachs ached from laughter. It wasn't a Bob Hope/Betty Grable review, but it was the best we could do under the circumstances. We were, of course, just laughing at ourselves and spitting into the face of death.

For some of us the relief was short-lived. Major Felker, our battalion executive officer, was now ordered to put together a small expeditionary force of about 300 Marines. This force, complete with amphibious tractors and supporting arms, was then embarked upon LSTs and put to sea with an escort of a couple of small warships. Their mission was to raise the American flag on more than twenty-five atolls in the Marshall Islands, including Bikini, Rongelap, and Uterik. The uncertainty of each landing with the very real possibility of a serious encounter every time was harder on the troops than the few small firefights they actually did encounter. But all in all, on Eniwetok and the lesser atolls, the 22d Marines ended up killing about 2564 Japanese of a total garrison estimated at 13,000 men scattered across the Marshall Islands, leaving the rest to thirst and starve on these tiny isolated dots in the Pacific.

While Major Felker's small expeditionary force is busy securing Bikini, Rongelap, and the lesser islands, some changes are taking place back on Roi and Namur. It is announced that our regiment is no longer an orphan. It is now part of the 1st Provisional Marine Brigade, together with contingents from the four Raider battalions that have been transmuted into a full infantry regiment, the 4th Marines.

The new brigade is headed by Brigadier General Thomas Watson, with our regimental commander, Colonel John Walker, now moving up as Watson's chief of staff. On the regimental level, the 4th Marines get Colonel Alan Shapley, a good heroic officer but who seems to us in the 22d Marines as a stick-up-the-ass Annapolis graduate. We, in the Twenty-Second Marines, get Colonel Merlin T. Schneider, a rough-looking redhead, also out of Annapolis but of an earlier vintage and one who fits in well with the more casual culture of our *fifi lemu* regiment from Samoa.

When Heavy gets the news of the new organizational structure, he takes the news as he is beginning to take all news, both good and bad. He says: "I'll drink to that." And somehow he always manages to have a bottle of the hard stuff on hand for just such occasions, or for no occasion at all. And whatever his small failings may be in the procurement or consumption of booze those failings are well compensated for by the talents of his drinking buddy Lieutenant Don Miller.

Don Miller is as big as Heavy but not as heavy as Heavy. He's a big farm boy from midstate Illinois, and he's our 81mm mortar platoon leader. As the 81mm mortar platoon leader, Don is part of Headquarters Company and when in bivouac hangs out at Battalion. It leaves him a lot of free time and puts him in an advantageous position to talk and trade gifts with visitors from other outfits, including swabbies and flyboys. Whatever it takes, Don always has booze and cigars, so he's one of Heavy's favorites.

But sipping whiskey is not yet an all-day occupation, so Heavy, Don and a few other former college jocks put together a couple of touch football teams and play beach football. Meanwhile, as one of the loners, I take to the ocean.

While in Samoa, I had sent home for a swimming face mask, but Samoa was a volcanic island so there were no beautiful coral reefs to explore. Now here I was in the Marshalls – amongst the greatest collection of colorful coral islands in the world. So while

Heavy, Don and their gang are busy with beach football and booze, I slip into the water carefully, wearing sneakers to protect my feet against deadly coral cuts. Then putting my mask on and leveling out to cruise the surface, I review an incredible underwater show. Here in this vast garden of multi-colored coral formations swim dozens of varieties of tiny, brilliant-colored, odd-shaped fish. As they dart about, in and out of the coral formations, I submerge and follow one group after another for as long as I can hold my breath. I discover a whole new world , a world of peace and quiet that leaves the war far behind. This silent new world will be my salvation between battles during the next two years.

Chapter 11

Tofa Micronesia – Talofa Melanesia

The Twenty-Second Marines had acquitted itself well in its first combat operation in the micro-island country of the atolls. Now, as a blood-tested regiment, it was time to prepare for some big-island objectives. So after a month of garrison duty on Namur in Kwajalein Atoll, the Twenty-Second was embarked on the USS Aconagua and shipped to Guadalcanal on April Fools Day, 1944.

At this time, Guadalcanal was out of enemy contention, but it was an excellent jungle island to be used as a training and staging base for future campaigns. It could supply all the miserable training conditions that the Marine Corps values so highly. Located at ten degrees below the equator, the Canal could provide the Corps with steaming-hot humid weather, thick impenetrable jungles, and water hazards in the form of crocodile-infested rivers. It was any Paris Island Drill Instructor's dreamland. It also seemed to satisfy both the Navy and Marine Corps commands as a staging area – a bi-Service meeting of the minds that had been seriously lacking during the battle for Guadalcanal.

We soon found ourselves in a very neat orderly tent city that was situated in the shade of a commercial grove of coconut trees. The trees had been planted for their copra before the war by our British landlords, and it was rumored that for every tree that the Marines had destroyed in winning the island back from the Japanese, the U.S. paid Britain a reparation of thirty-five dollars per tree.

Anyhow, this shady grove, set just a few yards back from the ocean, made our camp as hospitable as possible on this equatorial island with its mosquito-infested swamps and suffocating jungles of eight-foot tall bamboo and elephant grass. We soon discovered, however, that we had traded our *mumu* mosquitoes of Samoa for the deadlier malaria mosquitoes of Guadalcanal. We also discovered that we had traded our Polynesian and Micronesian natives for what seemed like a more primitive Melanesian group.

Melanesian means black, so as the name indicates, the Solomon Islanders are much blacker than the previous islanders we had encountered. They are essentially of the same ethnic stock as the Fiji Islanders; but in 1944, the Solomon Islanders were closer to their native origins and culture than were the Fiji Islanders. It was our uneducated belief at that time that the Solomon Islanders had recently been headhunters and cannibals – and for all we knew they still were. So we were somewhat concerned one Sunday afternoon, as three or four of us sat in our tent drinking warm cans of beer when the back flap of our tent was lifted up and two natives squeezed under it. They were barefooted and bear-chested, dressed only in old worn denim shorts, and they had adorned themselves with necklaces and pierced nose ornaments. One appeared to be a chief, and the other his flunky. They spoke to us in the Pidgin English of the South Pacific.

Spotting a box of 12 gauge shotgun shells on a portable map table, the chief picked it up and said "Me buy."

Of course, there was no way we could allow any of our ammunition to get into the hands of the natives, but we didn't want to agitate this chief. We wanted to keep him friendly. So, pointing to the box that the chief still held in his hand, I said: "Chief, no good without gun. You need gun." I knew, of course, that we had no shotgun in the tent.

The chief grabbed the box tighter and replied: "Me got gun."

Well, there blew my argument. That's when Heavy stood up and, towering over the lean muscular chief, he reached over and fingered an amulet that hung from the chief's neck, and said: "We trade." He pointed to the box and then to the amulet.

Immediately, the chief shrunk back as though confronted by a ghost, and handing the box back to Heavy, he shook his head and said: "No trade." Then after of moment of reflection he said:

"Where priest?"

It so happened that our battalion chaplain, a Navy lieutenant, was quartered in the next tent. He was a fiery young Frenchman who spoke American English with a French accent. He also was subject to the same human qualities as the rest of us – that included anger and humor. So, seeing an opportunity to get rid of the natives and pull a practical joke, Heavy eagerly pointed out the chaplain's tent to the two savages. Then we all followed them outside our tent and watched the chief and his flunky disappear into the chaplain's tent. We wondered what the natives wanted with a chaplain and what the chaplain would do with the natives.

In a moment the two natives came back out of the chaplain's tent, each adding a Catholic rosary to the strings of shark's teeth that hung around their necks. They were immediately followed by Father Bordenet, who seeing us standing there and laughing, let out a stream of French epithets and concluded in English: "Who the hell sent those guys to me?"

Well, it didn't take long for the Father to get even with us. He said for penance , we could help him build a chapel. He could get the materials from Headquarters, and it was up to us to get some experienced volunteer troops to do the work. In due time the chapel got built, but first we had a lot of tough training facing us before our next operation.

It had taken me 14 months to get promoted from second lieutenant to first lieutenant because (just like that popular song "There'll be no promotion this side of the ocean…") promotions never did seem to catch up with the guys who were actually fighting the war. However, by 15 March 44, while we were doing garrison duty on Namur I had been promoted to first lieutenant, and I had been assigned as a platoon leader and executive officer of Easy Company, which remained my assignment on Guadalcanal until June.

So on Guadalcanal during the months of April and May, as a platoon leader and the executive officer of Easy Company, I trained with Heavy Pfuhl in the same company. During those jungle exercises, Heavy was always a hard charging Gung Ho Marine. And now with his combat experience, he was a special inspiration to the new replacements coming aboard. But during free time, he knew how to relax and take the war in stride.

As a natural leader Heavy continued to organize the other former jocks in the battalion, playing team sports like touch football, baseball, and volleyball. But when he was not on maneuvers or playing games on the beach, he also continued to be good at locating booze and places to consume it in congenial company. On the other hand, I continued to be a loner spending my free time in the sea. And here on the Canal the underwater gardens were even more beautiful and more plentifully populated with exotic colorful fish than the waters of the Marshall Atolls.

The green water of the coral shelf extended only a few dozen yards out into the sea, and where it ended the water suddenly became cobalt blue and was thousands of feet deep, so of course there was usually no visible life beyond the shelf. However, one day while exploring the edge of the shelf, I was taken by surprise by a pod of porpoise that came swimming by me. They seemed to be very friendly and projected no threat as they passed me on both sides, but it made me wonder what would have happend if it had been a group of sharks. After that, I always swam underwater and kept my eyes open for intruders from all directions. The water was so clear that with my facemask I could see almost as well through the water as through the air.

I became so proficient at holding my breath and swimming underwater I learned to travel more than 50 yards underwater at a stretch, holding my breath for almost two minutes at a time. On one occasion, while trying to set my own private underwater swimming record, when I came to the surface, I noticed something floating about 50 yards away from me at the edge of the coral shelf. The object – which I assumed to be a log – was about ten to twelve feet long. Then I saw it move. As I started to go closer to investigate, I suddenly recognized that it was a very large crocodile. I beat a hasty retreat to the beach. Of course, we all knew that there were crocodiles in the rivers, but I didn't expect to see any in the ocean. I assume that this one had unintentionally drifted with the fresh water effluent from a nearby river into the sea by our beach area.

We were soon to learn that river crocodiles were not the only natural oddity on this island. We awoke one morning at dawn to discover that the entire ground around us seemed to be alive, moving inexorably into the sea. We slowly realized that the beach was a solid claw-to-claw carpet of thousands of slow-moving crabs. We were later told that we had experienced an annual migration of land crabs back to the sea, something like the lemmings of northern Europe. At any rate, they were there by the thousands, dying by the thousands, and contaminating our entire tent camp. It is not possible to describe the suffocating stench of those thousands of decaying critters. We rapidly organized a clean-up crew to load the mini-carcuses onto trucks and carried out of the area to a far distant dump. Despite such distractions of nature and my valiant efforts to spend all my spare time underwater forgetting the war – the war went on, and preparations for our next campaign soon intensified.

I remember the day that our entire regiment was called out in parade formation to be introduced to our new commanding general. Our new commander was Brigadier General Lemuel C. Shepherd, and his task was to join two veteran reinforced regiments, the 22d Marines, and the 4th Marines into the First Provisional Marine Brigade. We, of course, had just seized Eniwetok Atoll, and the 4th had recently returned from its occupation of Emirau.

I clearly remember the general standing before us in field uniform and paying us great compliments for the way the 22d Marines had taken Eniwetok Atoll in record time well ahead of schedule, and then acknowledging our regiment's twenty-six amphibious landings on the lesser Marshall Islands.

But I also remember squirming when he began to praise us too much. I remember him saying: "Men, most of you are very young; many of you are teenagers. But when I look into your faces, I don't see the faces of boys – I see the faces of veterans."

As the general made his remarks, I looked into the faces of the troops that he was addressing, into the faces of our Twenty-Second Marines. I knew that the general had come to us with some recent – and significant – combat credentials, and he had every right to speak to us as one combat Marine to another. But I wasn't sure that he really knew all that these teenage "veterans" had been through. Of course, he knew about Eniwetok.

Did he also know about their fifty buddies they had seen blown apart on Maui prior to combat through our own command failure? Did he know about the more than 400 Marines who had been so badly stricken with *mumu* on Samoa that they had been sent home as casualties? Did he know that many of us had already been overseas almost two years with no leave or taste of civilization? Did he know about the many men who had committed suicide because they saw no leave in sight or any Marine Corps rotation plan such as the other services had in place? Did he recognize that without any hope for life beyond the war, without a light at the end of the tunnel, individuals would look for their own ways out of that tunnel – often with results disastrous to themselves and others?

It didn't seem to me that the general was aware of all of this. I was convinced that he was a good man and a good Regular Marine Officer. But there's a great divide between a Regular Marine Officer and the rest of the Marine Corps, which during a war is made up of reserve officers and civilian enlisted troops. A Regular Marine Officer like the general is expected to be eager for victory in battle and the opportunity for winning honors, obtaining promotions, and furthering his chosen career.

That kind of motivation seldom applies to the reserves and the civilian enlisted. That does not mean that in battle any Marine is any less a Marine than any other, reserve or regular. My experience is that in the heat of battle all Marines do their job, and only a fool would be thinking of medals and promotions. But strictly as a morale factor, I was concerned that the general was miscalculating the mood and morale of our regiment. So everything that I have set forth here, I set forth at that time in an unsigned letter to the general, which I managed to get delivered to him outside of the chain-of-command.

I didn't like the idea of an anonymous letter, but I felt that the content and my advocacy for a rotation plan was more important than the format and protocol at that time. At any rate, I have every reason to believe that the letter served its purpose.

Shortly after the general received the letter, he made a trip to Nimitz's Headquarters in Hawaii, quickly followed by a visit with the Commandant. And within three months, the Marine Corps announced a new rotation policy similar to that of the other services, and it wasn't long before some 30-day leaves to the States were authorized. I don't think the general made those trips for the sole purpose of lobbying for a leave and rotation plan. But I believed then and I believe now that the general was the kind of man who, if he agreed with the premise of my letter, would have had the compassion and guts to make my argument on behalf of his fighting Marines.

Training in the Samoan jungles had been rugged, but training on Guadalcanal can be best judged by what happened to us on one memorable large-scale maneuver. The details of that maneuver have long since been lost to me and probably to everyone else who participated that day, but the impact of the exercise remains.

I think the maneuver was called by our newly organized 1st Provisional Brigade Headquarters to give us an opportunity to train as a brigade, or at least as full-scale regiment, rather than as individual battalions. Usually such large-scale operations are of more help to the senior command than they are to the assault battalions, but we knew that the colonels and the generals had to learn their jobs too and that our future engagements would require much larger forces than what we had employed in the atolls.

So it was on a hot muggy day (as every day on the Canal is hot and muggy) that we launched our biggest training exercise. Beach temperatures were probably in the 90s with 90% humidity, but the maneuver was not going to take place on the beach. The challenge for our regiment was to maneuver our three battalions through a jungle of elephant grass eight to ten feet tall as though we were operating on clear open fields. Of course, everything went wrong.

In eight-foot-high bamboo that rose two feet over our heads, there was no visual communications between units, field phone wires got tangled and snagged, and radios proved ineffective. Entire units got lost. Then as temperatures in the elephant grass were recorded as high as 135°F., four hundred of our men passed out, succumbing to heat exhaustion and suffocation, and had to be physically dragged out of the jungle grass to sick bay. When we realized what a disaster had struck us without any help from an enemy, I think we fully appreciated for the first time what our comrades in the 1st Marine Division had faced in their six-month-long battle to take the Canal from the Japanese in 1942 and 1943. Here during our maneuver, more than a year later, we were still finding remnants of that old battle – an occasional skull, a helmet here and a bayonet there – remnants from both sides.

After that one large disastrous jungle caper, we restricted future training to smaller unit sizes again, mostly company and platoon level operations. And for our kind of combat, that's where most of the action is, on a company and platoon level, with battalion and regiment supplying supporting arms and logistics. Because in most Marine operations, the generals must do all their work before the battle starts. If the operation has been planned properly, based upon valid intelligence, there should be little for the generals to do once ashore, other than direct the use of reserves, supporting arms, and the flow of logistics. That does not hold true for the Army when engaged in their usual long drawn-out campaigns that often involve deeper penetration into hostile territory and longer engagements than typical Marine amphibious operations.

So all through the month of May 1944, we in the rifle companies trained our platoons very hard, concentrating on tank/infantry tactics and small unit exercises. With our newly developed fireteam concept, the Browning Automatic Rifle (the BAR) became the core weapon of our four-man fireteams. Like the M1 rifle, it was a gas-operated 30-caliber weapon, but unlike the M1, it was fully automatic and capable of firing 300 to 500 rounds per minute. It was also heavier than the M1, so the wise platoon leaders usually assigned it to their biggest strongest Marines.

As a platoon leader and the executive office of E Company, I was busy most of each day with hard training exercises or company business, as was my good friend Heavy, the E Company platoon leader who had played the starring role in our Engebi and Parry operations. But on Sundays and other lazy days when no exercises were scheduled, we each continued to pursue our own ideas of recreational activity. In Samoa, my favorite activity was to take lonely hikes over the native trails that traversed the volcanic ridge running the length of the island. The view from the top of those green-covered volcanic ridges was spectacular;

looking out upon a multitude of different floral patterns that led down to the beaches of the beautiful blue Pacific.

Here on Guadalcanal there was no recreational incentive to penetrate the hostile jungle, no nearby hills to climb for a view, no reason to stray very far from our camp unless it was to visit another unit's camp. But the view from underwater was still so magnificent and the scene so peaceful that it was not only my escape from the war – it was my chapel and my open line to God.

Chapter 12

Two Months on the High Seas

W e knew that something big was coming up for us when they added the latest hand-to-hand combat training film to our usual evening schedule of "B" movies from Hollywood. Although it was an official military training film, it had been produced in Hollywood by professional filmmakers who had donned uniforms for the duration. Therefore, it was complete with all the hyperbolic Hollywood effects, and it scared hell out of us.

It was thirty minutes of non-stop bayoneting and throat-cutting. It was a furious battle with the outcome uncertain until the good guys finally overwhelmed the enemy by sheer determination and force of will. After it was over, Major Felker commented to several of us junior officers: "Our next one could be just like that."

"Would that be in the Marianas, Major?" Heavy asked.

"You know that that's classified" until we're aboard ship, Heavy," the major replied.

"And when will that be?" Heavy persisted.

"I'm sure you know that we've already started combat loading the APAs," he answered.

"Of course I know, Major," Heavy replied, "but I don't want to believe it."

Having finished off our training with amphibious exercises at the end of May, on June 4, 1944 we loaded our troops aboard the USS Leedstown for an unknown destination. As it turned out, we spent most of the next two months at sea on a circuitous route throughout the Marianas and Marshall Islands.

Although we didn't know where we were going, we knew it was going to be a big one. We could see that we were in the middle of a major armada. What we didn't know at the time is that we were part of a U.S. Joint Expeditionary Force comparable in size to the North Africa Landing with our 535 ships and 127,571 troops. The force was under the command of the two most experienced amphibious warfare experts – Vice Admiral Turner, USN, and Lt.General Holland M. Smith, USMC. Our targets were the three major islands in the Marianas – Saipan, Tinian, and Guam – from which our B-29 bombers could easily reach Tokyo itself.

The plan was for the 2d and 4th Marine Divisions to hit Saipan and Tinian June 15, and then the First Provisional Brigade and the 3rd Marine Division would strike Guam three days later. Two Army divisions, the 27th and the 77th were to be held in Force Reserve. Although the Marines respected the 77th Army Division, they had no respect for the 27th Army Division after its poor performance on Makin and Eniwetok, which may be a reflection on the command but is no reflection on the many brave individuals who served in that division. At any rate, the Guam landing was postponed due to the unexpected fierce resistance on Saipan from General Saito and his 32,000 men as well as the approach of the Japanese Fleet. With those complications, our First Provisional Marine Brigade was ordered to remain afloat as a mobile reserve for the Saipan operation.

During our many weeks afloat we stopped off briefly at Eniwetok for logistical replenishment, and we in the assault battalions were transferred from the APAs to LSTs, so many of our weeks afloat were in those giant shoe boxes. The LST officers' quarters were pleasant enough, as we were bunked with our Navy counterparts three to a cabin. But our troops were bivouacked on deck using their personal gear, shelter halves, and ponchos to create a topside campsite as best they could. That included their laundry, washed out in salt water and strung across the deck to dry. Aside from the poor troop housing accommodations aboard LSTs, their defense against attack was even worse. There were a couple of 20mm anti-aircraft guns, but of course, there was no defensive armor anywhere. Had the ship been made of cardboard it would have offered about as much protection against enemy strafing as the actual lightweight metal structure and skin provided. Whether you were on deck or below, if a 50-caliber bullet was coming in your direction there was nothing to deter it from its target. In convoy, it was planned that our carrier planes and the destroyer escorts and other picket ships that accompanied the troop transports and the LSTs, would intercept or shoot down any enemy marauders before they could reach us in the soft inner belly of our amphibious force.

So we took alarm when we heard that the battle ashore was going poorly for our forces and the Japanese Fleet was quickly approaching our Fleet west of the Marianas. Fortunately, we didn't realize then that something later to be called "the Great Marianas Turkey Shoot" was happening. In two days, we shot down 476 planes, at a loss of 50 of our own. Our submarines sank two large Japanese carriers, and our U.S. carrier pilots destroyed a third of their planes, leaving the Japanese only 35 planes operational. Of course, it only takes one operational enemy plane to kill you, and that's what we were worried about when we looked up from the deck of our LST and saw that we were coming under direct enemy aerial attack.

"Heavy, do you see what I see?" I asked Pfuhl, pointing to the horizon.

"You bet your ass! It looks to me like a half-dozen torpedo-fighters heading this way," he answers; "but they'll never make it," he adds. "Our escorts will get them."

Now we're both looking around for a place to hide, but we know there isn't any safe place. Right now we'd give up Navy comfort for a Marine grunt foxhole. None in sight. Our escorts knock out four Japs, but two keep coming, one on a direct beeline toward our ship. Enroute, it strafes one of our escort ships a few thousand yards out on our line and still it comes. I rush to the deck house and kneel down behind a solid-steel 6-inch stanchion reducing my vulnerability by that 6 inches and hoping that that's where the bullets will hit. But fate is more generous than I had hoped – some skinny sailor on our 20mm gun has brought down the bogey with no harm to our LST. We later learn that there was one casualty from the strafing on the escort ship, but we've been saved.

Then, as I stand up again, I realize that two of our guys are sitting in the deckhouse playing cards, seemingly unaware of the excitement. Here's Major Felker and Captain Lanigan in an innocent game of Acey/Deucy. With no place to go and no place to hide, they had decided they might as well just go on with their game. So that's what they did.

By July 9th, the bloody battle for Saipan was over, with 3426 Americans dead and 13,099 wounded. Enemy dead was estimated at more than 32,800, and the Japanese General Saito had committed *hara-kiri* and Admiral Nagumo had shot himself in the head. Now only Tinian and Guam remained to complete the Marianas campaign.

The one-month delay in the invasion of Guam was used to pound Guam with weeks of intense naval and air bombardment not previously equaled in the war. The underwater demolition teams (UDTs) who swam in to clear the approaches to the invasion beaches destroyed 900 log cribs and wire cages filled with coral. They also left a sign on the beach that said: "Welcome Marines!" But as always we knew that many enemy installations would escape destruction, and we expected that most of the 18,500 Japanese soldier and sailors would be waiting on their guns behind that facetious welcome sign.

As eager as we were to put an end to our many weeks at sea and recapture the U.S. territory where our 150 Marine comrades had been overrun by 5000 Japanese troops at the start of the war, we could not match the fervent desire for revenge that was burning in the souls of the Chamorro natives of Guam who had been impatiently awaiting our return for almost three years.

Although there were a lot of nasty rumors, we didn't know then in the week before our invasion of July 21, 1944 what was actually taking place on the island of Guam. It was only later that we learned how the desperate Japanese command, knowing that Saipan had fallen and that their fleet had suffered great losses, began to take out their revenge on the helpless Chamorro natives who they knew were praying for the return of the Americans.

On July 12, during our intensified bombardment of their defenses and just nine days before our invasion, the Japanese military inflicted a series of executions and massacres on the Chamorros. They accused Father Jesus Duenas, a Chamorro priest, his nephew and two other Chamorro men of being American spies, and then they tortured and brutally beat them beyond recognition. Following the torture, they were beheaded by a Japanese officer swinging his treasured Samurai sword. Then as our daily bombardment turned into a preinvasion barrage, their executions turned into four successive massacres committed against the native population on July 15, 16, 19 and July 20.

Through we had no full knowledge of these events or any verification of the many rumored atrocities at that time, we all sensed that in this campaign to recapture our barracks, our U.S. territory, and to liberate an innocent Chamorro population, there were powerful moral imperatives driving us.

Now with the continuous bombardment of Guam reaching full intensity, we knew our time was running out. We couldn't sail around in reserve forever. We knew we would have to make that landing pretty soon, and we began to talk about it, but it was all guess work until about a week before the invasion. Then we went into a final review of our maps and battle plans. That's when the officers in the assault companies and attack platoons implanted every detail of their mission into the heads of every Marine.

First, they spelled out the big picture to the troops. They told them that our III Amphibious Corps was commanded by Major General Roy S. Geiger and that it included the Third Marine Division and the First Provisional Marine Brigade, consisting of our 22d Marines and the 4th Marines, backed up by the 305th Regimental Combat Team from the 77th Army Division.

Then they explained the battle plan. The Third Marine Division would land on the northwest coast of Guam near Asan, establish a beachhead, and then seize Mount Tenjo. Meanwhile, our First Provisional Brigade would land on the mountainous southwest coast of the island between Agat and Bangi Point, secure a beachhead, and then execute a very difficult military maneuver of a giant two-battalion left turn to the north to close the mouth of Orote Peninsula and cut off a sizable force of Japanese troops defending Orote Airfield, the town of Sumay, and our old Marine barracks.

Enough for the big picture. What the troops really care about is their own tiny microcosmic part in the invasion. What part does our company, platoon, and squad play in all of this? That's when the platoon leaders like Heavy lay it out for the boys again. That's when they all have to come up with their third pregame pep talk. It worked twice on Eniwetok, and it will work again on Guam, but with an ever-diminishing effect.

Finally, on D-Day minus one, Heavy's talking to his guys:

"We land on Yellow Beach 2, south of Orote Peninsula near the town of Agat. Our First Battalion will be on our left, and the Fourth Marines will be on our right. Our third Battalion is in reserve. We'll head for Harmon Road by fire and movement. Gunter's platoon will be on our left. Bachelot, tie in with him. Roy you take the right flank. Billy, get in behind Roy. Crisp and Easy Three will be behind us. Any questions?"

"Heavy, do you think it will be lot worse than the last one?" a squad leader asks.

"Well, we're a hell of a lot closer to Tokyo than before. What do you think?"

"That's what I think."

Heavy continues: We're not going to win this one without taking some hits, but we beat their ass on Eniwetok, and we'll do it again here. And the sooner we do it, the sooner we get the hell out of here and back home. Anyone want to argue with that game plan?"

"If we make it, Heavy, are you giving us guaranteed leave?"

"Hell, if I was the general, you'd already have your leave. You've been over here in the jungle for almost two years and you've already made two landings. In my book that would send you home. But they're not using my book, and we've got this big game coming up, so concentrate on what's important. Scuttlebut is that the Japs have been mean landlords and are cutting people's heads off on that island. So now we're going to recover the premises. Let's go get our Marine barracks back!"

Chapter 13

Guam, Our Third Beachhead

The 22d Marines had made two major amphibious assaults against heavily defended beaches on Eniwetok. If we never did another one that would have been enough for us – but of course not enough for a nation at war. So we went through the motions again, preparing once more to throw our bodies against the evil enemy defending a hostile shore.

All during our strenuous field training exercises on Guadalcanal, from March 15 until June 1, I had served with Heavy Pfuhl in E Company as an infantry platoon leader; and, as the senior first lieutenant, I was also the company executive officer. However, on June 1st, three days before we set sail for Guam, the battalion commander called me to headquarters to tell me that he was transferring me to a position on his staff at Battalion.

Lieutenant Colonel Donn C. Hart, our battalion commander, was a handsome intelligent gentleman, well schooled in military operations, but not well suited to leadership in the field. I soon learned the he was a micromanager, unwilling to leave anything to chance, which in the field translates into reluctance to take risks.

"What is my job, Sir?" I asked the colonel when I reported to him.

"Jones," he replied, "Major Felker and I need an experienced first lieutenant like you up here at Battalion more than they need you down at the company level. As a battalion liaison officer your primary job will be to assist Major Felker with his XO duties. Once we're on the beach, where he goes, you go."

"Yes Sir," I responded, but then on D-Day I somehow ended up hitting the beach in the third wave in the colonel's LVT rather than the major's. I think that the colonel had been scheduled to go in a later, safer, wave and had traded with the major so that he could take command on the beach as soon as possible. So he and I were now in what should have been the major's boat.

The scene is familiar: three discernible waves of a hundred LVTs stretching to our left and right, all trekking in abreast toward the hostile shore at 3 or 4 knots. We're coming to claim one more beach in hell, a beach ablaze with fire and with a heavy curtain of smoke hiding much of our landing area.

The dive-bombers from our three carrier escorts have already

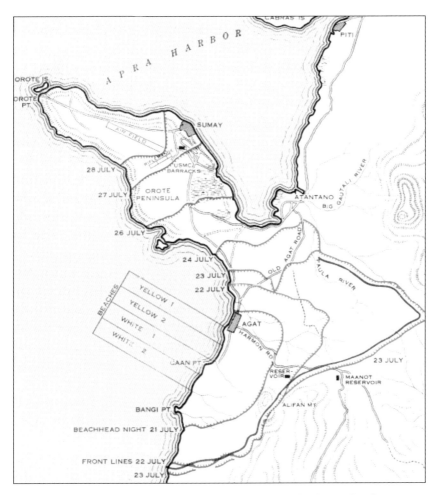

Second Battalion, 22d Marines, lands on Yellow 2 under heavy fire from Gaan Point. Wounded Sgt. George Weber knocks out enemy positions; author writes him up for Navy Cross. (Map from 6th Division History)

done their job. Now over our heads we hear the constant rustling of the large naval projectiles coming from our fleet of six battleships and six cruisers. They are supporting us with the war's most prolonged naval bombardment to date.

But we know what we're going into because our UDT guys have already been there. Their report, along with our aerial reconnaissance, tells us to expect a well-organized beach defense, with concrete pillboxes built into the coral cliffs, an elaborate trench system along the water's edge, machine gun emplacements, tank traps, several 75mm guns in concrete blockhouses, and beaches that are pocked with mines and studded with booby-traps.

As we slowly eat up the distance to the beach, we begin to see trouble ahead. The two waves directly in front of us are not only receiving the expected enemy small arms and machine gun fire, but they're also being targeted by a heavy duty coastal gun whose water hits are splashing all around them. Then I see the first solid hit on a boat in the first wave. The boat is crippled and the wounded men are struggling in the water. Next I see a boat in wave number two cross the critical line that is targeted by the enemy coastal gun. Boat number two is slammed out of action. We're in boat number three. It's obvious – we're next. I say a quick prayer and hold my breath waiting for the slam. It doesn't come. God's listening – we reach Yellow 2 beach.

When we hit Yellow 2, it is still being raked by crossfire from Gaan Point and Yona Island, which has already knocked out 24 amtracs and killed seventy-five Marines in the first two waves. An aid-station party is hit by a 75mm field gun on Yona, the wounded are attending the wounded while waiting for additional medical personnel to come ashore.

Now as we rush across the beach looking for a place to gather our battalion CP group, I see one of our company commanders, who has landed in the second wave, sitting on the ground giving orders to his troops. Then, seeing blood coming through his pant leg, I realize he's taken a bullet in the calf. I recognize the captain as Owen T. Stebbins, CO of G Company. I also recall that he is a devout Christian Scientist. "Stebbie," I say, "you've been wounded; you need to see a corpsman."

Amtracs carry assault waves to the beach south of Agat. (USMC Photo)

Tank covers Marines wading ashore past crashed Jap plane after their boat is hit. (USMC Photo)

"No, I'm okay," he replies, refusing to accept the reality of the flesh, "I can work from here on the beach."

"Stebbie," I persist: "you get a free pass on this one. Get out of here and back to the ship." The devout Christian Scientist ignores my advice.

Later, another wounded captain comes along with his left arm in a sling. It's Captain Don Goverts of Easy Company, my former CO. He's been shot through the elbow, but unlike Stebbie, he looks relieved for his free pass out of this one – relieved but still reluctant to leave his men.

Meanwhile, the colonel and Felker have gathered our headquarters group together and we all move inland about a hundred yards past the old Agat road, which is a dirt trail. When we pause in a grove of trees I look back toward the beach, and I see a squad of Japanese soldiers carrying rifles and heavy machine guns. They're marching north on the old Agat road acting as though they are on a routine patrol. They seem to be oblivious to the invasion. They're less than 200 yards away when I yell: "Japs!" and I lift my carbine to squeeze off a round, but our adjutant ıeflects my carbine upward, forcing a miss and says: "Don't shoot. They're Marines."

I'm pissed at him when the colonel looks over at me thinking I've shot at Marines. "They're not Marines," I insist. "Look at their helmets. Look at their rifles. Look at the way they carry them at the balance? When have you ever seen a Marine carrying an M1 at the balance?" Then I run off, pursuing the squad of Japanese soldiers by myself, armed only with a carbine and a fighting knife.

Fortunately for me, two of our riflemen know I'm right and they follow me with their M1s. We quickly catch up with the Japs, and we realize that it's a Japanese machine gun squad, looking for a place to set up their gun to rake the later waves of Marines still coming in.

"I take the first shot with my carbine and wound the squad leader. As the Japs scramble to hide in the brush, my two riflemen let loose with their M1 artillery, finishing off the squad leader.

Since our place is with headquarters, not to go hunting Japs, we return immediately. I report to the colonel in front of the adjutant that the patrol we fired on are Japanese, not Marines, and that it is a machine gun squad looking for a place to set up. The only problem is that I have not positively identified the bodies by close inspection, and I know this colonel will not accept an assumption without positive verification.

But we can't stop the battle while I go back for one more look. So we proceed inland, but I promise myself that I will find a way to make that verification before the battle is over.

It took a few more days before my duties took me back to the beach, but I went out of my way to find the dead body of that Japanese squad leader lying just where I had dropped him. It was verification enough. It didn't make me feel good to kill a man, but it was a man setting up a machine gun to kill us. And it made me feel a lot better to know that the body I found was not that of a Marine.

By afternoon, Easy Company had crossed Harmon road and was advancing northeast. The 4th Marines were to our right, and our 1st battalion was meeting resistance in Agat. Then enemy artillery started falling on us. When it first started, Major Felker and I were alone waiting for the rest of the CP group to catch up with us. The major stood about ten yards from me as we rested in a shady draw when the first round hit closer to the major than to me. I was looking for a direction to run when the second round hit exactly where I would have run to had I moved. That's when I realized there is no safe place to go when you're in the impact zone of an artillery barrage.

Still, I yelled at the major to do something that I had heard about in my Reserve Officers' Class at Quantico: "Why don't we call for counter-battery fire?" I asked. Of course, he had no more of an idea than I did how you would go about that when you don't know where the enemy's guns are. So we just stood there in a stoic stupor and waited for the artillery to lift or move along. And it did, only to start up again later in another place.

While I was digging my foxhole for the night, I was thinking about our landing. How was it that the two amtracs in front of us each took direct hits, and yet we came through unscathed? I promised myself that if I came out of this campaign alive, I would find out who was responsible for knocking out that killer gun on the point. He certainly deserved a medal in my book. He had saved that whole right flank and, not so incidentally, my life and the life of the colonel.

At the end of W-Day, we spend a spooky night with occasional mortar blasts and unaccountable sounds but with no major enemy challenges or *Banzai* charges against our position, but it doesn't go that well for our rear echelon and our flanking units.

For them it had started a few hours after the landing. Captain Charles Widdecke of the 1st Battalion, 22d Marines who is on our left flank runs into severe resistance on Bob's Hill over the town of Agat. His unit attacks and is pinned down for over an hour from withering machine gun fire while waiting for reinforcements. With the reinforcements, he attacks again, but Japanese fire from concealed weapons brings his attack to a hold. Then, as darkness falls and his men are digging in for the night, along come twelve Japanese soldiers carrying the machine guns that have held up the Marines' advance all afternoon. As they march boldly toward the Marines on an open trail, our bullets promptly riddle these inscrutable Japanese. (Were these the survivors of the patrol whose squad leader we had killed earlier?)

Meanwhile, on our right flank to the southeast, elements of the 4th Marines are dug in on a thin line extending 1600 yards from the beach to Harmon road. At 11:30 PM, Jap reconnaissance patrols draw fire from the Marines to locate their positions, which results in an extensive mortar barrage and an attack by the Japanese throwing demolition charges and small land mines as though they were grenades. Six Marines are bayoneted in their foxholes before the Japs are turned back. A second more serious attack then comes at 1:00 AM against the 1st Platoon of the 1st Battalion, 4th Marines, occupying a small hill named Hill 40. The platoon is forced to withdraw, but it reorganizes at the base of the hill and retakes it, only to be driven out again by a second counterattack. Finally, Lt Marvin C. Plock brings help in the form of two squads, joining the other men at the base of the hill and they take it for the third time. By morning 63 dead Japs are counted on the hill and another 350 between the hill and the beach.

But the enemy loves the night. So at 2:30 AM, a more serious counterattack is launched against our positions near a reservoir northwest of Mt. Alifan. This one is led by tanks and truck-mounted guns, with infantry following. In the middle of the attack with the enemy force visible only by the light of our flares and their gunfire, some unnamed bazooka man of the 4th Marines rises to his feet and knocks out the first three tanks before being shot down. His heroic sacrifice gains enough time for a platoon of our General Sherman tanks, led by Lt. James R. Williams, to reach the area and destroy the remaining enemy tanks before they can deploy, and without armored support the Jap infantry retreats behind Mount Alifan to reorganize for one more try.

Next they attack our positions on the lower slopes of the mountain under cover of a barrage of knee mortars and machine guns. Led by an officer waving a battle flag, they come through a draw shouting slogans, swinging Samurai swords, and throwing grenades. This attack is stopped by elements of our brigade reserve before it reaches our brigade's artillery positions.

At 3:00 o'clock in the morning, one more attack is launched. This attack against the 3rd Battalion, 4th Marines. The attack comes into a sector covered by Lieutenant Martin "Stormy" Sexton. The Japanese are tossing antitank mines, tumbling into foxholes, bayoneting our wounded. The main attack is halted, but many of our Marines run out of ammunition and can't stop the Jap infiltrators from reaching our pack-howitzer positions four hundred yards from the beach where the Japs are finally destroyed by our support elements.

We are not surprised nor do we feel directly threatened by hearing about all that action on our right and left flanks. In a battle the enemy usually picks on what he considers the soft spots. We are probably a little cocky to think that he wouldn't pick on us in the 2d Battalion 22d Marines, in the powerful center of our brigade line. He would more likely choose weaker spots, which usually means the flanks.

But by dawn, we are very surprised and shocked to hear that while we had spent a nervous but uneventful night at the front, an entire company of Japanese soldiers had managed to infiltrate around our position and reach our regimental command post to our rear. Fortunately, by the light of dawn, our regimental sentries discovered the enemy and gave the alarm. That's when the Marine

Corps tradition of "Every Marine is a rifleman" came into play. Instantly, headquarters personnel – including office clerks, runners, cooks, drivers – all seized their weapons and attacked the infiltrators.

Leading the attack were twenty-five men of the Regimental Reconnaissance Platoon armed with light machine guns. And leading the platoon was my mild-mannered little friend, First Lieutenant Dennis Chavez, Jr. who kills five Japs at point-blank range with a Tommy gun. When the smoke clears, three officers and 66 Japanese soldiers of an elite Imperial unit are found dead. Six Marines are wounded. My friend Dennis, who has just left our battalion Bn-2 job to take over the Regimental Recon Platoon, is the son of the senior senator from New Mexico. He is too old (about 30) and too small (130 pounds) to be a poster Marine hero, but he has turned down the opportunity of cushy job in Washington to be a combat Marine. I'm learning that heroes come from all segments of society, in all ages, sizes, and shapes.

In our front-line position, away from all the rear-echelon action of the night, we awake the next morning to the tinny noise of a Tunnerville-Trolley Japanese tank clanging down a trail on Mt. Alifan to our rear in the 4th Marine sector. It is the first time I have seen a Japanese tank in action, and I'm not very impressed. As a matter of fact, it's a pathetic sight. Here is this tiny Tinker-Toy tank going into battle against the 4th Marines with no infantry cover. Without infantry protection, this lone tank can be finished by any grunt Marine with a bazooka, a satchel charge, a grenade in the tracks, or with almost anything. It was a suicide run – far too slow and non-threatening to be called a suicide charge. So we are not surprised when we get the news that the 4th Marines have already knocked out four of these Nip tin cans, in that Japanese infantry-tank attack during the night, confirming our evaluation of their tanks.

We have mixed feelings about the battles of the previous night. We're thanking God for sparing us, but we feel a powerful empathy for our buddies who have suffered through that night battle. They put up a great defense, but now it's a job for the offense. So we are ordered to saddle-up, and our Second Battalion moves out — echeloned in depth, two columns abreast with the usual point, flank, and rear security guards. With no enemy in sight, the colonel gets more aggressive and sends Heavy, Ed Pesely, and Al Kirtz on combat patrol duty. Mission: on the way to closing Orote Peninsula, find the enemy before he finds us.

Although our patrols encounter little action on our second day ashore, the First Battalion, 22d Marines to our left meets moderate resistance north of Agat, and the 4th Marines behind us has to struggle against both the steep terrain and the enemy to take the heights of Mt. Alifan. However, by the close of the second day of combat, the brigade is well established ashore and prepared to launch its main drive to capture Orote Peninsula.

We are ordered to attack to the northeast along the Old Agat Road and seize the high ground overlooking the southern shore of Apra Harbor. During the next two days, while the First and Third Battalions are meeting significant resistance along the Agat/Sumay road as they fight to close the mouth of the

Tank-infantry team moves cautiously along Guam road before ambush at Road Junction 15. (USMC Photo)

peninsula, our Second Battalion is meeting only occasional sniper fire as we trek through some swampy terrain infested with mosquitoes on our way to our Apra Harbor objective.

By July 25th we are approaching our objective, the high ground overlooking Apra Harbor. Major Felker asks me to get Heavy Pfuhl. I find Heavy with his platoon taking advantage of a break to clean their weapons before the order to move out is issued. Heavy and I report back to Felker, and he orders Heavy to take a small patrol and locate Lieutenant Colonel Shisler of our Third Battalion who is somewhere in the midst of enemy territory on our left flank. After destroying a Jap machine gun nest and blowing a covey of Japs out of a cave with an explosive sphere, Heavy's patrol locates Lieutenant Colonel Shisler, and Heavy sends a team back to escort Felker and me to Shisler's position.

After Felker and Shisler confer, it is decided that a patrol should be sent ahead to scout out Apra Harbor before the main

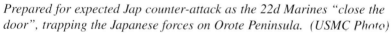

Prepared for expected Jap counter-attack as the 22d Marines "close the door", trapping the Japanese forces on Orote Peninsula. (USMC Photo)

body of either battalion is committed to moving on that objective. We know that when we try to close the mouth of the peninsula, we can expect a desperate attempt by the Japanese to keep that last escape route open. Unfortunately for Heavy, he and his guys are elected to carry out that recon mission.

Heavy's group moves fast and they reach their objective in twenty-five minutes, but the news isn't good. They scout out a company of enemy troops 400 yards down the road. After reporting to Shisler, Heavy contacts us by radio at our Second Battalion CP and reports to Felker. Since it's getting late, Felker tells him to join Shisler's battalion for the night. Their job is to protect the Third Battalion CP.

As we expected, the desperate Japanese are determined to keep their last corridor out of the peninsula open. They start at 2100 with their artillery blasting the front of both battalions, but with the main thrust against Lieutenant Colonel Shisler's Third Battalion. Within an hour, the Japanese artillery is followed up by the enemy probes, and by 2300 all hell is breaking loose.

Fortified with the usual sake, the Japs come at Shisler's battalion in a *Banzai* charge with rifles, bayonets, knives, and grenades. At the height of the turmoil, one of Shisler's companies that is catching hell calls for our artillery to move in closer to their front lines. Captain Frank of L Company distinguishes himself, standing exposed to enemy fire while spotting our artillery to within a few yards of his own position. With 26,000 shells thrown into the pocket between midnight and 3:00 AM, it is reported that arms and legs are flying like snowflakes. By daylight, over 400 enemy dead bodies are counted in front of our Third Battalion lines intermixed with scores of our Marine bodies. Fortunately, the dead doesn't include Heavy and his group, and Lieutenant Colonel Shisler sends them back to us with his commendations for their outstanding defense of his battalion CP on that fateful night.

Chapter 14

Road Junction Fifteen

The desperate effort by the Japanese to blunt our advance did not deter the brigade nor disrupt our attack plan. With the peninsula sealed we continue our advance on the 26th, heading west on the Piti-Sumay roads. We move out again echeloned in depth two columns abreast, one on each side of the road. F Company is leading the column, and Lieutenant Pesely has the point platoon. I'm with Lieutenant Colonel Hart at the forward battalion CP just behind the F Company CP group. We are about two or three hundred yards behind the point platoon. Nobody is firing at our column, and so we have no one to shoot at either.

It is an eerie truce after the vicious fighting of the night before. To our right front is a mangrove swamp, swollen from the torrential rains of the last few nights, but nobody challenges us as we march over a small bridge with dead Japanese floating in the water underneath. Strangely, it is quiet enough to hear the noises of nature without the usual barking of guns. And then the column suddenly comes to a halt. We all hit the deck, wondering why.

Soon Pesely appears, looking for the colonel, who is lying in a ditch at the side of the road next to me. Realizing we're not under immediate attack, the colonel sits up and asks:

"What's wrong, Ed? Have you run into something?"

"I'm not sure, Sir," Ed answers, "but…"

The colonel cuts off his reply. "What do you mean you're not sure? Are you taking any fire?"

"No, Sir, not yet, but…"

"But what, Ed?" The colonel is nervous and impatient.

"Well, Sir," Ed goes on, "when we got to Road Junction 15, my guys spotted a whole bunch of log bunkers and pillboxes."

"Well, are there any Japs in them?" the colonel asks: "is anyone shooting at you?"

"No, Sir," Pesely responds; "we fired a couple of M1 rounds into them and got no return fire, but my guys would like to hit those bunkers with a couple of 75mm shells before we try to move through that road junction, because if they've got some machine guns in there, they command that entire road junction."

"Haven't you got a half-track up there with you?" the colonel asks.

"Yes, Sir," Pesely responds; "Major Schuster's up there with a 75mm on a halftrack."

"Then why don't you go ahead and put a couple rounds in those bunkers?" the colonel asks.

"Schuster doesn't want to do it," Pesely answers; "he says the bunkers are deserted, and it would be a waste of ammunition."

"Well, you tell Major Schuster that we're not going to hold up the brigade's advance to save the cost of two rounds of 75mm. You tell him I said he should do what you want done regarding those pillboxes – and Jones," the colonel says turning to me; "you go with Ed and confirm my orders."

"Yes, Sir," I reply, and Ed and I lope off to the road junction. When we get to the road junction, all the men in the two columns remain in their alerted positions, sitting low in the ditches on either side of the road waiting for the word. Only Major Shuster is standing upright in front of his half-track, which is parked diagonally across the road junction from the plainly discernible enemy emplacements.

Pesely gives the major the colonel's message, which I emphatically confirm. The major, clearly annoyed, says; "All right, but it's a damn waste of ammunition." Then he lifts his right hand to signal his half-track gunner to place a round into the enemy fortifications. When he brings his arm down as a "commence fire" signal, dozens of enemy rifles and machine guns open fire at his command. The major ducks behind his half-track, and Pesely and I hit the deck and crawl into ditches on either side of the road. I scurry back through the ditch on my side until I am out of the field of fire. Then I rush to the colonel, and report our first enemy ambush. The thing I fear most is that the colonel might order a frontal attack through that road junction, with my good friend, Ed Pesely, leading the point. It would, of course, be a suicide order, and I don't think it's necessary.

One of the great advantages of my position as a battalion liaison officer is my unrestricted access to the ear of the commanding officer. It is like being an advisory minister to the king. I have little authority on my own, but I can often influence the decisions of the man with total authority. It is a good place to be when your best friend needs your help.

When the colonel learns of the severe resistance at the road junction, I can see he is visibly torn between taking immediate direct action by ordering his men to charge through that hell hole – and thereby winning favor with his superiors – or withdrawing and recouping for a later safer attack – and thereby losing credibility as a gung-ho Marine commander. I immediately give him my advice, which I hope is an acceptable third option.

"Colonel," I say; "Road Junction 15 is easily identifiable from the air; why don't we order an air strike?"

"That's a good idea, Jones," he replies; and he immediately gets on the radio to Regiment and asks for the air strike. Unfortunately, in war you seldom get what you need when you need it. That was especially true of air strikes on Guam. We had eight battalions in our brigade plus nine more in the Third Division, probably all asking for air strikes. At any rate, the colonel is told there are no planes available for us. But I still don't want Pesely and his guys charging through that road junction, so I go to my option two.

"Well at least Colonel," I say, let's pull back our troops and call in the artillery to blast those emplacements before we attack."

Whether the colonel paid any attention to my suggestion or not, he did follow that plan. He even went one step further. He decided to pull back and dig in for the night, and postpone the attack until morning – a compassionate, civilized, and sensible act that would cost him his command.

We had pulled back a few hundred yards from the heavy enemy fortifications at Road Junction 15 and picked the high ground opposite the mangrove swamp to dig in for the night. With a Marine credo of "after dark shoot everything that moves", we started out as usual digging our personal foxholes as fast and deep as we could to be finished before dark to avoid being shot by our buddies. But the enemy surprised us with one of his weird innovations.

Located in the dense mangrove swamp, the Japanese gunners could not level their weapons directly through the trees at the hillside where we were digging in. So they decided to use their flat-trajectory antiaircraft weapons for high-angle indirect fire to supplement their mortars. This resulted in a bizarre barrage of 20mm and 40mm tracer shells raining down upon our positions from above, rendering us defenseless in our shallow roofless foxholes. Added to that odd barrage were aerial bursts, which might well have come from our own artillery.

I noticed that Major Felker and the colonel, who were sharing a two-man foxhole, managed to pull a scrap of corrugated roofing material over themselves for protection from above. They escaped injury, as I did, but many of our men who escaped direct hits received shrapnel wounds from the aerial bursts.

The Second Battalion continues the attack through Road Junction 15 in the morning, but it looks like the regimental or brigade command expected more out of our colonel when we hit that resistance yesterday, because now he's gone and the sulky major with the halftrack has taken his place as our acting CO. Heavy's platoon is out front again, catching withering fire from Nip rear guard teams, as he moves through a coconut grove north of the road junction. He yells for armor, and he gets a half-track with a 75mm gun and two 50 caliber machine guns. They chase their targets through the afternoon.

Meanwhile, I'm still back in the coconut grove near the road junction with our battalion CP, and we're catching deadly sniper fire, but we don't know where it's coming from. We suspect it's from the mangrove trees in the swamp, but we can't see the snipers. Then unexpectedly one of the snipers slides down from a tree into three feet of swamp water. With his hands raised as a sign of surrender, he moves slowly toward us to within fifty yards of the road. A corporal, three riflemen, and I all have our weapons leveled at him, but I order them to hold their fire and allow him to surrender. But I also tell them to shoot if he makes any quick moves because we're familiar with their treachery, and they often carry concealed weapons and grenades. This one seems to be willing to surrender, and he keeps coming, hands high and moving slowly.

Just then I hear a burst from a Tommy gun, and I look around and see Heavy coming back through the coconut grove to warn us about the snipers. His burst was into the fronds of a coconut tree, and although no sniper falls out of the tree, a Japanese rifle hits the ground. "They're hiding in those fronds," Heavy says. Then, as he turns to go back to his platoon, he sees our Jap prisoner coming out of the swamp, and without taking aim he casually squeezes off a couple of rounds in the Jap's direction and continues on his way.

At least one of the rounds must have hit our prisoner because he now becomes enraged and belligerent, making grenade-throwing threats in our direction. I'm still hopeful of taking this prisoner, but then I am summoned to join Major Felker and move out, leaving the corporal and three riflemen behind to resolve the standoff. I order them to allow the Jap to surrender if he will, but if he won't surrender, I tell the corporal to form a firing squad and execute him rather then let him get away. I reason that with a firing squad, no single Marine will have the shooting death of an unarmed prisoner on his conscience alone. I move on past our dead at the road junction and never learn the outcome of the prisoner standoff at the swamp.

Meanwhile, Heavy has returned to his platoon and seems to be spearheading the chase. His platoon passes through Lieutenant Kirtz's G Company with the Third Battalion on the right and the 4th Marines on his left rear. Half-tracks and tanks are brought into the battle, and as night approaches our forces have broken the Jap's Main Line of Resistance across Orote Peninsula and we are approaching the high ground overlooking the Old Marine

Barracks. But as dark settles in, the 2d Battalion is in a precarious position, having seized the low ground below the Old Marine Barracks and with exposed flanks not yet tied into adjacent units.

That's when Capt John Waddill and I get the short-straw assignment of picking our way in the dark through no-mans' land to our front line companies to help the commanders tie in their flanks with each other and adjacent units.

Actually, I get the short-straw assignment because it is really Waddill's job as battalion operations officer (Bn-3) to consolidate the line, and he just takes me along for company. At any rate, when we get to the front, our situation doesn't look good. Our troops are dug in at the bottom of a hill with the silhouettes and chatter of the Japs plainly discernible as they scramble around at the top of the hill, obviously preparing for an imminent *Banzai* attack.

Heavy's left flank is wide open with the 4th Marines a good five hundred yards to their rear. None of our platoons are much better off. Waddill is a levelheaded common-sense guy. While I'm busy trying to figure out how to get our troops out of this mess, he's busy trying to make the most of a bad situation. He's moving around in the dark, risking his life to tie in the flanks of our scattered platoons and companies. Proving once again the validity of Marine doctrine that anything that moves after dark gets shot – the captain takes a mean M1 round in his leg and is out of action.

Meanwhile, G Company is taking heat too, and Lieutenant Kirtz catches serious shrapnel that almost tears his left arm off and sears his left side. It is clear to me that we are in an untenable situation. We have committed one of the dumbest maneuvers in warfare – instead of capturing the high ground and digging in for the night, we have captured the low-ground at the foot of an enemy-occupied hill and we are digging in for the night. I feel it is absolutely necessary to describe the situation to the Battalion and Regimental command posts, but we have no phone or radio contact so the word has to get back by foot.

With a captain who has just been shot by our troops while moving around in the dark in a small defined area, what are the chances that anyone can possibly make it back in the dark across thousands of yards of no-man's land without taking heavy fire from both the Japs and the Marines? I know the chances are slim, but I also decide that the chances for our troops are slimmer, positioned as they are at the bottom of that enemy hill. So with only a carbine and a .45 caliber pistol, I set out on a lonely trip across several thousand yards of no-man's land to make my report to Battalion.

I have only traveled a few hundred yards when the intermittent rifle fire starts up. It is obvious that there is still enough light for the enemy to see my silhouette as I hustle along the dirt road. Then the tracer bullets of heavy machine gun fire come at me. I dive into a deep truck tire rut and shove my head down into the mud while the tracers come lower and lower as the gunner corrects his elevation to hit me, the target. When I realize what he is doing, I leap out of the rut between bursts and dive into a new one several yards away. But at this pace, I will never get back in time to do our front lines any good, so I decide to run for it. I get up and start running, mindful to keep a dark background behind me to avoid providing the gunners with a silhouette target.

When I arrive at the battalion command post, our major XO is on the field phone with the regimental commander. I hear him say: "Colonel, I've got a lieutenant here who has just come back from the front. I'll let him tell you what's going on." And then he hands me the phone.

I pick up the phone and identify myself as Lieutenant Jones. "Lieutenant," the colonel growls," what's going on up there?" I immediately recognize the gravely voice of Colonel "The Red Beast" Schneider, our regimental CO. I know he's a 1923 Naval Academy graduate who's been with our regiment since Samoa and through the Marshalls. I know he can easily intimidate a lieutenant, but I also know that I have something important to tell him.

"Colonel," I report, "we're not in a good position. We've seized the low ground below the Old Marine Barracks, and the enemy has the high ground. When I left I could see the Japs massing at the top of the hill for what looks like a *Banzai* charge. We're dug in so close to the hill, we have no forward fields of fire for our automatic weapons. I think we should pull back a few hundred yards for the night, call in artillery, and attack in the morning." I know that the regimental commander doesn't need to get his battle plan from a first lieutenant, but it is my chance to propose the use of reason in lieu of senseless sacrifice.

"Lieutenant," the colonel shoots back; "the General says that a Marine can always hold any ground that he can take. We're not moving back a foot, do you understand?"

"Yes, Sir," I reply.

"But we can give you artillery right now," the colonel goes on, "if you can direct it because we have no artillery observers at the front."

"Sir," I answer; "I'm not at the front now. I'm at our battalion CP." For a brief moment I visualize having to go back through that no-man's land one more time. Then I realize – and hope that the colonel does also – that it would be useless because we have no communications from the front companies to our battalion or regiment.

"Lieutenant, get a map and call me the artillery coordinates from memory from where you are."

"Yes, Sir," I respond. Then the major hands me a map, a poncho, and a flashlight. I crawl under the poncho and shine the flashlight on the map, trying to locate landmarks from where I had just returned. Although there is a light rain falling, the poncho is used to keep the light in not to keep the rain out. Under those conditions, it is ticklish business to call artillery on an enemy position just a few yards in front of my buddies when a miss involving a few contour lines on the map will bring deadly fire on my friends. But the colonel insists that I do it.

Fortunately, the map shows the small contractor's shack located near the disputed hill that I can use for a reference point. So I go about my business of calling the coordinates, and the colonel passes them on to our artillery who then begins peppering the hill that the Japs hold.

Meanwhile, back at the front our artillery bursts on their hill encourages the Japs to make a premature *Banzai* charge. Thirty or forty of them come screaming down on our positions. They're throwing grenades, firing rifles, swinging sabers, and yelling obscenities, but they are met by some cool-headed Marines. One of the coolest is a tough little 135-pound Corporal Webster Bachelot. As a squad leader in Heavy's platoon, Bachelot has placed his own foxhole forward so he can be on guard at dusk while his squad digs in for the night. In that vulnerable position, he is the first to be hit when his squad comes under attack by a dozen of the Japs in a frenzied *Banzai* charge. He personally encounters the first four Japs with his rifle and bayonet, taking a Jap bayonet stab into his sternum but still finishing them off in hand-to-hand-combat.

Altogether, Heavy's platoon kills twelve Japs in that charge and chases a dozen more off to the west toward the cliffs at the end of the peninsula. Unfortunately, due to poor command coordination and without flanking tie-ins between adjacent units, Heavy's platoon loses four dead and five wounded. Because Heavy thinks it is an unnecessary loss, it is something that he bitterly resents.

Like all our platoon leaders, Lieutenant Kirtz in G Company also feels a strong affinity with his men. So on this seventh day of combat on Guam when he has been severely wounded by the hit on his left arm and side, he is reluctant to leave his depleted platoon. He is the 29th casualty of his 40-man unit. So even with a dangling arm and a bleeding chest, he feels guilty when his "golden wounds" send him directly to the Naval Hospital at Pearl Harbor where the doctors debate whether to cut off his arm at the elbow or the shoulder. His vote is to keep his arm and risk the gangrene, which they allow him to do. So he is returned to duty at the end of that war and in plenty of time for the next one in Korea.

After the battle for Guam, I wrote the following poem commemorating our first ambush that day at Road Junction Fifteen. Fifty years later, I was surprised to discover a copy of this poem on permanent display on the wall in the United States Marine Corps Museum on Orote Peninsula, Guam, USA. I also learned that a copy of this poem has been buried in a time capsule to be opened in 2044, on the 100th Anniversary of the Liberation of Guam.

Ambush at Road Junction Fifteen

I

We marched
in a line
a battalion long
And moved across
the dead fields
of marsh and mire.
No bird
no creature
stirred
with a song.
Ominous stillness
while Death
played at the lyre.

II

We crossed
a bridge
dead enemy beneath,
And advanced our column
to meet a somewhere
waiting foe.
No shot
no shell
did our guns
unsheath
Nor his destiny
could any man
know.

III

We halted
the column
men dropped
to rest
And on their faces
was writ

despair and desire
And in their hearts
were the thoughts
of the damned and the blest,
But their stomachs
were athirst
and on fire.

IV

We marched
again
along that road
Silently
on that trail
which led nowhere to Hell.
No Herculeans
these
following this mode
Green-clad youngsters
now yet alive
but on their way
to their last farewell.

V

We passed
their lines
many a pillbox
Not a challenge
issued forth
from the green
of the hills.
Every Nip
every Jap
mute as the rocks.
We sought an enemy
unknown
till he kills

VI

We reached
the junction
number fifteen,
a corner of a swamp
and stood listening,
a battalion
of U.S. Marines.
No band
no cheers
no glory or pomp
Not for us
the victory
just the means.

VII

We peered
with caution
at the positions
ahead
And awaited
the word
from higher command.
Then with a burst
came the flood
of sudden Jap lead
And hot
was the air
that shot and shell fanned.

VIII

We died
at the junction
or lay in our blood
beseeching the heavens
as we took
the enemy fire.
Through the grass
bullets whistled
and plumped into the mud
And the song
in the air
was the song
of the lyre.

IX

We marched
in time
beyond that place
and found another
and another
and another.
But no man
no lad
ever forgot the face
of the first comrade
who left him that day
for Death—
their brother.

Chapter 15

Vengeance Is Ours

It is confirmed that the higher command didn't like the way our colonel handled the Road Junction 15 impasse, and the word comes down that he has been relieved and the surly half-track major has been officially appointed as our new CO. None of us like the news because someone has removed a colonel with human feelings and jumped over a highly regarded executive officer to give us a not so highly regarded alternate major as CO. We're sure Schuster gets the nod because he is a "Regular" commissioned officer, not a "Reserve" like Major Felker and most of the rest of us.

But if most of us are simply displeased, Heavy is angry. He doesn't like the new CO. He blames him for the poor command control that resulted in his platoon's isolation and the beating his platoon took on the previous night. Still, the word comes down to him how important he and his platoon of thirty-five beat-up Marines have been in breaking the Japs MLR at Road Junction 15, then continuing pursuit of the Japs and holding off their frantic *Banzai* charges. It is recognized that his platoon was a significant factor in the action that became the turning point in the battle for Orote Peninsula. When the praise is passed on to his guys and one of his corporals magically pulls a fifth of Johnny Walker Red Label out of his pack, Heavy says "Let's drink to that."

But when they find some shade, open the bottle, and drop down to take a few swigs – the war interrupts again. Major Felker has asked me to send a runner to fetch Heavy. So Heavy, having left the bottle in the custody of his men shows up somewhat begrudgingly at our battalion CP. Felker gives him a mission. "Heavy," he says, "I want you to take a patrol into Sumay-town.

We've got a wounded man and four stretcher bearers pinned down."
The major pulls out a map and shows Heavy where they are.

"So I guess you want me to get them out," Heavy says.

"That's the idea," Felker replies, "but we'll be coming along
pretty close behind you with our forward CP because our battalion
has been ordered to take the Old Marine Barracks at Sumay."

As Heavy goes back to finish off the Johnny Walker before
tackling his patrolling mission, the major tells me to get our
forward CP party together and gather around his jeep. Altogether,
counting our communications guys, our intelligence section, our
forward observers, our riflemen and runners, plus the major and
me, there are seventeen in our group. When we get to the major's
jeep we see him standing in the shade of a huge Banyan tree. I
lead the group up to the major to receive our orders.

The major pulls out a map and starts talking: "Here's our plan
for the day…" Then he stops when he realizes that he's got the
wrong map. "Jones," he says to me, "go back to my jeep and get
the other map on the seat."

His jeep is less than thirty yards away, and on my way there I
hear the rustle of incoming artillery over my head with the
instantaneous loud explosion of a large caliber round behind me.
I turn to see that the blast has struck the Banyan tree I just left and
that the major – and all sixteen Marines in that group – are lying
prostrate on the ground, either dead or wounded. I grab the radio
in the jeep, call for corpsmen, and then rush over to find the major
still alive but badly dazed and confused. All the others are dead or
wounded.

Major Copeland, our Bn-3 officer comes up and takes over
Felker's job, and we proceed with our mission as though nothing
has happened. But a lot has happened to me. Why – out of that
whole group – was I spared in that split moment? Was I being
saved for a purpose? And if so what was that purpose?

Our battalion continues to move on toward the Old Marine
Barracks. We're anxious to recapture the barracks that was taken
from the 153 Marine defenders who were forced to surrender in
1941 by an overwhelming invasion force of 6000 Japanese. In
their brief defense actions before being ordered to surrender by
the island governor, U.S. Navy Captain George McMillin, four

Marines were killed and twelve were wounded before giving up their USMC barracks. Now it was our turn to take our barracks back.

Although we had breached the enemy's main line of resistance on Orote Peninsula, there were still heavy pockets of Japanese troops scattered across the remaining terrain that we had to cross to reach the Old Marine Barracks. The 4th Marines on our left, supported by tanks, pressed through heavy vegetation that concealed a line of pillboxes arranged in depth. When the tanks couldn't see what to shoot at, Marine infantry troops moved in front to lead them to their targets. A heavy battle ensued that took out four 4th Marine lieutenants, two sergeants, and two squad leaders. But when the battle subsided at 4:00 PM, 250 enemy pillboxes and emplacements were counted, and all the enemy defenders were dead.

Meanwhile, against moderate resistance, our Second Battalion continued throughout the morning to move toward our objective – the Marine Barracks. We soon discovered that we were by-passing many Japanese troops holed up in caves in the cliffs overlooking Apra harbor, so I was ordered to take a small patrol and go down to the beach below and follow a course parallel with the progress of our attacking forces up above. Our beach mission was to take prisoners if they would surrender or to blast or burn them out of the caves if they refused, because we were getting serious sniper fire from those caves.

Although we had Nisei American Japanese interpreters with our regimental headquarters, in a war what you need is seldom available when you need it. So I resorted to the use of my own limited Japanese language.

While on Guadalcanal, I had sent home for a Japanese grammar and studied it aboard ship, so I thought I knew a few phrases. Things like – "Put your weapons down. Put your hands up. Come here. We will not kill you." We soon learned however that our offer to prisoners could be a one-way contract. Even if we agreed not to kill them; they hadn't agreed not to kill us. So often they came at us with their hands up, and at the last minute they might pull a weapon or a grenade out of their uniform and attack. Anyhow, we didn't take any chances, so the surrender order went more like this: "Put your weapons down and come out with your hands up." Once they appeared, we ordered them to stop and strip before approaching us.

It was one of these incidents that was featured in the Stars and Stripes Service newspaper at the time. After one prisoner had come out of the cave and stripped, I wanted him to come closer with his hands up. So in my best Japanese I ordered him to –"*Kuru!*" He responded with –"*Koi?*" I repeated "*Kuru!*" which I understood to mean, "Come!" He responded again with "*Koi?*" It became obvious to me that he was correcting my Japanese grammar, so I obliged him with "*Koi!*" and then he came. (I later learned that I had been using the infinitive form instead of the imperative.) The Service newspaper caption read; "Prisoner Corrects Lieutenant's Japanese Grammar Before Surrendering." That incident had a better finish than one that was to follow later.

It is noon before I find a trail back up to the top of the cliffs to rejoin our battalion. I learn that our forward companies are already approaching the Old Marine Barracks against moderate fire. Most of the action is around the rifle range and the airfield so I run through mild sniper fire to be with our point platoon when it takes over the Old Marine Barracks. When I reach the Barracks, a corporal squad leader recognizes me as a Second Battalion officer, and he brings me a bronze plaque that simply reads, "U.S. Marine Barracks, Naval Station, Guam." The remaining barrack structures are simple skeletons of the original buildings. I ask the corporal where he found the plaque, and he says: "It was in a trash heap, Lieutenant; probably right where they threw it in 1941."

"Well, we'll be raising the flag and hanging it back up real soon," I said.

We had taken the Barracks but it would still be another day before the 4th Marines could make a final direct assault on the airfield and we could all move on to mop up the remaining pockets of enemy on the peninsula.

However, in the excitement of regaining our Old Marine Barracks, and in our eagerness to avenge the wrongs done to our out-numbered comrades who were overwhelmed in 1941, we couldn't wait for the battle to end to raise our flag once again over our property. So we held our own brief spontaneous ceremony, hanging up our plaque and raising a small flag. However, the official flag-raising ceremony came on July 29th, even though we were still in the midst of sporadic enemy fire at that time.

Because we had recaptured the site, our 22d Marine Regiment was chosen to provide the guard of honor, and our troops were

Vengeance is our as we raise the Flag at the Old Marine Barracks. Lt. Dale Bair, 2d Battalion, 22d marines, is the figure on the right (USMC Photo)

lined up in parade formation for the ceremony, which was being reviewed by Admiral Spruance, the three-star commander of the Fifth Fleet, and Lieutenant General Holland M. Smith, the three-star commander of the Fleet Marine Force, Pacific, as well as the regimental commanders of the 22d and the 4th Marines, and our one-star brigade commander, Brigadier General Lemuel C. Shepherd.

Lieutenant Heavy Pfuhl was also offered an official role in the ceremony but modestly declined saying: "They've got enough brass out there. They don't need my little second lieutenant bar to make it a good show." It was a good show – a highly charged emotional pause in the fighting, a moment of vengeful reflection of the two-year occupation of U.S. territory by an oppressive enemy. But our feelings of revenge paled by comparison with those emotions being felt by a thirteen-year-old Chamorro boy who was watching from a hiding place in the brush. This boy who had seen his compatriots beheaded by sadistic Japanese troops now vowed on this day to become a Marine. After the war he enlisted and rose through the ranks to retire as a general.

Chapter 16

It's Never Over Till It's Over

O nce we secured the Barracks and the 4th Marines secured the rifle range and the airfield, organized resistance on the peninsula was over, but the battle for Guam went on for another month. Isolated pockets of Japanese troops still held out in the many caves in the cliffs that ringed the island as well as in remote jungle areas. A few Japanese held out for many years.

After capturing the barracks and the deserted town of Sumay, we were pulled off Orote back to Harmon road near the town of Agat. Our battalion had fought hard and continuously on the attack for more than a week since our initial landing. And none of us had had a full-night's sleep in that time. We had survived catching a few moments of sleep in our foxholes whenever the chaos of battle, the torrential rain, and the persistent mosquitoes allowed it. But now we were in reserve, and we set up a base camp from which we sent out patrols to clean up the many pockets of Japs who were still fighting the war.

I was dead tired from that week without sleep, so I scrounged around our new area looking for a place to steal a nap. I came upon a small hut hidden in the brush. Then, with my pistol drawn, I carefully opened the door and looked inside. There were two bunks, a bare wooden table, and two wooden chairs. On the table was a bowl of rice, and when I reached the table I realized the rice was still warm. The enemy had left in a hurry. He could come back and cut my throat as I slept. But hell, I was dead tired, and I decided he wouldn't come back. I crawled into one of the bunks and pulled a Japanese Imperial Navy blanket over my mud-soaked clothes and fell into a deep sleep that lasted three hours.

When I awakened a scout from one of our patrols had just

come back with the news that his team had discovered a Japanese sake and beer dump a mile ahead of our position. It was late in the afternoon and not a good time to venture very far from our foxholes, but I knew if I turned down this opportunity to bring back beer and sake for our guys – my leadership credibility would be zero in this battalion. And, now as the newly appointed Headquarters Company Commander, I had a jeep and trailer available to me, which Heavy and the other platoon leaders didn't have, so I knew I had to make the run.

My jeep driver hitched up the trailer, and he and I and the scout who reported the dump all jumped in and took off at full speed. It was already starting to get dark when we arrived at the dump, and of course, our battalion wasn't the only one that had discovered the dump. There were three or four other jeeps and trailers loading up. But the supply was plentiful. There was case after case of Asahi beer in large quart-sized green bottles, and case after case of fine Japanese sake. We felt like pigs in the mud as we walked through the dump pulling out quart bottles of Asahi and breaking the neck off and chug-a-lugging the full contents. But we had to hurry to get back before dark and avoid getting shot by our own troops.

We loaded both the trailer and the jeep with as much beer and sake as they could hold, and we raced out of there. But then a few hundred yards ahead, we saw a roadblock. It was one of our own 2-1/2-ton trucks parked across the road. It was stopping the jeeps that had left before us, and an officer in a khaki uniform with full insignia was forcing them to unload their cargo onto his truck. I told my driver to creep up close enough so we could see the officer's rank and the ID on his truck. I was astonished to see that the officer was a lieutenant colonel and he had a truck from Brigade Headquarters. It was then clear to me that this was a hijacking. Using the authority of his rank and his position at Brigade Headquarters, he was taking beer and sake out of the mouths of the combat troops. I hadn't come this far to capitulate to rank and intimidation. I told my driver, "Rev this thing up as fast as you can and bust through the road block." He did, and we were on our way home.

When I came into our camp with over 600 bottles of beer and

sake, it was enough to distribute a bottle to every Marine in our battle-depleted battalion. Since there were those who didn't drink, those that did had a party. Fortunately, the Japs did not pick that night to attack.

After that beer run and the story of my running the blockade got passed around to the troops, my stock went up considerably. Heavy was the first to let me know. "Hey, Jones," he said, "that was my guy who found that dump. But I have to hand it to you. They never would have got it through that roadblock without you. That took guts. Do you know who you were bucking?"

"Some colonel from Brigade is all I know, Heavy," I answered.

"Yeah, but do you know who that colonel is?"

"I haven't got the faintest idea."

"That was Loopy Loomis you busted by," he informed me.

"And who the hell is Loopy Loomis?" I asked.

"He's famous in Marine aviation," Heavy told me. "He got his nickname by doing a loop through a hangar on a bet. He won the bet, but he was grounded for the rest of his career. Now I think he's an aviation observer attached to Brigade."

"Well, that's interesting, Heavy," I said; but last night he was just some guy trying to hijack our booze. And no way was I going to let him get away with it, and then come back here and face you guys."

"Smart move, Jones," Heavy said: "some of the guys used to think you were a snobbish loner, but you won some Brownie points yesterday."

Shortly after the beer-run episode, our new commanding officer, Major Schuster, brought us the news that our battalion had been selected to do a patrol in strength. He planned to leave one company in reserve at our campsite, and he would personally lead two assault companies on the patrol. We were to head into an area where it was reported that a force of two or three companies, about 400 Japanese troops, was still intact. The job of our patrol would be to find and destroy them – or pin them down until our reserves could help us.

Heavy did not take the news lightly. "I'll bet that sonofabitch volunteered us for that job," Heavy said: "it's just like that freakin

'Regular', always bucking for a promotion or a medal – and then sending me and my thirty-five beat-up Marines out to do the dirty work."

"Well, he's not *sending* anyone on this one," I pointed out to Heavy; 'he's *leading* the patrol. And I think your company's going to be in reserve," I added.

"Well, it's about time. We've been up front ever since we landed on that first beach on Eniwetok."

Early the next morning the major formed his patrol, and, true to his word, he took a position up forward with the point platoon. He also ordered me to stay at his side. The major had the only detailed map of the area we were to patrol All of our maps showed the general area, but only his had the latest intelligence input with newly discovered foot trails. Our mission was to take a foot trail from the high ground overlooking the sea down to a coconut grove on a beach area, then proceed along the shoreline with the sea to our left and steep cliffs to our right that were heavily overgrown with vegetation. The plan was that our patrol in force would outflank the 400 Japanese troops who were presumed to hold the high ground on top of the cliffs to our right. It was calculated to be a daring surprise maneuver that the Japs would not expect, because at the end of our beach trap there was only one foot trail up to the high ground. The enemy would not think it was suitable for a single file attack up a cliff against an entrenched force above. Even the suicidal Japanese would not have contemplated such a maneuver, so our success and survival depended entirely upon surprise.

The first surprise was ours when our scouts could not find that isolated foot trail that would lead us out of our beach trap. The trail was plain enough on the major's map, but our scouts could not find it on the ground. Our second surprise came when the major discovered that we had lost radio contact with our base camp. So now if we found the Japs – or they found us – we could not call in our reserves if needed, nor could we call for artillery or other support. Without communications, it was essential that we not deviate from our patrol plan of action. If we were to return by the route we came, our return in the dark would be unexpected by our troops and we would be dealt with as the enemy.

When it was clear that our scouts could not find the escape trail, I asked the major for his map and permission to scout it for myself. He agreed, and I found the trail within a few minutes. But finding it and climbing it were two different things. No wonder the scouts couldn't find it. They were looking for an identifiable trail. What I found was simply a route that had been taken over time by natives to make an almost vertical climb up a vegetation-shrouded volcanic cliff. It would be a difficult climb for a naked native; it would seem to be impossible for Marines heavily burdened with weapons and gear. I discussed the problem with the major.

"Major," I said, "I don't know if we can get a whole battalion up that single file trail with our weapons and gear. And if we get halfway up and the Japs discover us, they could roll one big rock down and wipe us all out. Or worse yet they may already have the top of the trail covered with a machine gun, just waiting for us."

"Without radio contact, we can't change our plans now. We'll proceed with our mission," the major said. Then he added: "Okay Jones, lead us to the trail."

I showed the point platoon where the trail began, and then the major and I followed closely behind them, with the rest of the patrol behind us. With some of our men carrying machine guns and ammunition as well as their personal weapons, it was necessary to take frequent rest breaks as we trudged up the cliff. At the end of one of these rest breaks, I noticed an assistant machine gunner get up and start out without his box of .30 caliber machine gun ammunition. "Hey, Private," I yelled at him; "you forgot your ammunition."

"I can't carry it no more, Lieutenant," he replied. "My arms are too tired."

I was so shocked to hear that, I wasn't sure what I had heard. "Did you say your arms are tired and you're not going to carry your ammunition?"

"Yes Sir," he answered, simply.

"Well, Private," I asked: "What are we going to do at the top of this trail when we're up against 400 Japs and we set up our machine gun and have no ammunition?"

"I don't know, Sir," he answered.

"Well I know, Private, you're going to pick up that box and carry it until your arms fall off. And if you don't, I might just shoot them off you now. Do you understand me, Private?"

Yes, Sir," he replied, and he picked up the box and moved out. Then it occurred to me why the Marine D.I.s are so tough on the recruits in Boot Camp. Somehow this Marine had gotten through without learning the basic Marine Corps lessons, but not very many do. And that's the way it's got to be.

Fortunately for us, we reached the top of the hill without being discovered, and no machine guns were needed. But our problems were far from over. The way back was over a clearly defined dirt road, but it led through heavy jungle growth on both sides, so we could still be ambushed at any turn. Also, we had not regained radio contact, so our exact position was unknown to our base camp. According to the original patrol plan, which they were following back at our base camp, if we did not find the enemy, we would continue our circle route and return to base camp down this road well before dark. However, it was now already getting dark and we had just reached the top of the trail, several hours behind schedule. Now we were an isolated patrol in enemy territory, and our artillery had started their standard operating procedure that required them to register their guns in on enemy approaches to our base camp. Of course, we knew what was happening when our artillery shells began bursting over our head. Our artillery was using aerial bursts to zero-in their guns. We also knew that the bursts would start far out and then gradually be brought in closer and closer to our front lines at the base camp. Unfortunately, we were in between the aerial bursts and the base camp, hoping to move fast enough to stay ahead of the fast encroaching artillery. When it appeared to me that the clumsy battalion, with all its gear, could not move fast enough to stay ahead of our artillery, I had a suggestion for the major.

"Sir," I said; "without radio contact nobody knows we're out here. They either think we've engaged the enemy and we're dug in someplace, or we haven't found the enemy and we're much closer on our return to camp than we are, so the artillery's going to keep closing in until it catches us."

"I'm aware of that, Jones," the major replies; "but we're

moving as fast as we can."

"Yes, Sir," I answered; "we are moving as fast as a battalion can, but we are not moving as fast as a runner can. Why don't you let me run ahead and warn our camp where we are and get the artillery stopped?"

The major didn't respond right away. He was thinking it over. A "Regular" officer wants a combat history of successful operations. So if I got through and stopped the artillery, he might be commended, but it would still look like a desperate ending with a lieutenant saving a patrol under his command. And if he sent me ahead and I got ambushed and killed, it would definitely be a negative in the record of a patrol under his command. On the other hand, if he continued to lead the battalion at a steady pace and even if a few of our stragglers were wounded by our own artillery fire, it would not reflect negatively on him, since unforseen circumstances had knocked out his radio contact.

"No, Lieutenant," the major decided: "we'll all go in together."

We hurried as fast as possible to keep a few yards ahead of the artillery, and finally we saw a truck in the dusk. It was one of ours returning to our camp. We yelled. They heard us and slowed down. Now we knew it was far too dark for foot troops to penetrate our camp lines without being shot as enemy infiltrators, so we grabbed on to the rear of the truck and in a single file, with each Marine holding on to the sheathed bayonet of the Marine in front of him like the trunk-to-tail ritual of performing elephants in a circus – we were pulled safely through our lines.

In the following days, even though our battalion was now in reserve, we continued to draw patrol missions as part of the so-called moping up phase of the battle. The difference between the new moping up phase and the previous combat operations was the lack of front lines. Earlier, on the battle for the peninsula, we knew where the enemy was, and we moved against him as one organized force against another, with the taking of various terrain objectives as our immediate goals. Now our goal was simply to find pockets of the enemy, often holed up in caves, and induce them to surrender or destroy them. But in-between such patrol duty our men were free to rest and relax as best they could. At one point, we were camped on high ground overlooking an enticing sandy beach when a group of four enlisted men in my Headquarters Company asked for permission to take a trail down to the beach and go for a swim.

"I don't think so," I told them. There are a lot of caves in that cliff that are probably full of snipers."

"Aw come on Lieutenant," they pleaded; "we've been living in the mud for almost two weeks. We need a bath bad. We want to take little swim and clean up. How about it, Sir?"

"Well, there's no way I'll let you go down there without your weapons," I told them. "If you want to go, you get your rifles; and then you treat that beach like a hostile beach. You keep each other covered."

"Yes, Sir!" they exclaimed in unison, and in a few minutes they were back with their rifles and on their way down the trail. I had just returned my attention to some administrative business when I heard the first shots ring out – the sound of an enemy .25 caliber rifle. Obviously, a sniper in a cave had spotted them. I raced back to the edge of the cliff at the top of the trail they had taken to the beach. There they were, pinned down on the beach about hundred yards from the cliff.

"Anyone wounded?" I yelled.

"No Sir," came the answer from the PFC nearest to the cliff, as he hugged the ground tightly.

I knew that we had combat patrols at the beach level working tight against the cliffs and sequentially blasting the caves, one by one, but now there were none immediately in sight. So it was up to me to get these men out of the spot they were in before they were all hit by sniper fire. From my position at the top of the cliff I could see several caves in the cliff directly beneath me, so I asked the nearest Marine:

"Can you see which cave the shots are coming from?"

If he could tell me which cave had the sniper, my plan was to tie a satchel charge onto a line and swing it into the cave from above. But, tragically, I had phrased my question badly. "I had said "can you see" instead of simply "do you know" which cave the shots are coming from. The word "see" suggested to him that he lift his head and look for the cave. The moment he lifted his head to look a sniper shot rang out, and a bullet struck him between the eyes, killing him instantly.

I felt as guilty as though I had shot him myself – why in hell did I say "can you see"? Why didn't I say "do you know"? But there was no time to mourn that one dead man when I had three more still pinned down who would also be dead soon if I didn't get them out. And the only way I could get them out safely was to get the Jap before he got them.

I ordered them – "Stay low and don't move: I'm going to get you out of there."

I explained the situation to the major and asked if we had patrols on cave duty working that way. He told me we did, and I got his permission to find them and lead them to our pinned-down men. When I caught up to the patrol they still had a few hundred yards to go and several other caves to blast before they could reach our group. But we hustled quickly past the intervening caves, throwing grenades as we went by, and we came to where the pinned-down Marines were still lying very low and stone-still, almost afraid to draw a breath. One brave Marine heard me coming and without moving he managed to speak up: "It's the first cave, Lieutenant," he said, "the farthest left."

It was the one closest to us. We blazed it with a flame-thrower and followed up with some heavy explosive charges. There would be no sniping from that cave again. But I dreaded the thought of the letter that I knew I would have to write to the family of the dead Marine, whose only mistake was wanting to take a swim in the ocean.

As we continued our patrolling in early August, we often spent the night in bivouac areas as an isolated battalion without the usual tie-in with other battalions. On one such night, the battalion commander orders me, as Headquarters Company commander, to coordinate the battalion defense. Because the major is in a hurry to get to Brigade Headquarters where the general is throwing a sake party for his victorious commanders, our new CO and his driver take off quickly in his jeep, leaving the details of our defense to me.

Shortly after the major leaves, one of our bivouac patrols comes back with the news that they drew fire from an enemy unit estimated as at least a squad or maybe a platoon strength. It is getting dark and a light rain has begun to fall. I don't have a lot of time left to organize our battalion defense, so I get right to it. With Japs all around us and with no flanking units to tie in with, we've decided on a perimeter defense.

We're going to put one line company in a ditch, running on our side of a road. It is our most vulnerable line, and since we believe it will be our main line of defense if the Japs attack, we place our.30 caliber heavy machine guns at both ends of the line with trajectories that criss-cross each other to provide a zone of fire that the enemy cannot pass through without casualties. Additionally, at one end of the line we also have installed a .50 caliber machine gun crew with their heavy-duty gun aimed down the road to take out any enemy vehicles that might come along. For the remaining three sides of our square perimeter formation, we place the other two line companies and I build my headquarters company line around Lieutenant Don Miller's 81mm mortar platoon and my three intelligence, communications, and quartermaster sections. It's a tight box with all guns pointing outboard, and I'm confident that the Japs won't easily sneak through this defense.

As the night comes on, we believe the Japs have formed a line on their side of our road because they've answered the shots of a few of our jumpy riflemen with their return fire coming from up and down the line. We're sure they're feeling out our flanks to make a *Banzai* end run. In the dark rainy night, we can't see them, but our machine gunners hear them coming through the brush onto the road and they let off a few bursts. Then sporadic fire from both sides develops into a mini firefight in the dark. Finally, just as quiet ensues, along comes the noise of a vehicle moving toward us down the disputed road. It's our major returning from the Brigade sake party in his jeep with the lights on.

"Turn those damn lights off or we'll shoot them out," someone shouts.

The driver realizes the danger, stops and jumps out of the jeep, and ducks into the ditch on our side. But the major who has seen a dead Jap officer with a Samurai sword lying on the road before the lights were turned off, gets out to retrieve the sword. At that precise moment the Japanese open fire all along the line. Our preset guns return the fire – and our commanding officer is ripped apart by a machine gun volley. Not even commanders are immune to tragedy if they violate either of the combat veteran's first two rules; (1) don't try to win any medals; and (2) don't hunt souvenirs.

By August 8, elements of our brigade had reached the northernmost point on Guam, and on August 10 the Corps commander announced that organized resistance on Guam had ceased. But although the island was officially declared secure, we continued systematic patrolling and we remained on the alert against attacks by large pockets of Japanese holdouts. Since it was necessary to maintain a continuous guard against such attacks, our new battalion commander, Lieutenant Colonel Horatio Woodhouse, had established several outposts. These outposts were hidden in the brush but commanded clear fields of fire on the most likely enemy approach routes.

The colonel would send an officer out to check the outposts every few hours. And when there had been no recent enemy activity along the inspection route, the officer usually went alone.

Even though the colonel had just joined us after the tragic shooting of Major Schuster, he already knew of Heavy Pfuhl by name and reputation. So when he saw Heavy return from a mopping up patrol along the nearby cliffs, he recognized him and said: "Heavy, before you settle down somebody has to patrol the outposts."

Heavy was tired and not thrilled to take that assignment. "You want me to go, Colonel?" he asked wearily.

"Well, I think they're your men on that outpost, aren't they?" he asked.

"No Sir, but I'll go. I just wish I wasn't so damn big and easy to pick out of the crowd," Heavy replied, momentarily envying the colonel's inconspicuous five-foot-six, 135-pound frame.

"Colonel," I interjected, "Heavy's done a lot of patrols, and I haven't done that many. I'll check the outposts."

"Thanks, Jones," Heavy replied," if it's all right with the colonel, I'm going to let you sub for me. The only run I want to make now is a beer run."

"That's up to you guys," the colonel said; "I just want one of you to go check on those posts now."

"Yes Sir," I replied. "I'm on my way." And I left.

Even though our area has been peaceful, I find that traveling alone through the brush to our first outpost is an intimidating experience. I feel that there are dozens of enemy soldiers all around me in the area and I know that our battalion is the only friendly force nearby.

When I come to the spot where the outpost is supposed to be, I learn that our men have done a good job of camouflaging their position. There's no one to be seen. I quietly voice the password of the day, which permits them to expose their position to me. It is obviously a nerve-racking assignment for them to sit there and wait for a possible attack by an overwhelming enemy force. The men are happy to see a visiting officer.

"Hi, men," I greet them. "have you seen any activity or have your heard anything?" I ask.

"Nothing, Lieutenant," the gunner replies. "We're just sitting here like a couple of duck hunters, but there are no ducks."

"Well, that's good, isn't it," I say. "You know, those Japanese ducks carry guns."

"That's what they say, Sir," the gunner answers with a grin, "but me and Gene are ready for them. Right, Gene?"

"Well, we've got a helluva good field of fire, Lieutenant," Gene answers, and he gestures with his hand at the broad clearing in front of their machine gun.

The cleared area is several hundred yards wide and deep, with only knee-high grass growing on it. But it backs into a forest grove of twenty and thirty-foot-high trees.

Suddenly, we are shocked as we watch a large force of soldiers emerge from that forest in a skirmish formation. Since our battalion is the only friendly force known to be in the area, and since I know we have no patrols beyond our outposts – this huge force that is coming in our direction can only be the enemy. Since they can't see us in our hidden position, we wait and watch. Then as they continue to approach us, barely two or three hundred yards away, my gunner whispers, "Should I fire, Lieutenant? Should I fire?"

"Hold your fire," I tell him; "if they're Japanese, we can't afford to miss, and if they're not Japanese, we sure as hell don't want to shoot."

"I think they're Japanese, Lieutenant," Gene, the assistant gunner confirms his buddy's suspicion.

They're close enough now, Lieutenant," the gunner insists; "I think I can take them out." And he nervously fingers his weapon.

"Hold your fire," I order. "They're not close enough until we can see who they are."

They continue to come at us, and we silently hold our breath. Finally, they are clearly visible. They are Marines!

Then I step out to reveal myself as a Marine and ask: "Who are you guys?"

They are from an entirely different regiment, whose commander has obviously not coordinated his patrolling with that of our regiment. Only when we reveal our gun emplacement to them do they realize how close they have come to disaster. Although, when I took on this patrol I violated one of the veteran's key maxims "Never volunteer for anything", my presence at the outpost at this critical time proves to be a godsend for that vulnerable company of Marines.

Chapter 17

Back Home to the Canal

I t had been about three months since we had left our base on Guadalcanal. We had spent the first two months at sea on transports and LSTs as a floating reserve for the Saipan/Tinian operations and in preparation for our own delayed invasion of Guam. Now that we had completed our month of fighting on Guam, we were back aboard ship heading home. Just imagine we were going back to Guadalcanal and thinking of it as "home!"

Much had happened in those last three months, and we had lost a lot of good men. Of course, we had also inflicted casualties on the enemy that were ten times greater than ours – a fact that didn't make our losses any easier to bear.

Our total Marine losses in the Central Pacific Campaign at that time, from the battle of Tarawa through the battles of the Mariana Islands then totaled 6,902 dead and 19,471 wounded – more than an entire Marine division. It was a sobering thought that the Marine Corps had already lost the equivalent of one-sixth of its ground forces, with the even bloodier battles of Iwo Jima and Okinawa still to come.

Now, safely aboard ship, Heavy and the boys in his platoon were in high spirits, recapping the highlights of their many narrow escapes on the Guam. No matter how tragic the loss of one's comrades, there is something exhilarating about being a survivor. And the fact that Heavy had personally taken out six nambu machine gun nests and was still here to tell about it bordered on the miraculous. Survival was certainly worth celebrating.

But my spirits were not so high as I reviewed our casualty lists and took advantage of my time aboard ship to write those sad letters to the families of my men who would not be coming home again. One of the saddest was to a rural address in Tennessee. It was, of course, to the home of the boy whose death I had witnessed as he followed my instructions trying to locate the sniper in the cave. The only thing I could think to say to alleviate the family's pain was that their son didn't suffer but died instantly from a clean shot between the eyes. But there was nothing to alleviate my pain when I received a return letter from the boy's mother *thanking me* for that information.

It was a real mystery how a guy like Heavy could lead his men through the fiercest fighting and come out intact while others far less exposed to front-line dangers would somehow catch a fatal piece of shrapnel or a stray round. Back at the Jungle Warfare School in Samoa — before my combat experience — I had thought there were rational measures you could take to improve your chances in war. It had seemed to me that the more you knew about tactics and the better your physical conditioning – the better your chances for survival.

With that in mind, I had trained my men mercilessly. I had even removed a physically weak squad leader in order to promote another man to that job because of his superb physical condition. Then one day on Guam, a convoy from the Third Marines had stopped for a brief moment and in the back of a truck were most of the guys from my Jungle Warfare School platoon.

"Hey, Lieutenant Jones," one of them yelled. They sent us all to the Third Marines as a platoon."

I was amazed because that's what I had wanted. I had trained these guys so vigorously so we could go into combat together as a team. At least it had worked out well for them, I thought.

"Are all the guys okay?" I asked.

"No, Sir," one of them replied; "we've lost a few. And Lieutenant," he added, "remember PFC Bloom? You said he was your toughest and best squad leader."

"Yes, I do," I told him, and then he gave me the zinger. "Well, all that hard training didn't do him much good, Lieutenant; he was the first to catch a bullet in the head when we landed on our first beach."

"I'm sorry to hear that," I told him; "but I see that training did some of you some good because you're still here."

The truck had then pulled away and left me thinking. Can any amount of learning and preparation really help you avoid your fate in war or peace?

Upon our arrival back on the Canal, it's like homecoming week as our rear echelon guys give us a great welcome. The first thing that strikes me is how fat Lieutenant Casey, our assistant quartermaster, has gotten in the three months that we've been away. During all that time he had nothing better to do than to sack out and chow down, and by the looks of him he took full advantage of both options.

Casey, a short red-faced Irishman, was of course just as short as when we left him, but now he was also very rotund, making him look shorter and as round as a butterball. He was not your typical poster Marine. But he was always good-natured, even when he got orders from our new lean colonel to diet, exercise, and lose 30 or 40 pounds fast. That was acceptable compensatory punishment for a Marine still grateful for having been left behind to guard our supplies while we hit our toughest beach to date.

But it wasn't long before the word come down to Battalion from Regiment that Colonel Schneider, who liked a drink as much as any man, was throwing a victory party at the regimental club. I passed the word to Heavy and the other company officers and then got out of their way as they set a new speed record on the way to the so-called "club".

The club was a plywood shack about 40 x 40, with tarpaper roof, screens and screen doors, and a makeshift bar and a few scattered chairs and benches. Nobody cared about the décor because there was plenty of booze that had been received and saved during our three months away in the Marianas Campaign. Heavy was foremost among those who tried to drink it all that night, but he had robust help from a likeable new lieutenant, Jack Fitzgerald, who had joined us on Guam, as well as his old stand-by drinking buddy whom he affectionately called "Whiskey Miller", our large amiable 81mm mortar platoon leader.

Despite the blaring noise of the regimental band marching around while playing the "Marine Corps Hymn", Ed Pesely and I found a relatively quiet corner to sit and talk while we drank a couple of beers.

"What did you think about this last one, Ed?" I asked him.

"It was bad," he said; "it was no quickie like Eniwetok."

"Yeah," I agreed. "And the next one could be worse."

"And I'm getting too old for this shit," Ed added.

"How old is too old, Ed?" I asked.

"Too old is twenty," he replied; and I'm almost thirty. The only officer in the battalion older than me is the new colonel – and he's only thirty-two. Hell, I put on my first Marine uniform in 1936 when you were probably a sophomore in high school. You know, I was pulling duty in Hawaii before Pearl Harbor."

"I know you were, Ed, and you've been out here a couple of years on this tour, haven't you?."

"About 26 months," he replied; but the scuttlebutt is that the Marine Corps finally has a rotation policy and some guys may be gong home soon. What do you hear at Battalion?" I couldn't tell him about my very strongly worded letter to the general, pleading for some kind of Marine Corps rotation or leave policy like the other services, so I simply said: "I have a hunch that the scuttlebutt might be right this time. I definitely know the general was told about the problem and I think he took some action before we went to Guam."

After the big party, we settle down to some housekeeping chores. Our energetic little French padre is determined to build a recreation area for the men. He visualizes a large lounge, a courtyard, a library, a barbershop, an NCO club, as well as a chapel and chaplain's office. The guys decide to call the area *FIFILEMU* (Take it Easy) in recollection of our Samoan days. And they build a huge three-dimensional sign spelling out the word in Samoan and placing it on top of the coconut-log gate into the area.

Other more mundane facilities also had to be built such as enough heads (latrines) to accommodate the needs of the hundreds of Marines in our battalion. Each company commander was assigned a specific place to locate his company head. There were three phases in the construction of every head. The first phase was the digging of a deep rectangular trench. The second phase was placing a twelve-hole box over the trench. And the last phase was placing a housing over the entire construction. As was

The 22d Marines' veteran Lt. Heavy Pfuhl, and his new good friend, Lt. Jack Fitzgerald, at the Fi Fi Lemu gate to the 2d Battalion Recreation Center on Guadalcanal. (Courtesy of Jack Fitzgerald)

customary, each company commander delegated the project to a trusted sergeant, which I did as the CO of Headquarters Company. Since there were four companies in our battalion, there were four such heads (outhouses) of identical size and shape lined up, about a hundred yards back, along our main battalion camp roadway.

Constructing four outhouses would seem like a simple enough project, but often the military has a way of complicating simple projects. The first mishap was a very large explosion that rocked the camp when a sergeant in Heavy's company used a large explosive charge as a short-cut to the digging of his pit. The colonel was not pleased and suggested finishing it with shovels.

The second mishap fell upon me and my company when our colonel came by for his pre-inspection before the Regimental inspection, and he was shocked at what he saw. Looking down the battalion roadway he saw three outhouses perfectly aligned parallel with battalion roadway, and the fourth – mine – at a forty-five degree angle with the roadway. Although such juxtapositioning would hardly matter to any Marine doing his business in that outhouse – it was, of course, a serious infringement on the law of uniformity to the military mind. Anyhow, the colonel said: "Jones, what the hell is that?" and before I could answer, he said: "Fix it! Before Regimental inspection."

Since Regimental inspection was only a few hours away, and there was no possibility that we could dig a new pit that was properly lined up parallel to the roadway in time, I told the colonel: "We don't have time to dig a new hole, Sir,"

"I didn't tell you to dig a new hole, Jones," the colonel replies. I just said 'Fix it'."

"Yes Sir," I responded, and I called my first sergeant. "Pennock," I told him; "the colonel wants our head to be lined up parallel with the other heads immediately before Regimental inspection."

"Yes Sir," Pennock said, and he departed, leaving me wondering how he was going to do it. No matter, I didn't invent buck passing in the military. I was just keeping the tradition alive.

The colonel was no more mystified than I when a short time later we paraded down our battalion street with the inspection team from Regiment and dutifully noted how beautifully aligned were *all four* of our battalion outhouses. After the inspection, I asked the first sergeant to tell me the secret. He led me to the head, opened the screen door and when we entered I saw a new creative architecture for a multiholed outhouse. Of course, the pit and box remained in the same misaligned position that they had been before, but now the outer housing had simply been properly aligned so it looked fine from the roadway. So who knew if the men using the facility were sitting on a box that was angled from corner to corner rather than the usual end-to-end?

Before we settle down to our usual get-ready-for-the-next-beach schedule, we have serious unfinished business from the last one. Our company and battalion officers are flooding our new colonel with recommendations for medals for the many heroic acts of their best men on Guam.

The colonel passes the buck to me. "Jones," he says, "you've been with this battalion since Samoa. You know the officers and a lot the men. I want you to screen all these recommendations and bring me your final list." Then he handed me the recommendations and a thick manual put out by the United States War Department that listed all categories of medals that could be awarded for heroic action in combat along with sample write-ups for each category.

"Here, Lieutenant," he said; "this is your guide for which medal to recommend for each level of valor." "Level of valor," I thought; "how do you split up unusual acts of bravery into levels?" Anyhow it was my job to go try.

After extensive consultations with the other company commanders and platoon leaders, I brought a consolidated list to the colonel of the medals that were being recommended. It was not what he wanted. He wanted to see the write-ups for each medal being recommended. He said: "Jones, how am I going to judge these if I don't see a description of the action?" One other thing, he warned me, "when you use that manual I gave you to write those descriptions, remember that's the Army talking, not the Marine Corps. So whatever the Army gives a Medal of Honor for, we give a Navy Cross, and whatever they give a Silver Star for, we give a Bronze Star – a Marine is expected to do more.

"Yes, Sir," I replied, and I was gone for another week before I returned with my recommendations complete with individual write-ups. At the top of my list were two recommendations for Navy Crosses. The first was to Corporal Webster Bachelot in Heavy's platoon. The way he had placed himself out front of the entire battalion at the most vulnerable spot on our line, and the way he and his squad had absorbed the brunt of a vicious *Banzai* attack, and the way he had taken a bayonet in the chest and then engaged and killed four of the enemy in brutal hand-to-hand combat – all of that in a significant battle that helped break the back of the Japanese defense – certainly seemed to Heavy and to me that he deserved the nation's second highest award, the Navy Cross. The colonel who had been at Brigade Headquarters at the time had personal knowledge of this action, and he approved our recommendation without discussion, but my second Navy Cross recommendation didn't pass so easily.

During the landing on Guam, I had promised myself that if I ever found out which Marine had silenced the enemy field piece in the cliff after it had destroyed the two boats in front of mine so that my boat could slip safely ashore – I would award him whatever medal I could. He had not only saved my life and that of our colonel, but he had also ensured the successful landing of the waves behind us and guaranteed the security of our tenuous hold on that flank of the beach.

So now that I knew he was Sergeant George Weber, I wrote him up for the Navy Cross. During the landing he was one of the few survivors of an amtrac in front of mine when it was blown up fifty yards from the beach. In spite of a bad head wound, he crawled into a shellhole near a Japanese gun that was sweeping the reef and began tossing grenades, silencing the first gun. Then he continued his grenade attack, silencing all the guns bearing on our flank of the beach before picking up his rifle and joining his squad advancing inland.

The colonel agreed that Weber's actions were certainly heroic and deserving of a medal, but he was hesitant to recommend two men in our battalion for the Navy Cross. "Why the Navy Cross?" he asked; "Why not the Silver Star?"

It was not a good time to state the simple truth, but I did anyhow. "It was only because of Sergeant Weber that our battalion command boat, with Colonel Hart and me in it, ever made the beach," I stated.

"Well, it was a commendable action, Jones, but we don't give Navy Crosses just because a Marine saves a lieutenant's life, even if it's yours."

"I understand, Sir," I replied, but he not only saved our lives, he saved a beachhead."

"That's enough discussion, Jones; put him in for a Silver Star."

That was a direct order, so when our recommendations went to Regiment, I had to recommend him for a Silver Star rather than a Navy Cross, but I hadn't been specifically ordered to rewrite my elaborate write-up which was written with the words traditionally reserved for Navy Cross recommendations. Consequently, within a short time, after all the other recommendations had been approved by Regiment, that one recommendation was bucked back down to our battalion commander with a note from our regimental commander, that asked simply – "Why wasn't this man recommended for a Navy Cross?" Needless to say, I swiftly returned my original recommendation to Regiment, and Sergeant Weber received his just award as well as my eternal gratitude.

For leading the First Provisional Marine Brigade in its successful Guam operations, Brigadier General Lemuel C. Shepherd received the Distinguished Service Medal and was promoted to the rank of major general. He was also authorized to form the new Sixth Marine Division in September of 1944. This was accomplished by adding the 29th Marines to the Brigade's 22d Marines and 4th Marines.

But only the man wearing any medal knows whether he earned it or not, and the Secretary of the Navy thought enough of the brave actions of all the men in our First Provisional Marine Brigade to bestow upon all of us the U.S. Navy Unit Commendation: "For outstanding heroism in action against enemy Japanese forces during the invasion of Guam…"

The rewards to the outstanding enlisted men who had distinguished themselves in combat were not limited to medals alone. Several of them were recommended for field commissions, including Navy Cross winner, Corporal Bachelot. Some others found themselves reassigned to the States. It seemed like my letter to the general suggesting a combat rotation plan or some kind of relief from the Marine Corps policy of "stay-and-fight-till-you-die" had produced mixed results. Anyhow, it turned out that our enlisted veterans with two years overseas were being reassigned to stateside duty, but not the officers. Someone in the Corps (probably Academy graduates and Regular officers) had decided that all officers lusted for all the combat duty they could get. So officers with more than two-years over here were simply to get a quick 30-day leave to home and civilization. My two good friends, Ed Pesely and Heavy Pfuhl, were happy to hear that they qualified. And although I was a few months short of qualifying, I was vicariously thrilled by their excitement..

As usual, Heavy took the news of his upcoming leave as an

occasion to celebrate, so one afternoon after sharing a bottle of scotch with the new officer-nominee, Corporal Bachelot and a couple of the Stateside-bound men, Heavy was wheeling his way back to his tent when he encountered little Dean McDowell.

Lieutenant McDowell was a physically-fit athletic Marine who was barely more than half the size of Heavy. As the stepson of a Navy admiral, he seemed to be too much of a regulation-book Marine to please Heavy. So Heavy took every opportunity to tease the little lieutenant. This occasion started no differently than any of the others, but it had a very surprising ending.

In a playful mood after his session with the bottle, Heavy couldn't resist the temptation to interrupt the little lieutenant's purposeful marching stride as he was making his way to the officer's mess tent. Heavy simply stepped in front of him, blocking his way. And when McDowell tried to sidestep the big guy, Heavy purposely blocked that maneuver as well.

"Come on, Heavy, let me get by," McDowell said.

Heavy gave him a kind of boozy grin and said:

"What's your hurry, Deanie?" And as he continued to block McDowell's way, McDowell tried to push past him, with a hard shove. Heavy didn't like the shove, so he assumed a playful boxer pose and said: "Are you going to fight me, Deanie? Come on let's box." And with that Heavy laid a couple of easy open-handed slaps on McDowell's cheeks. Then to the shock and dismay of all of us watching this uneven encounter, McDowell threw a right hand punch at Heavy's chin, and the big guy dropped to his knees.

It shocked us as much as it did Heavy. We knew we had to get McDowell out of there before Heavy realized what happened, so we hustled McDowell off to the officer's mess while Heavy was shaking his head and exclaiming: "That little bastard closed his fist on me. He got me with a sucker punch. Where the hell did he go?"

While one group of us got Heavy to his tent, another group in the officers' mess was hearing McDowell's explanation of what happened. It was a very straight-forward but naïve statement: "Heavy was fooling around with me," McDowell reported, "so I had to drop him." We tried to explain to McDowell: "We got you away with your life this time, but never try to 'drop him' again."

In the Marine Corps, like the Old West, any little guy like McDowell who had got away with a sucker punch on a big guy like Heavy had better become invisible fast. But unlike the Old West a Marine can't just leave town – not without orders. Fortunately for McDowell, Heavy soon got his orders for a quick thirty-day leave as his reward for surviving thirty months of jungle warfare that included three assault landings. So the big guy left town leaving the little guy to strut around camp unassailed – at least for thirty days – and he could hope that thirty days of civilization would send Heavy back as a mild-mannered civilian.

Ah, that was the rub. When I had written my letter to the general pleading the case for a rotation policy I had not thought of short leaves home as being a solution to the tragic state of troop morale. I had expressed my view that what was needed was a rotation policy of transferring combat troops home after a period of eighteen months like the other services, or a two-year jungle combat tour at the maximum. War in the Pacific was never like Europe. In the jungle, half your time goes to fighting your environment, and half your time to thinking about things back in civilization and wondering if you'll ever see it again. Without a firm rotation policy, our own commanders had unintentionally been subjecting our troops to insidious psychological warfare.

Finally, many of the original troops who had been oversees with the 22d Marines for 30 months were being transferred to stateside duty, but not the officers who were simply offered a short thirty-day leave. Whether thirty-days leave at home was a sensible alternate plan to a rotation policy or not, that was the plan now offered to some of our officers. To pluck war weary Marines like Heavy Pfuhl and Ed Pesely who had been overseas two-and-a-half years from out of their combat jungle environment and give them a brief taste of home and then dump them back into the jungle was not an option I had contemplated. Of course, short R&R leaves to some nearby civilized locations within the Pacific Theatre would have been welcomed, but the thirty-day home leave was like giving the last meal to a condemned man. Worse yet, it also put his family through that excruciating ordeal, even as they wept tears of joy with their temporarily reprieved serviceman.

Without the benefit of my gloomy sour-grapes analysis, it was in November of 1944 that Heavy Pfuhl, Ed Pesely and a handful of other 22d Marine officers found themselves happily seated aboard a PBY on the first leg of a trip that would take them to the country and family they hadn't seen in two-and-a-half years. Meanwhile, I (with three assault landings but slightly less than two years overseas) remained in the jungle and chalked up my six-hundredth day on primitive islands without leave or relief.

Chapter 18

The Calm Before The Storm

While Heavy and Pesely took their pleasures at home in the States, for those of us with less than two years of Island time it was business as usual on the Canal. It was a brief quiet time, like the calm before the storm.

In August, while still on Guam I had been re-assigned from a battalion liaison officer to CO of Headquarters Company, 2d Battalion, 22d Marines. That was the job I had on October 16, 1944 when Private Bobby Faolea of the British Solomon Island Labor Camp was struck and killed by a Marine hit-and-run ambulance driver. It seems that PFC White, an ambulance driver with our Regimental Medical Company on detached duty to our battalion as part of my Headquarters Company, was the one being held by the Provost Marshal for that hit-and-run fatality. This situation brought me quickly to our colonel's office.

"Jones," he said, "What do you know about this hit-and-run accident?"

"Only what I've heard from the Sergeant of the Guard, Sir," I answered. "The driver was taking a couple of stretcher cases to the field hospital in the dark when some natives suddenly crossed the road in front of him. The light was poor. He couldn't stop. He hit him."

"Well, Lieutenant, there's more it than that. He didn't help the victim. The victim died, and then the driver lied about the accident to our MPs. So now you have a hit-and run manslaughter case on your hands."

"On my hands, Sir?" I asked.

"Yes, Lieutenant, you're Headquarters Company Commander, he's assigned to your company, so I'm naming you as the Junior

Member of the court that we have to convene. That means you will be the Court Recorder, and it will be your job to conduct the case."

"But, Sir, I don't know how to conduct a court martial. I'm not a lawyer, and I have no relevant training."

"Lieutenant," the colonel persisted, a Marine officer can perform any assignment he's given, and here's the book on Navy Regulations and Court Martial Law. Read it and prepare the case. Also, make sure you maintain a liaison with your British counterpart in the Solomon Island Governor's Office."

"Aye, Aye, Sir," I responded, and I took the book and left.

"Until now I didn't know there was a British compound nearby. All I knew was that we were living in tents on a jungle island. But my jeep driver took me to the British compound which was a beautiful island-type structure somewhat like the one that the London Missionary Society had constructed at the Leone Girls' School in Samoa – only this was much bigger with gated grounds.

A barefooted, bare-waisted native soldier from the Fiji Islands with chevrons on his *lava-lava* stood guard at the gate. His wooly black hair, black skin, and native features were indistinguishable from those of the local Guadalcanal natives, but when he spoke there was a great difference. Instead of the Pidgin English spoken by the local natives, he spoke impeccable English with an upper-class British accent that he learned from the British officers that he served. After a proper military greeting, he passed my jeep through, and we pulled up to a broad wooden stairway that led onto a wide veranda upon which sat an English officer at a breakfast table set for one.

The officer was a major dressed in summer uniform, which for the British meant a short-sleeve khaki blouse and khaki shorts with knee-length khaki stockings. A black native in a white *lava-lava* who was waiting on him greeted me and led me to the table. The major remained seated as I introduced myself.

"Sit down, Lieutenant," he said. "Won't you have a spot of tea?"

"No sir," I answered. "I just wanted to meet you and discuss the court martial case."

"The court martial case?" he asked. "What court martial case?"

"Well, I assume you know about the accident?"

"Well of course I know about Bobby, but I didn't know there was a court martial involved. You mean you Yanks would court martial one of your own men over the accidental killing of a native?" He seemed dumbfounded.

"Maybe not, Major, if it was a simple accidental killing, but in this case it was hit-and-run and then lying to his superiors to cover up. The Marines are pretty strict about honesty and taking responsibility."

"All this over the accidental death of a native" he asked still dumbfounded.

"We're not doing it solely to avenge the death of a native boy, Major; we're doing it to maintain integrity and discipline in the Corps," I told him.

The major offered his full cooperation in the matter and simply asked that he be given the complete minutes of the court martial for his records. I returned to camp, reported to the colonel, and he set a date for the proceedings.

As Court Recorder I served as the prosecutor. A captain served as the driver's defense attorney, and a major was the Senior Member of the court. Although I could have charged the driver with manslaughter, I had no intention of doing that. He was a scared young man in a hostile native environment, and black natives in the black of night are not easily seen. The accident seemed to be a truly unavoidable accident, for which he might be excused.

The vexing question was why didn't he stay and assist the victim, or take the victim to the hospital? However, he already had a full jeep load with two Marine stretcher cases, and he did stop but was afraid to dwell for fear that the other natives might turn on him. Still, there was no excuse for lying to the Marine MP sergeant who later – in the safety of our compound – asked him if he had struck a native. He strongly denied it, despite the obvious damage done to his vehicle.

The Senior Member of the court made it known that he would

like to see the proceedings acquit the Marine of all guilt, but as prosecutor I felt I had to be the one to uphold some standard of Marine discipline and integrity. If this Marine could get away with lying here and now and shirking his responsibilities in a rear-echelon camp, how could he be trusted not to do the same in our next combat situation? I felt he had to have some punishment, no matter how slight, to let him know lying to his superiors was not a penalty-free option. I prosecuted him accordingly and the court found him guilty on two minor charges. We reduced him from PFC to Private and fined him $50.

The senior member, the major, chastised me for not following his lead and spinning the proceedings to result in full acquittal; but the colonel agreed with my decision and complimented me on my conduct of the case.

The court martial was not a task I was qualified to perform, but orders are orders – at least they were then – and we had no Unified Military Code of Justice for the Armed Forces at that time. As a matter of fact, we didn't have any "Armed Forces" as an entity. What we had were two independent services – the Army and the Navy, with the Marine Corps and the Coast Guard reporting to the Navy and with the Air Corps part of the Army. No, there was no separate Air Force in World War II.

In November 1944, while Heavy, Pesely, and the other 30-month veteran officers were enjoying their brief reprieve, we continued with our usual training and administrative routines. About a week before Thanksgiving, the sergeant major showed me an order that had just come down from Division Headquarters. It stated that all battalions would designate one major as the unit transport quartermaster, and that officer would be relieved of his battalion duties and be assigned to Division to go to Transport Quartermaster School in preparation for serving as a battalion transport quartermaster (TQM) on our next combat operation.

"Okay, Sergeant Major," I said: "I'll take this order to the colonel since our three majors come under my administration as CO Headquarters Company."

When I showed the order to the colonel, he was not happy. "Jones," he said, "I only have three majors and I can't spare any of them for any damn quartermaster school."

"Well, Sir," I asked, do you want me to check with Division and see what the alternatives are?"

"Hell no," he replied," they're not going to give us any alternatives. I'm going to give them the alternative. I'll give them an officer as experienced and as capable as any in the battalion, but he won't be one of my three majors. I'll give them a company commander."

"Yes, Sir," I said, "which company?"

"Yours," he replied.

"But I'm only a first lieutenant, Colonel, and they asked for a major," I reminded him. "Don't you think they'll at least want a captain?"

"You're my most senior first lieutenant, Jones. You've had every job in the battalion except mine, the XO, and the Bn-3 operations. You've been a platoon leader and executive officer of a line company; you've been the Bn-1 Adjutant; you've had the Bn-2 Intelligence Platoon; you've had the Communications Platoon; you've been the Bn-4 Supply officer, and now you're Headquarters Company Commander. Hell, in the Army or the Navy, you'd have your gold oak leaves by now. Anyhow, you're the guy I'm sending up there."

"Aye, aye, Sir," I replied. "I'll report as ordered."

I reported with all the majors from the various battalions to the first day of Division Transport Quartermaster School, which was held aboard an Admiral's flagship. All I remember about that day is that I was seriously outranked by almost everybody except for a couple of Navy enlisted stewards who were on hand to serve coffee to the brass. What I learned that day was that the Navy was taking our next combat operation very seriously. It was obvious that the next one would be a lot more complex than any of our previous operations. Therefore, it was expected that for the next three or four months, each of us transport quartermasters would devote his full time, plus that of an assistant, to learning the job and planning the combat loading of his reinforced Battalion Landing Team (BLT) and all of its equipment aboard troop transports. Combat loading, of course, meant that every piece of equipment, plus the expendable supplies required for a successful amphibious assault, must be precalculated and loaded to fit precisely according to a meticulous plan aboard each specifically designated APA ship.

The colonel was pleased to get my report and to learn that Division had accepted me as our qualified BLT#2 TQM. He then allowed me to select one of our newly-arrived second lieutenants as my assistant. I chose Second Lieutenant Robert Small, who was not a small man and who was a little older than most second lieutenants. Small was about my age, married with two children. I picked him because he seemed to be a conscientious officer who I thought would work well on our very important but tedious assignment. And since he was married with two children, I knew he had been safe from the Army draft and therefore was a true volunteer who had willingly joined the Corps.

It was only a week or two after we had started our daily sessions at the TQM school when I noticed a new cargo ship had arrived and was anchored closer than usual to our battalion campsite. Curious about what kind of ship it was, I asked one of the TQM Naval officers about it. He told me it was an ammunition ship loaded with ten thousand tons of high-explosive shells. I would have thought no more about it except for how close this ship seemed to be anchored to our camp, seemingly only a few hundred yards off the beach where our battalion tents were located.

At that time I was bunking with Lieutenant Castagna, the new battalion adjutant. There were two folding field cots in our tent, and even though we were living at the Equator, I slept in my skivvies under a woolen GI blanket, since, of course, we had no such luxuries as sheets.

Suddenly, in the middle of the night, I was jolted awake by a brilliant flash of light, followed by a thunderous roar. The light was so bright it penetrated the heavy canvas of my tent, and the entire sky was on fire. Soon things were falling all around us, metal scraps and pieces of debris, some as large as locker boxes.

"My God;" I yelled at Castagna, "what the hell was that?"

Then we both ran out of the tent to look. The 10,000-ton ammunition ship was gone. It had literally disappeared in a flash. The next day at TQM school we had a serious subject to discuss – the safe loading and unloading of high explosives. It seems that the explosion (equal to that of a 10-kiloton "A" bomb) was caused by the careless dropping of a net full of high-explosive shells into the hold of the ammo ship. The officer in charge and the careless workers on that shift would never have an opportunity to make that mistake again, and then it was clear to me why the Navy felt that my unglamorous TQM job rated a very senior Marine officer. No details are routine and nothing is trivial when you're handling 10,000 tons of high explosives.

Chapter 19

An Ill Wind Building

U ntil September 1944, the 22d Marines and the 4th Marines had been two highly individualistic regiments that had been loosely thrown together to operate as a brigade for the Marianas Campaign. However, in September 1944, when the 29th Marines was added to General Shepherd's brigade roster and the 6th Marine Division was thereby formed, with the supporting arms of artillery, tanks, and engineers, we were now a formally organized U.S. Marine division. We were the only one in the history of the Marine Corps to be formed overseas and, as it turned out, to never set foot in the Continental United States.

At our battalion level, life went on as usual. We continued to train in the sweltering jungle. A certain percentage of us got injured or sick and were sent away. Another percentage of us was still showing up at sick bay with *mumu*, malaria, or some other tropical fever and were being sent home. And new replacements were coming along to fill in for our battlefield and training casualties. Perhaps only a third of our original officers from Samoa had lasted this long, so even such newcomers as Lieutenant Jack Fitzgerald, who had joined us as recently as the end of our last campaign on Guam, was now an old salt in the 22d Marines.

But it was the eager new second lieutenants I felt sorry for, especially the football players, like Teddy Ogdahl, one of the several new replacement lieutenants assigned to Easy Company after Guam. Teddy had been an All-American back before joining the Marine Corps. On his first day with the battalion, as I watched him trot self-confidently to join his new platoon, it was clear to me that here was an innocent young man who thought that combat was simply going to be another football game played on the rival school's turf. If he lived through his first landing he would soon learn that, unlike football, combat is a game played for keeps.

With our new division status, we are not only getting new replacements but we are also getting new equipment, new uniforms, new supporting units, new training schools, even a new simulated Japanese village. Soon Heavy and our rifle companies are performing in battalion, regimental, and divisional exercises – all prescribed by an energetic little G-3, Lieutenant Colonel Victor Krulak, at Division Headquarters.

But since I was now assigned to Division as the BLT #2 TQM, I was excused from the battalion field exercises. Instead, I was now holed up with my assistant, Lieutenant Small, applying what we were learning at TQM School to the very real task of planning our battalion logistics for our next combat operation. Since our job involved a serious "need to know", we were among the first to learn that our next operation would be an attack on Okinawa, an integral part of the Japanese homeland. Knowing first hand how fiercely the Japanese had defended their outlying buffer territories like Saipan – we knew we would be facing an enemy with suicidal determination on a home island like Okinawa.

As we get closer to the date of embarkation, Lieutenant Small and I are busy sliding tiny cut-to-scale templates of every piece of our battalion gear into position on the diagrams of every individual hold and deck cargo area on our APA. It's a tedious and exacting task, but it gets us out of the daily jungle grind. Of course, Liuetenant Small hasn't been exposed much to the daily jungle grind, because he's newly arrived from the States, and this is his first combat theatre assignment. Except for the war stories he's heard from us, he has no feeling for what the war's been like for the past two years that we've been here. However, even an innocent optimist would know that the combat mission we're loading for is now going to be a big one with high expectations of severe casualties. As that dawned on my assistant, he started peppering me with some very nervous questions.

"What was it really like on your first landing?" he asked.

"Well, as I've told you before, it was very scary in the boats going in, and very confusing on the beach. But I think on your first one you get by on your ignorance."

"What does that mean?"

"On a hot beach landing, it means that you're going to learn more about combat in the first few minutes than anyone has been able to teach you outside of combat; and you'll be too busy reacting to the enemy and learning how to stay alive to think about anything else – even how scared you are."

"What about your family," he asked; "do you think about them?"

Now I began to see what was bugging him. I remembered that he was a married man with two small children. Then I realized what a handicap it was for a Marine to be married with a family. Fortunately, most of our guys were very young and single.

"No, Bob" I don't think you'll be thinking about your family on a hostile beach. You'll be totally focused on self-preservation – saving your ass. You'll think about your family on the boat going in, and you'll certainly think about them after it's over. But not on that beach in the thick of it, where you would trade a pass through the pearly gates for a muddy shellhole."

"I think my family means more to me than self-preservation, Lieutenant," he said glumly.

"Well, Lieutenant, "I answered," a dead Marine is no good to the Marine Corps or his family, so you better put first priority on self-preservation. Of course, that's self-preservation while you're performing your mission," I added: "not in lieu of getting the job done."

After the lieutenant and I finished our day's work, I returned to my tent to find Heavy and Pesely looking for me. "We're heading to the OC. Why don't you come along and tell us what's happening at Division."

The OC was an island shack made out of two-by-fours, a wooden floor, a tin roof, and canvas sides. In one corner of the shack was a wooden table, and a dozen fold-up camp chairs made famous by Hollywood directors. As we reached the table, we saw that it was already loaded with empty beer bottles and the chairs were filled with one captain and a bunch of lieutenants from the Second Battalion who were busy emptying more beer bottles. We got some beer and joined the group.

Clockwise from Capt. John Lanigan (seated left forefront) are Lt. Rusty Green, Lt. Bob Carey, Capt. Benny Hoover (standing), Lt. Dale Bair, Lt. Tom Jones (author), Lt. Hank Lassiter, Lt. Curl Tuell, Lt. Ed Pesely, Lt. Swindell, and Lt. Dan McFadden. About half of these beer drinkers made the landing on Okinawa, but none who made it on to Okinawa made it off the island unscathed.

"Jones, what the hell are you guys doing up there at Division?" someone asked.

"We're loading ship," I told them.

"Hell, you've been loading ship for three months, Captain Lanigan said with a smirk. "While these guys have been out eating mud," he added gratuitously.

"I think you know, Captain, I've eaten my share of mud in the last two years," I reminded him. "And I'll be on the beach eating it again with you when we make this next landing. But me being on the beach in the first couple of waves this time isn't as important as making sure you get the ammunition, water, and supplies you'll need to stay alive on that beach."

"I don't think you're going to be on the beach at all," the Captain replied. "The colonel told me that someone had to stay here on the Canal in charge of our rear echelon camp."

"Did he say that it would be me?" I asked.

"He didn't say who it would be, but since you're the TQM, you're the likely prospect, aren't you?"

"No," I replied. "He hasn't said anything to me about it."

"Don't fight it, Jones," Heavy spoke up. "If you don't want that assignment I'll take it. I've had enough of this hitting-the-beach crap. You and I and Pesely, Dale and the captain, and a bunch of us here have survived three beach landings already. What are the odds that any of us are going to make it through a fourth, especially against old Tokyo Rose's home garden – Okinawa?"

"Well, I'm with you, Heavy," I said; "I don't feel like we owe anybody anything, especially another bloody landing. I'd just as soon stay here, but the colonel isn't offering, and I'm not asking."

After a few more beers, Heavy got into a macabre guessing game. "Well, who's going to get it on this next one?" he asked. Then he turned to the captain and said – "It doesn't look too good for you, Captain."

The captain grinned away the drunken prophecy, but Heavy continued down his clairvoyant list. "Jones," he said, "I see you on a stretcher but you're just going to get nicked, a little shrapnel in the leg. "Ed," he turned to Pesely. "You're going to get the hell shot out of you, but they can't kill an old Marine. You'll retire on 30. "Dale," he said to Lieutenant Bair, "you crazy gung-ho sonofabitch, you're going to get yourself killed. You ought to sit this next one out." And so he went on down his list, predicting disaster for almost everyone there. Finally, the captain interrupted Heavy's drunken oration.

"You're full of crap," Lanigan told him.

"Okay, Captain," Heavy replied," but I'm putting money where my mouth is – I got a hundred bucks on every one of my predictions.

"I'll cover all your bets," Lanigan replied, "because even if you're right, I'll be dead and there'll be no payoff. I can't lose; you can't win."

"Well maybe I'll be wrong about you and win on all the other counts," Heavy responded cleverly.

"It's still a good bet for me," Lanigan explained; "it's worth a couple hundred bucks to see your bet on me come up empty."

By that time, everyone had had so much beer that I'm sure only the captain remembered the great prophecies by the football clairvoyant.

Since we were getting very close to our actual embarkation date, it was necessary for me to spend some time with our colonel to discuss in detail the priorities he wished to assign to each category of cargo, because, of course, we would have to load last those items that were first to be unloaded on the beach. As a general rule, ammunition and water were the highest priority cargo because they would usually be needed first. However, every landing and each beach required careful study with final decision making by the commander of the landing team. As commander of BLT #2, Lieutenant Colonel Woodhouse sat with me in a number of sessions while we thrashed out the priorities he wanted assigned to the combat cargo for his team.

From our experiences in the Marshals and the Marianas, we had learned the critical importance of flamethrowers when attacking an underground force who fought from caves and interconnected tunnels. Therefore, flamethrowers were the number one priority on our colonel's list. Number two priority was the usual water, and number three was a surprising item simply identified on the secret order I signed on 27 March 1945 as "(1) Net of Secret Weapons." I didn't know then, and I still don't' know today what those weapons were, but they were higher on our priority list than napalm, nitrogen cylinders, wire concertinos, wire stakes, barbed wire, sandbags, "K" and "D" rations, and communications wire. During one of these sessions with the colonel, I asked him about Captain Lanigan's remarks indicating that an officer would have to stay on the Canal in charge of the battalion's rear echelon contingent.

I asked the colonel directly: "Do you want me or Lieutenant Small to stay on the Canal in charge of the battalion's rear echelon?"

"Yes," he replied; "one of you will stay here."

"Which one?" I asked. Having survived two major campaigns and three assault landings, which many of my friends did not survive, I was not eager to tempt fate with this fourth ominous campaign. Of course, I was ready to accept the colonel's decision, but it turned out that he didn't want to make that decision. He simply replied to my question "Which one?" by saying — "It's up to you, Jones."

That put me in a terrible place, much worse than if he had simply made the decision and had left me only to follow orders. Now I had the choice or ordering myself or my assistant into a deadly fierce combat operation. But it also meant that I was the only Marine in our battalion who could choose whether to participate in this campaign or not. The colonel couldn't even grant that option to himself, but he had granted it to me.

That night I sat down with Lieutenant Pesely and kicked around my options.

"What should I do, Pesely?" I asked him.

"Don't sweat it," he told me. "Let the new guy go. You stay here. You've seen enough combat. He hasn't seen any. Like Heavy said the other night, some of us are bound to get hit bad this trip, and all of us old timers are due to run out of luck. You can be lucky once, or twice, or three times – but I don't know about four –that could be the jinx. Hell, if you've got a chance to sit this one out, do it. I would."

"But, Pese," I reminded him; "you didn't do it on Eniwetok. You were TQM for that operation, and you went with us. You didn't stay on Maui."

"No," he answered, "but I wasn't given the choice. The colonel said 'go' and I went."

"I wish he had just said 'go' to me," I responded. "It would have made it a hell of a lot easier. Anyhow, I've got to deal with it in the morning."

The following morning, I called Lieutenant Small into my tent to talk. We were the only two in the tent, and he sat on a cot opposite mine. He spoke up before I did. "Lieutenant," he said, "I heard the scuttlebutt that one of us will stay behind as the officer in charge of our battalion rear echelon contingent. Is that true?"

"That's what I want to talk to you about, Bob," I told him. "As you know, I've been out here for two years and I've been in two major campaigns and have made three assault landings against hot beaches. I've never had a leave, and I'm pretty worn down. To tell you the truth, I'm not eager to make this next one. A lot of us old timers have a bad feeling in our bones about this one."You, on the other hand," I continued, "have only been here a couple of months. You've never been in combat. Your luck is shiny new and unused. Ours is pretty bedraggled and worn down. I suppose you joined the Marine Corps to get into the war, and this may be your last chance to do just that."

"Gee, Lieutenant," he said despondently, "I hope you haven't already decided to send me. You're right, Sir, I haven't been in combat and I did voluntarily join the Marine Corps, but now I realize I wasn't thinking about my family. My wife never wanted me to do it, but I was stubborn. I didn't know what it would really be like, to be away from home, to be away from my wife and my kids, and maybe to die and never see them again. I'm not afraid for myself, Sir, but when I think of what it would do to them if I were killed out here. Who would take care of them, and what would they do? That's what I'm afraid of, Sir; I'm not afraid of combat."

"Well, you should be afraid of combat," I told him; "we all are – except the crazies. But we do our job the best we can."

"Yes, Sir," and if you tell me to go, I'll go Sir. "I'll go and be the best Marine I can be."

"I know you would, Bob," I told him, "but forget it. You're not going. I am."

"Yes, Sir," he replied elatedly. And he remained elated until our ship sailed from the Canal, leaving him behind in safety for the sake of his family.

Chapter 20

Okinawa and the World's Greatest Armada

"What the hell got into you, Jones," Heavy said the first time we met on deck aboard the APA that was carrying us to a rendezvous staging area for the greatest armada that the world had ever seen.

"What are you talking about, Heavy?" I asked.

"What I'm talking about is why are you here? I expected to see Bob Small here and you still on the Canal living it up with double beer and booze rations. The colonel gave you a choice, didn't he?"

"Yeah, he gave me a choice."

"Well, you sure made a hell of a poor decision. I know which way I would have decided."

"You really don't, Heavy, but I do," I told him. "There's no way you would have sent your platoon in on this one with some green second lieutenant while you sat back on the Canal."

"Maybe not when my platoon was all my old guys from Samoa, Eniwetok, and Guam, but we've got a lot of new guys now. I'd just as soon let them find out how it is for themselves, along with the new lieutenants. We know how it is. We don't have to find out any more."

Then, getting back to his point, he said: "you know how I love a good scrappy game of football, but this war is a nightmare. It's like a game where no matter how many yards you make on a play they keep moving the goal post so that it's always a hundred yards away. You should have benched yourself on this one, Jones, and let the new guy carry the ball."

"Heavy," I reminded him, "remember your prophecy for me?

I am just going to get a light nick in the leg. I figure I can handle that much."

"Well, I give good hunches," Heavy concluded; "but I don't give any guarantees."

About that time, Pesely came along with the news that we were picking up ships like a snowball on a downhill roll. We now knew that we were headed for Ulithi Atoll as our final staging area for the forthcoming invasion of Okinawa. It was hard to believe the rumors that there were more than a thousand ships in our convoy because we could only see the few around us. The thousand ships were dispersed miles apart. The troop ships were in the safe center of the convoy, and the various warships – from the small gunboats, minesweepers, destroyer escorts, to the destroyers, cruisers, battleships, and the aircraft carriers – were all deployed in some complex naval battle formation covering an immense part of the ocean.

However, when we finally entered the Ulithi Atoll and anchored our massive armada, the calm flat lagoon was soon converted into a forest of ships so great in number no one could possibly count them. Records now show that there were 1440 warships and merchant ships of all kinds and sizes. It was in fact the greatest armada in the history of the world, compared to the 130 ships of the invincible Spanish Armada in 1588 or the 800 warships of our Normandy invasion in 1944. There were so many ships that not all could anchor in the huge Ulithi lagoon at once. Timing, movement, and positioning of these great ships had to be as tightly choreographed as a theatrical production, and one part of the task force had to stage in the Leyte Gulf of the Philippines, eight hundred miles away.

Despite the incredible congestion of a thousand ships anchored in the Ulithi lagoon, every effort was made to give the men aboard those ships a brief respite on the tiny atoll islands. Boat after boat of officers and troops were ferried to the shores of the tiny sand spit islets for a last drink and song before the big one.

Most of our group ended up on an insignificant coral islet called Mog Mog which rose maybe ten or fifteen feet above sea level at low tide. Anyhow, it looked good to us. The few tropical grass-roofed structures ashore had been converted into outdoor bars, where the enlisted men – most of whom were minors – were treated to a few beers, and the officers were allowed some harder stuff.

Heavy in his usual propensity for stumbling into the unusual goes ashore on the Flag island by mistake and finds himself in the company of the famous combat correspondent, Ernie Pyle, and the former heavyweight champion boxer, Jack Dempsey. Heavy wastes no time promoting the Marine Corps to Ernie Pyle, and Jack Fitzgerald commiserates with Dempsey over his one-time loss to King Levinsky. Then they proceed to get as drunk as the circumstances permit before struggling to find their way back through the forest of ships to the USS Wayne.

Meanwhile, on little Mog Mog Island, I have a couple of drinks and take the first boat back, but after searching for our ship for about an hour, I realize that our Navy coxswain hasn't the faintest idea where the USS Wayne is anchored.

"Coxswain," I tell him, "pull alongside any ship and get directions from the officer of the deck." In theory every ship in the lagoon had a specified mooring location, and each ship was apprised of the locations of all the ships. That was in theory. In fact, we had to search through this dense forest of ships for another half-hour before we found the USS Wayne.

On March 26, while we were having our doomsday celebration on a couple of sand spits in Ulithi, the Navy had already launched its final softening up barrage on Okinawa which would continue through the 31st. The 16-inch guns of three Maryland-Class battleships; 14-inch guns of two New Mexico-Class and the older New York, Texas and Tennessee Class: plus the 12-inch armament of the Arkansas were all pounding the island in a continuous barrage. To this battleship power the Navy added the guns of seven heavy cruisers, three light cruisers, twenty-four destroyers, and about 50-rocket and mortar ships.

During this time *Kamikazes* hit the American invasion fleet by coming in underneath the radar at dawn and dusk. They managed to crash six ships and damage ten before L-Day, including Admiral Raymond A. Spruance's flagship Indianapolis. Altogether, the Navy blasted Okinawa with 27,226 rounds of

5-inch and larger shells before the main landing. Minesweepers destroyed 257 mines, and UDT swimmers blew up 2700 posts embedded in the reef landing area. Carrier aircraft flew 3.095 sorties, and by March 29, two days before the L-Day landing, Okinawa's air strength had been eliminated.

On the morning of March 27, as we were steaming out of Ulithi heading to Okinawa for our April 1st L-Day landing, seven *Kamikazes* attacked our naval forces that were softening up our beaches. Diving through a curtain of antiaircraft fire, one *Kamikaze* crashed on the main deck of the battleship Nevada, knocking out two 14-inch guns, killing 11 men and wounding 49. A second *Kamikaze* dove at but missed hitting the Tennessee; a third missed the Cruiser Biloxi, but a fourth hit it and the bomb failed to explode. The fifth hit the destroyer O'Brien, killing 50 men and wounding 76. The sixth crashed onto the deck of the minesweeper Dorsey, and the seventh *Kamikaze* missed all the ships but presumably managed to hit the water and destroy itself.

That premature enemy raid by seven *Kamikazes* on March 27th was followed up on the March 28 and 29th by a determined Japanese aerial attack against the U.S. minesweepers operating close to the coast. Results were one lost minesweeper and ten lost Japanese aircraft. Although the Japanese continued to operate aircraft from Okinawa airfields for only two more days, the local fighters plus sporadic appearances of Japanese bomber and torpedo planes and occasional *Kamikazes* was enough to trigger the immense antiaircraft firepower of our huge armada. So even before the serious *Kamikaze* attacks started on April 6 and 7, every appearance of an enemy plane caused an uproar of the antiaircraft guns of our entire task force, and the sky became an umbrella etched by the trajectories of thousands of tracer rounds. It soon became apparent that we were in almost as much danger from the flying shrapnel and falling unexploded rounds from our own ships as from the enemy action.

Because Iwo Jima was originally scheduled to take place about the same time as the Okinawa campaign, the traditional "D-Day" was pre-empted for the Iwo Jima operation, and for Okinawa our "D-Day" was designated "L-Day". Heavy was quick to observe the ironic convergence of circumstances – that in the

year of our Lord, 1945, Easter Sunday, "Love-Day", and April
Fools Day were all destined to fall on April 1st. Of course, as
usual, the joke was on us.

By the time we arrived on March 31st and stood several miles
off our invasion beaches on the west coast of Okinawa, there were
badly damaged ships all around us, including the aircraft carrier
Franklin, with a hole so big we could see through it midship from
starboard to port. The hole seemed big enough that you could
drive an 18-wheel truck and trailer through it. In a pre-invasion
raid on 18-19 March, it had been hit by two bombs and set afire,
but even with that damage and the loss of 724 crew members, the
ship had miraculously stayed afloat, and remained with its Task
Force. Even though our carrier planes had already eliminated any
Japanese aerial threat from the airfields on the island, we were
still only 350 easy fighter-distance-miles from the main islands of
Japan.

As Battalion TQM, I was still aboard the APA that had taken
us off the Canal, with responsibility now for launching our

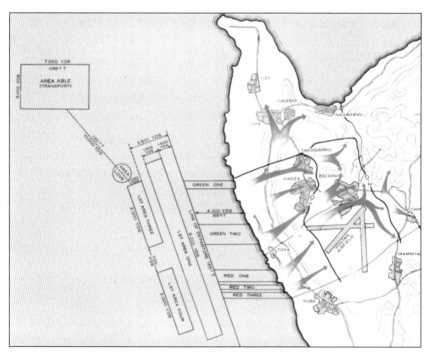

On L-Day, 1 April 45, assault battalions of the 22d Marine Strike Green Beaches.

combat cargo and our supporting troops. All of our line companies had been transferred to LSTs before we left Ulithi, and I could see dozens of those small shoe-box ships ahead of us, forming up to position themselves properly for the pre-dawn run-in and the dawn invasion. It was a strange feeling being on this APA transport with battalion support units instead of up there on one of those attack LSTs. I had never gone in later than the third wave on my previous three assault landings – that means within six minutes of the first man on the beach. Now I was under orders not to go in until I had personally supervised the unloading of all our priority cargo and had sent it on its way to the beach. Psychologically, I was way beyond the stage of wanting to hit any hostile beaches in the early waves. I no longer had to prove anything to anybody, but it still seemed like I belonged up there in those LSTs with my buddies – not on this damned transport.

By dawn on Easter Sunday, all the ships of the landing force had moved into their final positions to launch the greatest amphibious operation of the war. Our Naval task force continued its merciless bombardment of the island. Five hundred carrier planes, including four Marine squadrons, strafed and napalmed the landing beaches. Ten battleships, 9 cruisers, 3 destroyers, and 177 gunboats pounded those beaches with 3800 tons of shells.

The III Amphibious Corps, consisting of our 6th Marine Division and the 1st Marine Division, was assigned the northern end of the 10th Army Beachhead; and the Army's 96th and 7th Infantry Divisions were assigned the southern end. Approximately 50,000 U.S. troops were to be landed on L-Day to face an entrenched Japanese force of more than 100,000 defenders.

In his book, "The Battle for Okinawa", Colonel Hiromichi Yahara, the senior staff officer for the Japanese commander, Lt. General Mitsuru Ishijima, states; *"On the morning of April 1, in the twentieth year of the Showa era, the island of Okinawa is rent by an earthshaking bombardment, vast and oddly magnificent in its effect, in preparation for the American Army's landing attack."*

The colonel goes on to note: *"At this time the commanders of Japan's 32nd Army are standing on the crest of Mount Shuri near the southern end of Okinawa's main island, quietly observing the movements of the American 10th Army,* According to the colonel, *"they gaze calmly at the enemy landing force disembarking twenty kilometers away.*

Continuing his account, the colonel states: *"Since early dawn, the silhouettes of enemy troopships have darkened the coastline. Ten battleships and ten cruisers form the core of the attack force: Some two hundred lesser ships line up offshore. Stretching from Manihira to Heianzan, Kadena forms a seven-to-eight-kilometer-long coast zone. There the heaviest gunfire is concentrated. Smoke and debris from the explosions and fires rise up to the sky. The enemy aircraft, looking like hundreds of over-size bees conceal themselves in the convenient smoke screen before carrying out their bombing operations..."*

"At 8:00 AM the enemy infantry disembarks from the thousand-odd landing craft, thrusting onto the shore. The sweep of the ordered military formation is impressive. It is as if the sea itself were advancing with a great roar...They take cover. They are probably anticipating the famous Banzai charges repeated time and time again throughout the Pacific island operations...But the Japanese atop Mount Shuri show no signs of using such tactics. The group simply gazes out over the enemy's frantic deployment, some of the officers joking, a few casually lighting cigarettes. How could this be? For months now the Japanese army has been building its strongest fortifications on the heights of Mount Shuri and its adjacent hills. Here they will lure the American forces and confound them. Hence their air of nonchalance. The battle is now progressing as expected.

"All the Japanese command need do is to await the completion of the enemy's landing at Kadena and watch them head southward...As their troops land with almost no resistance from the Japanese force, what must the enemy commander and staff be thinking? I'm unable to suppress an ironic chuckle."

If the Japanese command really felt and acted the way he describes it, they were colossal idiots who didn't belong in this big league game. It would be like some college baseball team playing the New York Yankees and celebrating victory with their first man on base in the first inning. In the face of hundreds of ships and aircraft and the incredible bombardment they were experiencing without any significant countermeasures by their own Air Force and Navy, how could they foresee anything but their inevitable total defeat? Of course, the colonel claims he was one of the few command officers who expected final defeat, but he seems happy enough about this new defense strategy that would allow them to buy time for the homeland while exacting exorbitant casualties on the invaders.

Certainly, their new defense strategy was a pleasant surprise for Heavy, Pesely, Bair, McDowell and all of our guys still alive after our previous three landings against hotly defended beaches. It seemed a little ironic to me that the only landing where I wasn't in the assault echelon was the only one where nobody was on the beach shooting at us. It was the only one where we could stand up and walk in. Of course, we wouldn't know that until after our first wave hit the beach.

Meanwhile, during the bombardment and while the hundreds of amtracs were making their landings all up and down the west coast of the island, I was still functioning as the 2d Battalion TQM aboard our APA transport, kicking Marine and Navy ass to make sure that my L-Day high-priority supplies were getting ashore as I had ordered. I was determined that there would be no hundred-pound sacks of flour getting ashore before the ammunition on my watch – as had happened elsewhere.

In addition to the combat cargo aboard our APA, I was also responsible for dispatching a small detachment of black Marines. They were the drivers of our amphibious trucks (DUKWs) Their job was to drive these heavily loaded amphibious vehicles from our APA transport several miles to the beach and land without benefit of direct infantry support. The thought was that the first waves of Marines to land would have already secured the beach sufficiently that by the time any truck drivers came ashore the enemy would be neutralized. Of course, a careful study of Tarawa and any number of other beaches would have dispelled that notion. Anyhow their orders were to get those trucks onto the designated beach, and my orders were to brief them and emphasize the importance of their mission – and especially the importance of hitting the right beach.

The morning of the invasion, I called the group of healthy looking young black Marines together. For a black to be a Marine then meant that he was highly motivated, and he was hand picked. What especially caught my notice was their cool sense of humor. They were nervous. They were eager. But they had been poorly briefed so they weren't sure what they were supposed to do. I pulled out a large map showing our battalion landing area, and I pointed to an area on the map labeled "Green One". I noted that the line of departure from the LSTs to the beach was 4000 yards and that our transports were positioned well behind that line, so they would have a run of several miles in their slow-moving amphibious trucks, making them vulnerable to shore fire all the way in.

I don't like that, Lieutenant," one of the young blacks spoke up with a grin. "Looks like we're going to be sitting ducks," he said, with a play on the acronym DUKW (pronounced 'duck') for amphibious trucks.

Since we didn't know the new Jap strategy of allowing us to land on undefended beaches, I told them: "By the time you get in, the enemy will be too busy fighting the Marines ahead of you to worry about you guys in your trucks. But you do have to worry about hitting the right beach," I added. Then I pointed out that our battalion was the northernmost unit of the entire Tenth Army, with only Japanese forces on our left flank and no friendly units within a thousand yards of us on the right flank. There was no room for error. If they missed Green Beach One, they would just be a bunch of truck drivers alone with their cargo in Japland. That got their attention.

One southern black said: "Yeah, that would be just like me getting caught in my truck at midnight in the white part of town." The brothers chuckled knowingly. Another black from Harlem said: "We ain't missing no beach, Lieutenant; just tell us how to find that sucker."

I explained the beach marking system and reminded them once more that if they missed, miss to the right because there they could find friendly forces about a thousand yards away. Then we carefully lowered each DUKW into the water. The trucks were so heavily loaded that the cargo with a tarp pulled over it projected a couple of feet out of the well of the truck, and when we launched the trucks into the water from the lowering crane, I held my breath fully expecting them to sink right to the bottom of the sea – driver, truck, and cargo together. Miraculously, they stayed afloat, bobbing dangerously with the ocean swells. At least they stayed afloat until they were out of my sight and I could take a deep breath again. Even though these young blacks were not combat troops, I was impressed by their positive cool attitude as they headed – unescorted by infantry – for what they expected to be a very hostile enemy-held beach.

Chapter 21

The Enemy's Invisible Defense

As Battalion TQM I could not go ashore until all of our vital combat cargo had been unloaded and beached. For me that meant working aboard ship for the first twenty-four hours and not reaching the beach until L-plus-1. It was the first time in my four landings that I came ashore safely in a Higgins boat instead of storming the beach in an amtrac. And it was the first time on any beach where no one was taking a direct aim and trying to eliminate me from planet earth.

Reporting to the Beachmaster who stood among mountains of equipment and supplies, I quickly took charge of a 2d Battalion jeep and a 2-1/2-ton truck that we had combat-loaded back on the Canal. Along with a couple of drivers and riflemen riding shotgun, I headed inland and north to try and catch up with our battalion which had far exceeded their L-plus-1 objective. We didn't catch up to the battalion until late afternoon on L-plus-2. By then the 2d Battalion was digging in for the night a few miles below the Ishikawa Isthmus.

Although the battalion was moving rapidly against almost no resistance, it was moving cautiously because no one yet knew what the new Jap strategy was. After our fierce battles in our three previous campaigns, we knew the Japanese were not going to sit back for very long and watch us take over an island that was the sacred territory of the homeland. We also knew that there were approximately a 100,000 Japanese soldiers somewhere on this island – we just didn't know where. We assumed they were all around us and watching and waiting. But waiting for what?

Of course the Japanese knew where they were and what they were waiting for. Here's what Colonel Yahara writes about us at that time:

Contrary to their expectations, the enemy meets no resistance from Japanese troops. They will complete their landing unchallenged. Advancing with such ease, they must be thinking gleefully that they have passed through a breach in the Japanese defense. They will be wrong. In that eerie atmosphere are they not suspicious that the Japanese army has withdrawn and concealed itself in the heights surrounding Kadena, with plans to draw the Americans into a trap? What a surprise it must all be. It is amusing to watch the American army so desperately intent in its attack on an almost undefended coast, like a blind man who has lost his cane, groping on hands and knees to cross a ditch.

Since we didn't know where the Japanese army was, it was a scary trip for me with my little two-vehicle convoy and four enlisted men to zoom ahead of Regimental Headquarters through unsecured territory looking for my battalion. But even under those tense circumstances, I was thrilled by the beauty of this quaint oriental countryside. Moving quickly against no resistance, our forward battalions had left much of the bypassed territory completely undisturbed. Therefore, as we came along a day behind them we saw native Okinawans tending to their rice paddies and their livestock. They were dressed in traditional oriental peasant garments with the typical broad brimmed *minogasa* (coolie hats) and *monpe* (work pants) against a background of the *matsu* (pine) trees and thatched roof houses. Around every bend was a new pictorial vista that reminded me of every classical oriental watercolor I had studied in art classes.

When we eventually caught up to our battalion, we discovered that they had not yet engaged the enemy. When I reported to the colonel, he asked about the progress of Regimental Headquarters. I told him they hadn't moved far from the beachhead at the time I passed through.

"Jones," he told me, "we're moving so damn fast, I'm afraid we're going to outrun our supplies. So I want you to assist the Bn-4 on our long-distance logistics. Keep your jeep, your drivers, and your riflemen; and as soon as we've used up the supplies in your 2-1/2-ton truck you go back as far as you have to and get it loaded again."

"Aye, aye, Sir," I said, not relishing the idea of going back and forth through no-man's land with a couple of riflemen. But with our battalion of a thousand men on the move and with no supplies catching up to us from Regiment – I knew it wouldn't be long before that trip would be necessary.

However, we were in good supply for the next few days even as we continued our fast-paced progress toward the town of Nago and the Motobu Peninsula. On about the 6th of April we were camped in the countryside just short of Nago. Although we still didn't know where the Japanese troops were, and although the few Okinawan's we succeeded in questioning assured us there were none in the North and that they all fled to Naha in the South – we didn't believe them. Since we expected trouble in Nago and out on the Motobu Peninsula, the colonel ordered me to remain in our countryside position in command of the battalion rear echelon until he ordered us forward. That left me with some logistical equipment, reserve ammo, general supplies and a handful of men. It also left me with the responsibility of setting up a perimeter defense around our encampment.

The center of our encampment was a high-quality, thatched-roof, deserted farmhouse belonging to what I assumed to be a relatively affluent Okinawa farmer. I quickly organized my small party of Headquarters Marines into several 4-man fireteams and sent half of them out to patrol the immediate area, especially some of the caves in nearby hills likely to hold Japanese soldiers. It wasn't long before my men brought back three generations of an entire Okinawa family. There was the forty-year-old-father, the wife and five kids from ages eight to two, and the seventy- year-old grandpa and grandma.

"Where did you get them?" I asked the corporal team leader.

"Hiding in the caves, Lieutenant," he told me. "They were afraid to come out, but once we grabbed on to one of the kids, they all came out. They're lucky, too, because my guys didn't want to take any chances. We saw somebody run into the cave, but it could have been a Jap. My guys wanted to throw a grenade in, but then a little kid darted out and we nabbed her."

"I'm glad it went that way," I said; "do they speak English."

"No, Sir," he answered. "At least not to us."

"Eigo O hanashi Masuka?" I asked the father in Japanese. He shook his head "No" indicating that he didn't speak English.

Since it was imperative that we communicate, I hauled out my military Japanese language phrase book and went to work. The first question, of course, was: "Where are the Japanese soldiers?"

He pointed to the south, saying "Naha" and motioning with his hand that they had been here but they had left and fled south.

Then, because I knew our battalion was on its way to Motobu Peninsula without any clear idea of what they might find there, I asked *"Iku nin no heitai ga arimaska?"* and I pointed to my map and said *"Motobu?"*

His answer was the same as before. He indicated that all the Japanese soldiers had fled to the Naha area in the south. Of course, I didn't believe him because this would be the expected answer that the Japanese would have instructed the locals to say. Still I wouldn't be satisfied until I got a truthful answer. And although I needed that answer soon because my battalion was headed toward that peninsula and possibly into a Japanese trap and ambush, I decided to try kindness rather than force.

First, with the help of my Japanese phrase book and a reasonable adeptness at sign language after living among various natives in the pacific for the past two years, I told him that he and his family were welcome to return to their house and live inside while we Marines would sleep outside in the rain and mud.

He was visibly moved by this shocking proposition. Not in his wildest dreams could he ever have imagined a Japanese officer proposing such a thing. When the Japanese army took over an area, they ruled and the natives obeyed. What he didn't know is that I was also ruling and he would obey but on a different set of terms than he expected and for reasons he didn't know.

The rules, I explained to him, were as follows: "You and your family sleep in the house but no one gets up and moves after dark – not you, not the children, not the grandparents. The Marines have one important rule – anyone who moves after dark gets shot, even a comrade Marine! Do you understand?"

He shook his head, indicating that he understood. That meant he understood that no one was to move, but the quizzical look on his face made it clear that he did not understand why. Why did the

Marines want to sleep outside in the mud and why let him and his family sleep in their house and then shoot them if they move? To him it was a "puzzlement". However, he explained our rules forcefully to his family.

To me it was a no-brainer, although I heard some grumbling about the plan from a couple of my guys. Unlike the farmer, we weren't in our own back yard. We were still in combat on some exotic island, surrounded by an enemy force of unknown numbers. So, of course, we would make our usual perimeter defense of foxholes in the mud, with all our weapons pointed outboard in a 360° circle around the farmhouse. Fortunately for our small force, the *Banzai* attack that we had prepared for didn't materialize. We were pleased to see dawn and know that we had lived another day, but we still didn't know the whereabouts of the enemy.

Upon waking up, the first thing I did was to confront the farmer again with the same question I had repeatedly asked him: "Where are the Jap soldiers?" And I got the same answer as before. "Down south near Naha." Again, I didn't believe him, but how could I get the truth without physical violence?

Just then a flight of fighter planes appeared overhead. It was clear that they were American planes, and the farmer instinctively started to run toward the nearby caves. Then he stopped abruptly with a sheepish smile on his face as he realized that if they were American planes they would not be bombing their own troops. Since he was now with us, he no longer had to worry about American planes. Now he would have to run when he saw Japanese planes. How fast tides change in war.

As the American planes flew by, the farmer nudged my arm, pointed at the planes and said: "America and Okinawa, Okay: Tokyo, phooie!" trying to make it clear to me that he had no love for the Japanese government.

On our second morning on the Okinawa farm, we got the word from the colonel to join up with the battalion which was fast approaching the neck of Motobu Peninsula, still with no credible intelligence information on the enemy forces awaiting our troops in that area.

When I told the farmer that we were leaving, he looked

unhappy to hear that. By now we were calling each other by our names. "Lieutenant Jones," he said; "where you go?"

"We go north, Taro," I told him, pointing northward.

He hesitated for a moment, got an even sadder look on his sad face and said, "Lieutenant Jones, no go", and he point northward.

"Why, Taro?" I asked him.

"Many soldiers there," he replied again pointing north.

Now I knew he was ready to tell me the truth. *"Iku nin no heitai ga arimaska?* I asked the same question I had been asking for two days. This time I got an entirely different answer.

He answered in Japanese with a number I couldn't understand. I gave him a pad and pencil and asked him to write the number. First he wrote it in Japanese script that I couldn't read, so I wrote something in arabic numerals, indicating what I wanted him to do. He quickly understood and wrote the number 1500. Wow! That was a revelation. Fifteen hundred soldiers was the better part of a Japanese regiment – no small force to stumble on to accidentally and unprepared without that information.

I thanked the farmer and wished him well. As I walked toward my jeep, he yelled after me: "Lieutenant Jones, no go north." He seemed to be genuinely sad over the fate that he assumed awaited me. Then he offered me his prize possession as a parting gift. It was a beautiful white goat that stood munching weeds on a hillside. Knowing that marching troops have no way to keep a goat, he made a motion with his hand across his throat to explain he meant for me to kill and barbecue it and enjoy a hot meal on him. I declined the goat but I thanked him for his offer that was as graceful a gesture as anyone under those circumstances could possibly make.

More importantly – as fast as I could get it to him – I passed this new intelligence information on to Lieutenant Colonel Woodhouse, our battalion commander. As far as I have been able to learn, the farmer's estimate of 1500 soldiers was the first accurate intelligence estimate of the enemy force on Motobu Peninsula, probably saving many lives of Marines who might otherwise have walked unprepared into a deadly trap.

Chapter 22

Kamikaze's and the Suicide Defense

M uch has been written about the costly Japanese
Kamikaze suicide air attacks which failed to turn the
tide of battle on Okinawa, but, more important to the
ultimate defeat of our enemy, was the traditional Japanese suicidal
mentality. Every Japanese soldier and sailor was only too willing
to die for the Emperor. That was an entirely different war fighting
psychology than ours, which was best expressed by General
Patton when he told his troops: "I don't want you to give your life
for your country; I want you to make those enemy sonovabitches
give their lives for their country!" With their sacrificial
psychology, the Japanese had organized an elaborate suicide plan
they called "Ten-Go". It was a last ditch effort to destroy the
Americans on Okinawa.

Ten-Go was supposed to be a combined and coordinated tri-
Service operation with mass *Kamikaze* attacks from the air and
surface and submarine attacks from the sea with what was left of
the Japanese Imperial Navy. The flagship of the newly repaired
Second Fleet was the world's largest battleship, the 863-foot
Yamato, armed with 18-inch guns capable of hurling a shell of
3200 pounds a distance of 22 miles. It took a crew of 2800 men to
man it. With a cruiser, five destroyers, a few submarines, and a
number of *shinyo* and *kaiten* suicide boats and manned torpedoes
– the Ten-Go suicide task force was sent toward Okinawa with
just enough fuel for a one-way trip. The fleet never made it to
Okinawa, and on April 7, 1945 after three hours of steady attack
by 300 US carrier-based planes, the *Yamato* was sunk.

At that same time, on April 6 and 7, the Japanese had also
launched their first major *Kamikaze* raid against our forces with

699 planes, half of which were suiciders. The Japanese planes were more successful than their surface fleet, sinking six of our warships and seriously damaging ten. Although we, the ground troops, knew nothing about the fleet battle except the scuttlebutt that the *Yamato* had been sunk, we were only too aware of the *Kamikaze* attacks. For the first time, we saw more enemy planes in the air over Okinawa than our own, and we could see the *Kamikazes* diving through our antiaircraft umbrella and setting fire to ships in our fleet. It was the only time when we grunts would not have exchanged our muddy foxholes on the ground for the sailors' clean bunks aboard ship.

By now our battalion had advanced several miles beyond that hot action back on the landing beaches, but now we knew there were 1500 Japs dug in on Motobu Peninsula waiting to greet us. Then orders came through for our Second Battalion to continue with our fast-paced advance toward the northern tip of Okinawa, while the 29th and the 4th Marines plus the 1st Battalion of our regiment were ordered to attack the 1200-foot Mount Yaetake on the peninsula.

Advancing far ahead of schedule as much as five miles a day, our Second Battalion continued its march to the North. We were encountering only minor sniper fire with occasional harassing high-explosive bursts from remote artillery emplacements, but the enemy gun crews had very accurately zeroed-in on critical military targets like small bridges, narrows in the road, and places where they hoped to impede our rapid advance.

Since I was still bringing up our battalion rear-echelon, my small detachment was the last to pass through the small deserted towns along our route. I placed my jeep at the very end of the entire battalion in a rear guard position with our extra truck and supplies just ahead where I could maintain a watch against any breakdowns or trouble. But as we passed through one small town (probably Nago) my jeep driver came to a screeching halt. He jumped out of the jeep and hurried down a deserted dirt road between some crude Okinawa buildings. Disappearing momentarily, he then came running back out to our jeep with a gallon jug in his hand.

"What the hell is that, Snuffy?" I asked him. His last name

was Smith, and I never knew his first name because everyone called him "Snuffy".

"It's a jug of whiskey, Lieutenant," he said, with a broad self-satisfied smile on his face.

Snuffy smith, my 2d Battalion, 22d Marines, jeep driver from Kentucky who could smell a whiskey still a mile away and could fashion a crutch out of an axe handle. (USMC Photo)

"Well, that's great, Snuffy," I said, but how in the hell did you know there would be a jug of whiskey back there?"

"Aw, Lieutenant," he answered; "I'm from Kentucky, and I can smell a whiskey still a mile away." He wasn't the smartest Marine I ever met, but he was the kind of a solid salt-of-the-earth Marine you could depend on.

As we continue to walk, truck, and tank our way up the island against light sporadic pockets of resistance, our battalion begins to take on a strange appearance. Gradually, we are beginning to look like some kind of "Horse-Marine" unit. All of our heavy weapons guys have somehow commandeered dozens of the tiny Okinawa horses into service as pack animals. Our heavy machine guns and their heavier tripods, as well as our mortars and ammunition boxes normally hand-carried by our troops, are now packed on the backs of these local midget horses.

In keeping with the overall miniature scale of the island, the local farm horses at that time looked more like Shetland ponies than the Belgian draft horses we were used to at home. But their size was appropriate to the landscape of the island, as was the size of the Okinawan people who were themselves a head shorter than the small Japanese soldiers. The typical one-family Okinawan farm was not like ours of forty acres and a mule, but it was a half-acre and a pony. On these tiny plots, the Okinawan managed to raise livestock, grow rice and vegetables, and eke out a living for a complete family. As a six-foot Marine, the deeper I penetrated into the Okinawa countryside and was thrust into the midst of these small creatures on this exotic land, I knew what Gulliver felt like among the Lilliputians.

Although our "Horse Marines" were very happy to unload their burdens onto the backs of the midget horses, by the time we had acquired about a 150 of these little beasts of burden the word comes down from Command to free these animals immediately because we are upsetting the entire agricultural economy of the island.

We are moving so fast, we have soon used up our on-board rations and have outrun our supply lines. The colonel gives me a mission: "Jones," he says, "take that jeep and truck of yours and high-tail it back to Regiment and get us some supplies."

"Where is Regiment, Sir?" I asked.

"Someplace the other side of Motobu," he told me; "and they won't be moving up until they can pull the 1st Battalion out of that fight. Just go find them," he ordered. "We don't need much ammunition yet, but we need a lot of five gallon cans of water and gas, and we need rations. Check with the company commanders before you leave," he added.

"I am soon on my way back through no-man's land with my two-vehicle four-man caravan. It had been easy enough going through this countryside against light resistance as part of a thousand-man battalion combat force. It was a lot spookier going back now with my little group. Three carbines and one M1 rifle constituted our total armament, plus a .45 caliber pistol I carried in a shoulder holster. Even if we could get through the mined roads and make it back over the targeted bridges, our only chance was to avoid a firefight with the many stray Japanese patrols and positions that I knew we had bypassed.

Though it was a thirty-five mile treacherous run, we make it back to Regiment. Unfortunately, the regimental supply officer has bad news: "Sorry, Lieutenant," he tells me, "I have no supplies for your battalion. Whatever I have is for this Motobu fight. You can't be out of ammunition because you haven't hit any resistance yet."

"But the men have to eat and drink, Captain," I tell him and we need gas for our vehicles. What happened to our regimental supply line?" I ask.

"We can't make it through to your battalion right now by truck," he tells me. "The Japs are interdicting any serious road traffic with artillery. But when your outfit gets to the top of the island at Hedo, we'll try supplying you by ship and air drops" he said. Then he adds: "How the hell did you guys get through to us?"

"Speed and luck," I answer "mostly luck."

I knew that returning to Battalion with an empty truck and waiting for airdrops wouldn't satisfy my colonel, so we rev up our two pitiful vehicles and head all the way back to the landing beaches. Now I'm getting desperate because I'm not sure we can make it to the beach dumps, load up, and get back to our lines before dark, but I have no options.

It's already afternoon when we get to the beach. It seems like total chaos, with mountains of various supplies scattered here and there, including hundreds of fifty-five gallon drums and five gallon cans of fuel, five gallon cans of water, stacks and stacks of ammunition, and cases of field rations. I immediately order my three men to load up our 2-1/2 -ton truck with some of everything while I go looking for the beachmaster to give us a hand.

The beachmaster is a very nervous major who verbally pounces on me before I reach him. "What the hell are those guys doing over by your truck?" he asks rhetorically.

"Loading it," I answer simply.

"And who are you?" the major asks.

"Lieutenant. Jones," I tell him.

"Well, Lieutenant, where's your requisition slip?"

"I don't have one, Major," I answer.

"Then go back and get me one, or tell them to start unloading that truck," he responds succinctly.

"Major, I reply insubordinately, "I'm not doing a seventy-mile roundtrip to get a requisition slip. My colonel sent me here for supplies, and I'm going back with supplies."

The seventy-mile roundtrip catches the man's attention. "Seventy miles", he says; "where the hell is your unit and what outfit are you with?"

"Near the top of the island, thirty-five miles from here. I'm with the Second Battalion, Twenty-Second Marines," I tell him.

"Hell," he responds; "you guys are combat troops. Take all the supplies you want." Then he sends three of his men to help my guys load our truck.

Once our truck is loaded, I jump into my jeep and tell my driver to get rolling. "We've got to find Battalion before dark, Snuffy," I tell him, or you know what we're up against."

"Yeah, Lieutenant," he answers; "I don't want to bust through any Marine lines after dark." Then he guns our jeep and takes off like a scared rabbit, with our 6x truck bouncing along the dirt road behind us.

Between *Kamikaze* raids, the area around the beachhead was pretty safe, but as we continue to the north past Nago and Motobu

Peninsula we are back in unsecured territory that has been hastily bypassed by our fast-moving infantry companies.

Soon we start to pick up occasional sniper fire, which we ignore, but we can't easily ignore the artillery bursts bracketing us at every bend in the road and at every bridge that the enemy has previously zeroed-in.

Coming upon a particularly dangerous looking bridge located a quarter of a mile ahead of us, we watch as a friendly vehicle runs off the road to avoid a three-shell enemy barrage. Snuffy comes to a quick, halt, forcing our truck driver behind us to slam on his brakes. "What do we do, Lieutenant?" Snuffy asks. "They got that bridge zeroed-in."

"I know they have, Snuffy," I tell him, "but we have no choice. We've got to find our battalion and get this load through our lines before dark. Make a run across that bridge at full speed," I order, and I motion the truck driver to follow us.

We're lucky. We take a six-shot barrage, with the shells bursting all around us, but by the time the last two hit the bridge, we're safely across and on our way.

"That was a close one, Lieutenant," Snuffy says, "but we're home free now."

"Are we?" I ask him; "we've got no idea how far the Battalion has moved since this morning, and it's getting dark fast."

To complicate matters, we had now run out of what had been a reasonable dirt road. We're now traveling on a one-lane pathway just wide enough to accommodate our 6x truck, with a precipitous hill on one side and a steep embankment that leads down to the ocean on the other. We can't afford to overshoot our lines because there is no way to turn our big 6x truck around on that pathway.

Until now I had not really considered the possibility of overshooting our lines. When I'd left that morning in broad daylight our battalion of several hundred Marines was easy to locate, but now with the light gone, it's a different story. Suddenly, I realize that we must have passed our lines long ago. So now we're simply four Marines in a truck and a jeep lost in the dark in the middle of hostile enemy territory. To make matters worse, there's no space to turn the truck around and go back.

I confer with the truck driver. "You know we've got to go

back," I tell him. Then I ask: "Can you turn this thing around?"

"No, Sir," he says, "not without falling off the cliff."

"Well, that ain't' a real good option," I say. "If you've got any other suggestions, let's hear them."

"Only one thing, Sir," he answers. "I can back this sucker up."

"How far?" I ask.

"As far as we need to go to get our asses behind our own lines, Sir," he responds.

"Then let's get to it," I order. "Snuffy, turn the jeep around."

Turning the jeep is easy, but getting it past the truck isn't possible. "Okay, Snuf," I tell him; "we'll have to follow them on the way back."

"Lieutenant," the truck driver yells. "I think we've still got a problem. If I can't see the bends in the road behind me, we still might fall off the cliff."

"Well, men," I say, "you know as well as I do that if we turn on our lights we're sitting ducks for the Japs. Every rifle, machine gun, and artillery piece on this end of the island will be blasting away at us. Worse yet," I add, "we're not going to be able to see our own guys who are dug in and camouflaged, and you know what'll happen when our guys see lights shining ahead of their front lines."

"What are we gonna do, Lieutenant?" the truck driver asks.

Nobody says anything, but I suppose they're thinking that's why you lieutenants are getting the big bucks of $135 per month to make decisions like this.

"Well, our mission hasn't changed," I say; "the colonel told us to go get supplies and get them back as fast as possible. So we're turning on the lights and taking our chances."

Snuffy turns the jeep lights on. They are aimed at the truck now in front of us and the road behind it. The truck driver slips into reverse and presses the metal to the floor. I estimate that we're going almost as fast in reverse as we had in forward gear on our way out. My two drivers do a superb job in literally back tracking several miles until we hear an American voice yell out.

"Shut those goddman lights off before we shoot them out!"

Now we know we're home with mission accomplished.

Chapter 23

The Isolated Battalion

The next morning after we had distributed our fresh water and rations to the companies, I reported the details of my beachhead expedition to the colonel. When he heard that there would be no more supplies coming up by road, he got on the horn with Colonel Schneider, the regimental commander, who promised him that we would be supplied by sea and airdrop as soon as we took Hedo, the northernmost tip of the island.

The colonel then calls in Captain Stebbins of Company G and tells him to form up a patrol in force and move ahead to reconnoiter the Hedo area before he moves the rest of the battalion up. To give him some big-gun support, a Navy patrol boat has been assigned to follow along the shore road, staying in radio contact with Stebby's outfit.

Just before reaching Hedo, Stebby looks up to see a flight of six U.S. carrier-based fighter planes coming out of the clouds to attack his ground patrol. His men frantically try to wave off the attackers as they level off and make a strafing run, with tracers and .50-caliber bullets ripping up the road. Stebby's men dive into the ditches and withstand repeated strafing attacks and the dropping of napalm bombs. But even though the attacks continue until the planes exhaust their ammunition, only three men on the ground receive minor wounds.

Since we were many days ahead of schedule in reaching Hedo, our pilots had assumed that any soldiers spotted on the ground would be enemy troops. That incident strongly confirmed two lessons we had already learned: one, which was discouraging, "always beware of friendly fire"; and two, which was encouraging, "you can't defeat an infantry force from the air."

Since the stiffest resistance that Captain Stebbins' patrol met was from our own aircraft, the colonel promptly moved the battalion forward and occupied Hedo Point, the northernmost tip of Okinawa. So on April 14, the day following the friendly fire incident, we began receiving the first in a series of airdrops, true to Captain Cruikshank's promise to me. He had also promised me we would be supplied by sea with drums of fuel for our tanks and trucks.

The colonel orders me to put together a work party and stand ready on the Hedo beach on the lookout for a supply ship. When we get to the beach, there is one small patrol vessel standing off a safe distance beyond the breakers, with two more farther out to sea. When we signal the close-in vessel it immediately dumps its cargo of dozens of 55-gallon drums of fuel into the sea, and then it turns and flees as fast as possible in the direction of the southern landing beaches and the protection of the fleet.

I quickly lead my work party of a dozen men out into the ocean to herd the floating drums ashore. Fortunately it is a mild surf, but unfortunately it is also damn cold as we wade fully clothed up to our neck in the freezing water and wait for the bobbing drums to drift in to where we can grab them and beach them. Once ashore, we load them on to trucks and move them inland a few hundred yards to where we are establishing a battalion supply dump.

Surveying the dump, it occurs to me that with our tanks, our trucks and jeeps, a few dozen drums of fuel and a substantial stack of air-dropped ammunition and rations – our dump is already an enticing target for the *Kamikaze* raids.

With that thought in mind, I hear the droning noise of an aircraft engine. Looking up I recognize it as too large for a fighter. It is either a bomber or a cargo plane. It's a relief to see that it is one of our cargo planes dropping us another load of supplies. But the relief is short-lived because almost immediately – very high in the sky and way out over the sea – appears a flight of four enemy zeroes looking for targets of opportunity.

Now, I think, where the hell are our Corsairs when we need them? Where are those flyboys who were so busy shooting up Stebby's troops yesterday?

It looks as though the enemy has the sky to himself and can choose his targets at leisure. Then the four zeroes break formation and each of them selects a target. Three of the zeroes are going out to sea, targeting the supply boat that has brought us our fuel and a couple of patrol boats that have accompanied it. But the fourth zero is coming inland in our direction, and I realize that my jeep driver, Snuffy, and I are standing in the middle of the only likely land target they can see. The two of us fall prone, helplessly hiding behind a 3-foot mound of loose gravel. Then comes the first miracle.

Out of the clouds, high above the four zeroes comes a flight of Marine Corsairs riding to the rescue. It is a magnificent sight, as our planes, with their .50-calibers rattling, easily power-dive onto the tails of the four zeroes. Even though the zeroes manage to make tighter turns than the faster Corsairs, their turns come too late and each of the three *Kamikazes* over the sea crashes in flames before reaching their targeted ships. But that leaves the fourth plane still coming at us.

To avoid eating up the tail of the zero he is chasing, the Corsair pilot behind the plane coming at us has to turn off abruptly, leaving us to the mercy of the *Kamikaze* that continues to come at us. Finally, we can see the 500-pound bomb under the plane and the face of the Japanese pilot still steadfastly coming our way. Then comes the second miracle. The zero does a sudden wing-over to the right and explodes a hundred yards away.

We immediately run over to where the *Kamikaze* has crashed and see that it has blown a huge crater in Captain Stebbins' Company G area, but since the company is on patrol, there are no casualties. We extricate the torso of the pilot from the plane. The limbs are missing, but we find his right leg a few yards away in a boot, along with a map outlining his one-way flight from Kyushu to Okinawa. The pilot was a young teenager who gladly died gloriously for the Emperor, as did a thousand other of his *Kamikaze* compatriots.

What we found in the pocket of his jacket was probably more indicative of his age than his culture. We found a miniature leather sheath that measured perhaps a half-inch by an inch. There were Japanese characters stamped in gold leaf on the leather, which we later translated into the name of some obscure religious cult. But from the sheath itself we extracted a very tiny but perfectly sculptured bronze penis. It seemed these religious cultists were phallus worshippers. It wasn't a Samurai sword souvenir, but the men proudly presented this military trophy to our leader, the colonel.

What happened next was unique for World War II. It was more like something out of the First World War. The leader of the Corsair flight circled overhead and came back to us where the zero had blown up. He threw out a tiny parachute with a scribbled message wrapped around a small weight. "Hope this makes up for yesterday." Oddly, my friend, Captain Stebbins, never knew about that incident until 1995 after I finally located him and found his phone number.

On April 20th, our Sixth Division Commander, General Shepherd, announced the end of organized resistance in the northern two-thirds of Okinawa. In a message to us at that time he said: *"Within a period of twenty days, the Sixth Marine Division effected a landing on a hostile shore, captured an airdrome, and fought its way over rugged terrain against enemy resistance a distance of 84 miles, securing an area of 436 square miles of Japanese territory."*

Meanwhile, during that same period, the President of the United States had died, the wartime Japanese Koiso cabinet was replaced by the Suzuki, cabinet, and developments in Europe were pointing to the fast-approaching collapse of Germany. And yet the battle for Okinawa was far from over.

Nevertheless, a mini-victory was celebrated on April 22,when the Commandant of the Marine Corps, General A. A. Vandergrift, visited the Sixth Division Headquarters at Nago and observed the raising of the American flag that signaled the conquest of the northern part of Okinawa.

Of course, we the troops knew that the main battle was still ahead. Word had already come up to us how rough the going was in the South. We heard rumors that the 27th Army Division (formed around a Brooklyn National Guard nucleus) hadn't moved in three weeks and were sustaining unnecessarily high casualties. Our previous experience with that division in the

Marshalls led us to believe that their tactical hesitancy was maximizing their casualties and minimizing their gains.

At any rate, they were ordered to relieve us in the north, and we were to be trucked down south to join in the real battle for the island. When those orders were received by our battalion commander, Lt. Col. Woodhouse, he sent for our battalion executive officer, Major Courtney, and me.

"Jones," he told me, "we have orders to move south, so you won't have any more 70-mile logistics trips to worry about. So from now on you'll be working for Major Courtney." Then addressing Courtney he said: "Major, take Jones and a couple of riflemen and go find our Army relief and plan our withdrawal." The major and I then set out in two jeeps, each of us with a driver and a rifleman looking for our Army relief. We located a couple of Army half-tracks on a dirt road parked alongside a three-foot high stone wall. I could hear the soldiers on the other side of the wall, but I couldn't see them because they were on lower ground below the wall.

The major's jeep pulled up several yards ahead of mine, and he got out and walked around the far end of the stone wall and down a sloping pathway. I however, decided on a spectacular Marine entrance to impress the Army, so I simply vaulted over the three-foot stone wall hoping to land impressively at the foot of the Army battalion commander. But in mid air I quickly discovered that there was a ten-foot drop onto a pile of boulders on the other side of that three-foot wall. I crumpled into a foolish heap, as our Major Courtney looked with embarrassment at his idiot liaison officer.

As I immediately stood up, I realized that I was in excruciating pain, I had torn the ligaments in my right knee. However, the pain of embarrassment at least momentarily outweighed the pain in my knee as I forced myself to stand quietly at ease while the two majors ironed out the details of our withdrawal.

Fortunately, as they walked away together, my jeep driver had come over to the place in the wall where I had made my dramatic vault and looked down and saw me standing by the pile of boulders.

"What happened, Lieutenant?" he asked.

"Snuffy," I yelled at him: "bring that damn jeep down here right away."

"Yes, Sir," he replied and he was down alongside of me before the two majors had finished their discussion and returned. By then, with Snuffy's help, I had managed to get back into my jeep.

When Major Courtney returned, he said: "It's all settled, Jones; let's go back."

"Yes, Sir," I said, and Snuffy and I and our rifleman took off. On the way, I said: "Snuffy, I need a crutch. I can't walk on this damn knee."

"Well, Lieutenant," he answered. "We don't have any crutches in Supply, but I'll find you something when we get back."

When we got back to Battalion Headquarters, Snuffy drove directly to our supply dump. In a few minutes he came back to the jeep with a three-foot long axe handle.

"Here, Lieutenant," he said: "I got you a Kentucky crutch. Back on the farm when I wrecked my leg, I just hobbled around for a few days with an axe handle. It worked just fine for me."

"Just show me how to use it, Snuffy, and we'll give it a try." So I got out of the jeep and began taking lessons from my driver, who quickly showed me how to get around on one leg and an axe handle, Kentucky style.

My little accident didn't slow our move onto the lines in the south, but everyone in the battalion was so busy making the move that no one paid any attention to my predicament. With my jeep, the help of my driver, and the axe handle, I was able to make myself useful in the Supply Section, as well as to continue to run the necessary errands for Major Courtney. Of course, I did everything I could to prevent anyone, other than my driver, from seeing me hobbling around on the axe handle.

As the rains came and turned the entire island into a quagmire, it became more and more difficult to slog through the mud on my axe handle, so it was inevitable that the colonel would eventually spot his axe-handle liaison officer hobbling across the road. When he finally did, he yelled: "Jones, what the hell happened to you?"

"I twisted my knee, Colonel," I told him.

"When?" he asked.

"A couple of days ago up north."

"Have you been to the aid station?" he asked

"Not yet," I told him; "we've been busy moving."

Then he said the thing I didn't want to hear, what I had been avoiding all along. "Get your ass back to the aid station now. You're no good me to me the way you are."

On any of our three previous combat operations, a trip to the aid station might have been a welcome relief, but not on this operation on Okinawa. Here your best chances seemed to be in a snug foxhole with your unit, not in a vulnerable tent with a big red cross painted on it. Not with the Japanese *Kamikaze* mentality and hundreds of those bastards flying around looking for targets of opportunity. But orders are orders so I went back to the aid station, expecting them to wrap me up with an Ace bandage and send me back to my unit. But that isn't what happened.

First, I was embarrassed to hobble in on my axe handle and be put on a cot next to the truly wounded. Then I was surprised when, after a quick examination, they stuck me on a stretcher and loaded me into an ambulance with several other stretchers.

"Where are we going?" I asked the corpsman, afraid that I already knew the answer.

"All long-term wounds go to the hospital ship," he answered. A tent with a red cross painted on it was bad enough, but who needs to be on a big white ship with a giant red cross under spotlights at night during constant *Kamikaze* raids. In fact, I had recently seen a dispatch from Admiral Nimitz' headquarters that reported an aerial encounter on April 18 when a Japanese suicide pilot deliberately crashed his plane into a brightly lighted, plainly marked hospital ship, the USS Comfort, killing 29 and injuring 33.

But once you were in this medevac process there was no court of appeal. Fortunately, the ship didn't stay in *Kamikaze* territory for long. By dawn we were on our way to a hospital on Saipan.

Chapter 24

The Big Picture

Agrunt in a foxhole has little time to contemplate the Big Picture. He and his foxhole are the center of the universe, but as he moves to the rear his viewpoint quickly broadens yard-by-yard and mile-by-mile. So here I was many miles from my foxhole on Okinawa, flat on my back with plenty of time to contemplate the Big Picture.

In the last few weeks, our President had died; the Japanese had thrown out their wartime cabinet; and the Germans had surrendered – yet my buddies were still fighting for their lives and dying on Okinawa. Much of what I didn't know then, I later learned from an account by Colonel Hirimochi Yahara. He was the senior staff officer in charge of operations on Okinawa for Japan's 32d Army – its last fighting Army.

For example, Yahara reported that on April 26 Prime Minister Suzuki made a special radio speech to encourage the troops and civilians on Okinawa to continue the fight. This was despite dismal failure of an ill-fated Japanese attack on April 12 that resulted in the loss of four battalions. This was followed by another Japanese attack on May 4th that cost the lives of additional 5000 men.

So by mid-May, with the news of Germany's capitulation, Colonel Yahara has written that he knew it was nonsense to continue the war, but the war was to continue anyhow until the total defeat and destruction of the Japanese 32d Army on June 21, 1945. And although we were killing ten Japanese for every American killed – for the enemy to continue to fight this hopeless battle after their defeat was clear by mid-May was an unnecessary and obscene squandering of human lives on both sides. Of course, the troops on the battlefield didn't know the situation then – and, like troops in every battle, they would have been powerless to do anything other than continue to fight and kill each other had they known the Big Picture then.

The enemy strategy at that time was later well described by Colonel Yahara in his book "The Battle for Okinawa". The Army's ground strategy had been outlined after the enemy's defeat in the Marianas by General Atoyima, Vice-Chief-of-Staff of the Imperial Headquarters Army Department:

First, we cannot hope to match the enemy's strength on the ground, at sea, or in the air. Therefore, we should attack the enemy from "underground."

Second, in order to prevent the enemy from using his superior ground, sea, and air strength to the full, we should make use of the cover of night to pull up behind the enemy or penetrate enemy lines. Enemy troops would be thrown into a state of confusion, unable to distinguish friend or foe.

Third, the greatest threat above ground is enemy tanks. We have only a few antitank guns, and these would be quickly destroyed by the enemy's bombardment. If a poor man fights with the same tactics as a rich man, he is sure to lose. Therefore, the Japanese army has formulated new "patented" antitank tactics. These involve hand-carried makeshift explosive devices containing ten kilograms of yellow powder. Our experiments have shown ten kilograms of powder to be enough to blow up enemy tanks of any size. Delivery of these explosives would be in the nature of a suicide attack, of course. Soldiers assigned to this duty should be promoted three ranks.

But, of course, the senior officers of the Japanese 32d Army knew that more than an Army ground strategy would be necessary to defeat the powerful American amphibious force. So the plans adopted for the decisive battle of Okinawa were based on the policy of Imperial Headquarters to use the Navy and Air Force to crush advancing forces at sea, even though after the fall of the Marianas, the 32d Army no longer had much faith in their Navy and Air Force.

Assuming that the Imperial Navy and the Air Force would not be able to prevent the American's from establishing a beachhead,

Colonel Yahara set forth this plan.

1. The effects of bombardment by the American navy and air force could be nullified by keeping our forces in underground tunnels that would withstand enemy bombs and gunfire. Against steel, the product of American industry, we would pit our earthen fortifications, the product of the sweat of our troops and the Okinawan people.

2. The Americans might put as many as ten divisions into the field, but no more than a few could land initially. There would doubtless be confusion in the ranks, as the troops would be exposed on a narrow strip of land without fortifications.

3. Holed up safely in our fortified area, we could, as our chief of staff put it, "laugh in the face" of the enemy's bombardment. We would be able to maintain firepower and organization and keep order in the ranks.

4. Because our army was on the defensive, we could concentrate large- caliber artillery guns in the field. We had 400 guns of 7-1/2 centimeter bore or above; of these, 120 guns were 15 centimeters or above. The firepower of these powerful guns directed at the enemy's narrow beachhead from the tunnel emplacements would have a devastating effect.

In modern warfare, tanks and artillery wield greater offensive power than infantry. Unfortunately, 32nd Army had only one regiment of light tanks; we did, however, have considerable artillery strength. With an eye on this, I devised tactics for effective bombardment of the beachhead. On the basis of these tactical concepts, I made recommendations to the central command for further artillery reinforcements. Stressing the necessity of unified command operation facilities, I made a strong case to headquarters and succeeded in having the 5th Artillery Group placed under direct army control.

5. In the Pacific islands so far, American landing forces had first secured a beachhead and then progressed step-by-step toward an advance a few days later. We could not discount the possibility that the enemy might stage an advance immediately after landing, with numerous tank units breaking through infantry resistance and striking at artillery positions. If this happened, our army would be at a disadvantage. If, however, we increased the longitudinal depth of infantry tunnel positions and made substantial preparation of antitank warfare, the infantry lines could hold out for the two days our army would need to prepare for a counteroffensive.

6. Given the enemy's sea and air supremacy, it would be difficult to move large fighting units through the narrow corridor of land connecting Nakagami in the southern half of the island with Shimajiri in the north. For the following reasons, I believed that this problem could be solved:

   a. The distance to be crossed was no more that twenty-five kilometers.

   b. Units could be moved under cover of night. Units unable to complete the move at night could adopt the procedures devised in Manchuria for troop maneuvers under enemy-controlled skies. The 9th and 24th Divisions had been thoroughly drilled in these maneuvers in Manchuria.

   c. Because the invasion would proceed from water to land, enemy aircraft would be based on aircraft carriers and would probably make no more than a few night air sorties.

   d. We could prepare four north-south roads for troop movements, place repair materials at those key segments most likely to be bombarded by the enemy, and construct alternate roads.

   e. Underground positions would be constructed beforehand for units to take up after maneuvers.

   f. The 9th and 24th Divisions and artillery units would undergo drills to master these maneuvers.

   g. Munitions would be stockpiled separately in the north and in the south.

Not all parts of the Japanese plan were implemented, but the significance of building and fighting from underground fortifications cannot be over- emphasized. It was just that concept that allowed a Japanese military force of about 100,000 isolated troops to hold out for 82 days against a far superior American force of 180,000 assault troops, supported by a dominant air and sea armada.

What I didn't know then but my buddies were painfully discovering is that the Japanese had spent the previous year creating 60 miles of interconnected underground fortifications, enough to provide protection for their entire Army of 100,000 troops. And because these Japanese defenders used direct fire and mutually supporting reverse slope positions, combined with interconnecting tunnels, it made it possible for our troops to be on top of a hill and still not control it.

Although the full force of the enemy we were fighting was never exactly clear to us at the battalion level, we had heard that there was a General Ishijima in command of the Imperial Japanese 32d Army defending the island. But in our minds it was never us in the U.S. Tenth Army against them in the Japanese 32d. It was simply us in the Second Battalion of the 22d Marine Regiment in the 6th Marine Division against whoever was trying to hold those hills that we were ordered to attack.

Now that I was comfortably bedded aboard this luxurious hospital ship, safely out of the concentrated *Kamikaze* zone, I began to have feelings of remorse. I knew that our guys were being committed to the hot combat zone by now, and here I was being fed hot chow by the first beautiful white women I had seen in two years. On the one hand, it seemed like a fair turn of fate – that after two years in the jungle and four combat landings – I was given a momentary respite. On the other hand, I felt like I belonged on the line with my buddies. I certainly didn't think I belonged in the hospital with the truly wounded. But nobody was asking me what I wanted.

Instead, they ran my knee through the X-ray machine and told me it looked like a box of cracker jack with a prize whistle inside. Anyway, they told me it would take surgery, or six weeks, or both, to heal. And they wound my knee up and gave me a crutch to hobble on.

At the field hospital on Saipan, they simply confirmed the shipboard prognosis and then told me they weren't doing elective surgery on knees but were restricting surgery to emergency and serious cases. Then they wound my knee a little tighter, gave me a new crutch, and told me to relax and listen to the war on radio. Who the hell can listen to a war their buddies are fighting on radio? In some strange way, I wanted to be back on Okinawa with my ax-handle crutch helping out the best I could.

The docs told me I wasn't going anywhere for awhile, so I read more news clippings, listened to the radio, talked to the newly arrived wounded, and followed the battle as best I could from 1500 miles away.

By now, of course, I knew that the Okinawa campaign was our biggest and most significant operation to date, but I didn't know yet that it would later prove to be the bloodiest single battle of the Pacific War and the second bloodiest battle of the entire World War II. With 243,000 killed in eighty-two days of fighting – combatants and civilians on both sides – the battle for Okinawa was by the war's end to be second in battle deaths only to the longer and bloodier battle for Stalingrad.

Chapter 25

The Little Players

By the night of May 9, Marines of the 22d were positioned on the cliffs overlooking the Asa Kawa River, taking a shelling from 150-mm enemy artillery. Their mission was to provide fire cover for a predawn attack across the river on May 10 by companies from the 2d and 3rd Battalions. When Colonel Woodhouse told Major Courtney to send Jones to G Company and bring Captain Stebbins back for a conference, the major reminded him that Jones had been evacuated on a stretcher.

"Hell," the colonel replies, "I just sent him to the aid station; I didn't send him home."

"No, but the docs did. At least they sent him to Saipan, according to our doc. But I'll get Stebby."

When Courtney arrives with Stebbins, the colonel lays out the plan for the predawn attack. With the word "predawn", Stebby's antenna goes up. "Predawn" means "dark", and Stebby knows that isn't good. Stebby reminds the colonel that in every one of our campaigns to date, our Standard Operating Procedure has been – "Anything that moves in the dark gets shot."

"Yeah, I know, Stebby," the colonel replies; "but the Division will attack at dawn, and your orders are to move out at 0300."

"Yes, Sir," Stebby answers dutifully – "0300."

Captain Owen T. Stebbins, commanding G Company was one of our old-timers who had not only made all our major assault landings in the Marshalls and Marianas, but he had also been picked to make a number of lesser landings in the Marshalls as part of the mop-up operations. Despite his long tenure with the regiment, he had been wounded and evacuated (against his will) on hitting the beach on Guam, so Okinawa was his first command of a company on an island big enough to allow him to excrcise company-level control.

After a month and a half on Okinawa, Captain Stebbins has proven himself to be a cool competent commander who is well liked by his troops. His mission now is to wade his company through the thigh-deep water of the Asa Kawa River while K Company of the 3rd Battalion on his right uses a newly constructed bridge for a simultaneous crossing. Just as each of the two battalions succeeds in pushing their two assault companies across the foggy river before dawn, a two-man Japanese suicide team rushes the bridge with explosive satchel charges, blowing up the bridge and themselves.

At daybreak the Marines see that they are facing a series of terraces and hills, and the Japanese see that they are facing a Marine attack. The Japanese react powerfully with large mortars and fierce small arms fire from automatic weapons. As G Company approaches some small huts near a stand of trees, they run into intense fire from rifles and nearby machine guns. Stebby's veterans soon realized that some of the fire is coming from hidden "spider holes" like those we had encountered on our first engagement on Engebi in the Marshalls. But here on Okinawa the Japanese have covered these one-man fighting holes with camouflage made of twigs and reeds from the local vegetation.

As G Company continues its advance through heavy eye-level weeds and brush, they are taking casualties from the enemy's camouflaged positions, so they resort to flamethrowers, bazookas, and rifle grenades. Even then the heavy underbrush often deflects the bazooka and rifle grenade projectiles, sending them off as harmless unexploded ricochets. As usual, they will have to physically overrun the Japanese positions to put an end to the casualties they are taking from enemy emplacements they can't see.

Captain Stebbins has correctly determined that our battalion is fighting through a classic enemy delaying action designed to inflict enough casualties to slow down our attack while allowing their own troops time to fall back to other better-constructed defensive emplacements.

G Company is only able to cover a few hundred yards during the day, but the cost in killed and wounded is already 29 men and one officer. Since the Company had been lucky in the first month of fighting up north, with only the loss of 22 men wounded, these new losses seem heavy for a single day of combat. But in less than a week, they would measure losses on a scale no one could yet foresee.

While my battalion was grubbing along, crossing rivers, and taking small insignificant terrain features, all the Marine brass, including our Division Commander, our Corps Commander, and even the Commandant of the Marine Corps were trying to convince Lieutenant General Simon Bolivar Buckner, the Commanding Officer of the 10th Army, to allow us to make an end-run around what seemed to be the Japanese "Main Line of Resistance". The proposal was to use the 2d Marine Division, which was the 10th Army Reserve, to open a second front with an amphibious landing on the west coast of Okinawa behind the Japanese lines. And even one of Buckner's own more venturesome commanders, General Andrew D. Bruce, CO of the 77th Army Division had proposed such a landing.

But Buckner was stubborn and ultraconservative. He seemed to be oblivious to the combat experiences of his own 27th Army Division. In a joint operation with us on Eniwetok, the 106th Infantry Regiment of the 27th Infantry Division performed miserably. They were taking casualties and still lying on the beach and failing to move in until we came to their rescue. We had to climb over their backs, and then threaten them if they didn't follow us in.

Now, here on Okinawa, on April 20th, when this same 27th Infantry Division ran into a Japanese defense point named "Item Pocket", they battled the pocket for five days before taking possession. Without carrying the attack to the enemy, they sustained heavy casualties, and two of their companies fled in panic after being surrounded and cut off.

There has always been a certain amount of inter-Service rivalry, and when kept within bounds it is probably healthy. It is difficult for any Marine to say that he thinks that a soldier is as good as a Marine. At least you don't say that in a barroom of mixed-Services. But in our hearts we respect a brave warrior regardless of uniform. Accordingly, many Marines learned to respect the 77th, the 7th and the 96th Army Infantry Divisions, but that was not how we felt about the 27th, nor the 10th Army Commander.

When I visualize the difference between the old school, General Buckner Army philosophy and that of the Marine Corps, I visualize an Army battalion like a standard 2-1/2-ton truck inching its way through the mud; then I picture a Marine battalion like a 4-wheel-drive Hummer speeding along with no brakes and no reverse gear. At any rate, it was the Army in charge on Okinawa, and Buckner was no General MacArthur, so there was no Inchon-type second landing behind enemy lines. The Marines, along with the doughboys, had to mount a slow, methodical, frontal attack against the entrenched enemy's main line of resistance.

Once the top Army brass had dismissed alternative tactics, much of the job of frontal assault fell heavily on the three-infantry battalions of our 22d Marine Regiment. The assault companies of all three battalions distinguished themselves by crossing the Asa Kawa estuary and attacking fiercely-defended, cleverly-camouflaged enemy fortifications. It took two days of hard fighting by Captain Warren F. Lloyd and his C Company to win the ground, which included a major fortification dubbed "Charlie Hill". The hill, named by the captain in honor of his company, was captured at the cost of 35 killed and 68 wounded.

Lieutenant Paul Dunfey of K Company, 3rd Battalion, who had led the first reconnaissance patrol across the river, later received a horrific abdominal wound that would cost him his life. And yet Sergeant Ray Gillespie, also of K Company with an equally horrific abdominal wound, somehow survived. It seems to me now that, unlike civilian trauma cases, in a war you can never predict survival based solely on the physical severity of combat wounds. Something beyond the physical is often at play.

As I lay in the hospital with my minor but incapacitating injury, I queried the wounded survivors who were being brought in daily. I was eager for the battle news, especially the news of our regiment and my comrades in the Second Battalion.

It was a trying time for me. I had no burning desire to go back and kill Japs. But then neither did my old buddies who had served in the Eniwetok and Guam campaigns. Nobody who had already spent a couple of years out here with scores of combat days and nights in a Marine infantry battalion needed any more combat days to feel like he had contributed enough. So what was bugging me? I was probably the only veteran in our outfit who, back on the Canal, had been given an "option-out" but who had volunteered to go along.

Of course, the new lieutenants, the former football stars coming in as replacements, were all eager to lead their platoons to victory – like Heavy had once been. Even some of our veteran lieutenants and captains who had been previously wounded and quickly evacuated on former campaigns, did not feel the same combat ennui now that some of us felt. Some of us, like Heavy, who had suffered through every day and night of all our previous campaigns, were now far more war weary than those with just a few days of actual combat experience. I came to believe that exposure of the human body to infantry combat was something like exposure to radiation – the effect is cumulative and every human being has his limit. Still, I felt guilty because, unlike Heavy, I hadn't spent all my combat time in a forward infantry platoon, so I felt like I had no right to claim I had reached my limit.

Of course, what I felt didn't matter to anyone but me. I was now caught up in the medevac situation—the doctors would decide when I would be released and where I would be sent next. Meanwhile, I tried to make peace with myself as I hobbled around the hospital on government-issue crutches, waiting for the next news from the front lines.

Chapter 26

Stumbling into Chaos

Chaos: confusion or confused mass of formless matter and infinite space, supposed to have existed before the ordered universe.

On the morning of May 12, Captain Stebbin's usual optimistic upbeat mood is severely shaken when a mortar bombardment makes a direct hit on his G Company command post. With three more dead and two more wounded from the blast, his company is now down to 60% of its authorized strength. Nevertheless, G Company moves out on schedule as soon as their tank support arrives. On Stebbin's left, First Lieutenant Frank Gunter's E Company is covering the regiment's left flank. These two assault companies move against some small hills that show no visible signs of the enemy. They try to ignore the small arms fire that they are taking from hidden enemy positions.

While G Company is moving against light resistance, E Company suddenly encounters persistent accurate fire from a Japanese heavy machine gun emplacement. A platoon sergeant reaches Heavy Pfuhl back at the E Company CP and asks for a tank to take out the machine gun. Then Heavy and the sergeant advance with the tank to the front. The sergeant is quickly struck by three slugs in the neck, side, and leg, and Heavy takes a single bullet through his right thigh, lower testicle, and left buttocks. He pulls the sergeant to a safe position and calls a medical corpsman. Lieutenant Pesely arrives with F Company and he and a corpsman evacuate the sergeant, dig out Heavy's slug and sprinkle some sulpha powder on his wounds. Heavy then continues his advance directing the tank fire to the target and taking out that Japanese nuisance only to run into more hidden Japanese emplacements. This slows E Company's attack and allows a gap to develop between them and the First Marine Division to their left rear.

At the same time, Stebbins' G Company has been moving ahead rapidly against much lighter resistance, with Captain Ahearn's F Company following closely in reserve. Then Lieutenant Colonel Woodhouse decides to assign G Company a new objective. Looking across a barren landscape of minor brush and scrubby trees, the colonel points to three insignificant hills, smaller than Charlie Hill seized the previous day by Captain Lloyd of the First Battalion. Stebby is told that his new mission is to take that little 50-foot hill in the middle.

During the briefing, the colonel first assigns numbers to the three hills, and then to avoid confusion he decides to name the middle one "Sugar Loaf." Compared to other G Company missions, this one looks to Stebby like a piece of cake. "It was just an attack against a routine strong point," he later told me. So the colonel assures him he will have the support of a platoon of tanks and tells him to go take that piece of cake.

It is doubtful that the colonel had been briefed by Division about a captured enemy document that indicated that the high ground they were attacking was defended by *a network of small-group positions organized for AT (antitank) defense*. But even with that information, none of the American forces knew at that time how inadequate our intelligence data was. They could not know then what Colonel Hiromichi Yahara would report after that battle: *"Not only did our troops fight brilliantly, but they were helped by terrain favorable to our defense. The fortifications at Amekudai (Sugar Loaf) were ideal. Our stronghold on the escarpment was located within deep depressions, which led to a network of caves and tunnels. These kept our troops relatively safe from artillery attack. From the top of the heights we had a bird's-eye view of the enemy. We had observation posts at Shuri with the Army Artillery Group and at Shikina with our brigade artillery, and Lieutenant Commander Nii's naval gun units assisted our forward positions at Amekudai (Sugar Loaf)."* What I suspected from the safety of my hospital bed at that time, but could only confirm after the battle was over, was that my few good buddies from way back in the Samoa days were throwing their bodies against one of the most impregnable fortifications of the war. So with limited intelligence data but with great faith and courage, the Second Battalion, Twenty-Second Marines, pursued its objective.

Two clean-cut all-American boys are leading the assault platoons in G Company – First Lieutenant Ed Reuss and Second Lieutenant Robert Nealon. Captain Stebbins follows closely behind his two assault platoons, well forward of his company CP. At first, G Company has the protection of a natural draw, while both F Company and E Company are catching machine gun and mortar fire from Shuri Heights. However, the luck of G Company begins to run out when they come out of the draw into the open terrain where they come under heavy fire from that little hill to their front.

Stebbins tries to direct his platoons to take full advantage of their tank support, but the tanks turn out to be magnets for the enemy's heavy artillery and high-velocity 47mm antitank fire. Two tanks are stopped in their tracks, either hit directly or stalled, and the infantry has to move on without them. Stebbins, a faithful Christian Scientist, tries to ignore the worldly realism as he passes the disemboweled bodies of two of his men who had been advancing behind the stopped tanks.

Stebbins then sends a runner up to Lieutenant Reuss' platoon to tell the lieutenant to pull his platoon over to a safer position and hold until the captain can get some tanks up to support his advance. Instead the lieutenant comes back to say he can hold where he is and doesn't want to move because he has several men wounded and trapped on the lower slopes of the objective hill.

Although the captain admires the lieutenant – a husky former football player and brave Marine – he also knows he is impetuous and inclined to take risky actions, seemingly in the belief that there is some kind of protective shield over heroes. It always took a little longer for the former football heroes to come to grips with the reality of the battlefield. Unfortunately, as brave a Marine as he is, Lieutenant Reuss does not heed a friend's advice: "You're not running for a touchdown when you command a platoon in combat. You've got 40 men to lead and protect." And so the lieutenant dies using himself as a playful, teasing target, jumping up and down to attract enemy gunfire to locate their positions. He knew he was tough, but he didn't know that he wasn't tougher than bullets. He died of three painful gunshot wounds in the abdomen. Platoon Sergeant Ed DeMar, a levelheaded veteran Marine takes over the lieutenant's platoon.

Meanwhile, Stebbins, who has cautiously maintained a lean OP of just himself and a runner to avoid looking to the enemy like a commanding officer, stands up to survey the scene before sending for the tanks. He is instantly riddled in the legs by Jap machine-gun fire, and his runner is killed.

Now Stebbins is alone and crippled, with no runner and no radio. Unaware that Lieutenant Reuss has been killed, he begins crawling along a drainage ditch the length of three or four football fields towards his company CP to let someone know that the assault platoons desperately need tanks.

While Captain Stebbins has been busy running the forward OP, First Lieutenant Dale Bair, a woodsman from Pocatello, Idaho, is at the company CP coordinating the battalion's 81mm mortars and 105mm artillery support for the infantry assault. Without radio contact with the front lines, Bair nevertheless continues to lay mortar fire on the Japanese positions in front of Lieutenant Reuss's platoon, now commanded by Sergeant DeMar.

Stebbins is picked up by medics and debriefed by Colonel Woodhouse who then personally calls on Bair and orders him to reorganize the assault platoons and continue the attack to take that stubborn little hill.

Bair confers with veteran Sergeant Ed DeMar who tells him that his platoon is down to half strength. "Well, we've got orders to take that hill," he tells the sergeant "because E Company is pinned down up there and taking a lot of wounded." He tells DeMar that the attack will take off at 1600 when their tank support arrives.

He knows that E Company has already taken significant casualties that included not only Lieutenant Pfuhl who has been wounded but stays with the battle, but also Lieutenants Nick Thorne, Dean McDowell and Teddy Ogdahl. Even at this time before the battle reaches its ultimate frenzic pitch, the lightly wounded without orthopedic or deep organic injury are simply patched up and kept on the line. So it is that Lieutenant Bair leads the depleted G Company in the attack, with him leading the first platoon on the right, Sergeant DeMar leading the third platoon on the left, and with the second platoon providing a base of supporting fire. Upon reaching the four supporting tanks that are waiting for them in a hollow out of sight of the enemy, Lieutenant Bair gives the signal to start the attack

Those not yet too frightened to breathe now hold their breath as they move out into fierce enemy small arms and automatic weapons fire coming from the hill directly in front of them and the two hills on their flanks. With Marines dropping all around, a PFC notices a Japanese soldier run toward a tank with an explosive charge only to be cut down by the gunner in a following tank. Soon two of the four tanks had been stopped, but even without tank cover the exposed Marines continue their attack. Sergeant DeMar is losing men on all sides as he reaches the base of the hill. Then looking up toward the crest, he sees Lieutenant Bair signaling him to stop the fire coming from the first tank. At that moment he sees Bair lurch forward wounded in his left thigh while at the same time DeMar takes shrapnel in his own left thigh. DeMar's leg collapses, and he falls to the ground. Another sergeant gets to the tank and tells them to hold fire. Then Captain Morell gets out of his tank into the chaos of the infantry firefight. He notes that amtracs bringing troop reinforcements into the battle are quickly stopped, and the replacement troops are being cut down as they come pouring out of the amtrac ramps. Some of these boys who were in high school 90 days ago are now dead before they fire their first shot in anger.

The battle continues. DeMar drags himself and his useless leg up the hill where he can see Lieutenant Bair to his right cradling a light machine gun in his arms, like Victor McLaughlen in an old World War I movie.

Dale Bair is a tobacco chewing, six-foot-two, 225-pound lumberjack from Idaho. He has a quiet, modest, but I-mean-business attitude. He is a good man to have on your side, but he is a very dangerous enemy as the Japs are now finding out. There he stands at the crest of the hill ignoring the wounds in his arm, his chest and his legs as he fires burst after burst at the Japanese to cover the withdrawal of his pinned-down troops.

Among his pinned down troops is PFC Jim Chaisson, a man far too old at 34 to be an unranked enlisted Marine and certainly far too old for the job at hand. But the "old" Marine defies age and logic and performs on the hill that day with sufficient energy, guts, and Marine courage to win a Navy Cross. Jimmy is all over the hill, helping with the wounded, reporting to Battalion, and incidentally fighting the Japs. Of course, he earns a Purple Heart – but then who didn't? It is the easiest medal to earn on Sugar Loaf Hill.

Chaisson and other lightly wounded Marines crawl back off the hill in the indentations made by the tanks. Their more seriously wounded are loaded onto the tanks, where many of them are then fatally wounded by Japanese snipers as the tanks make their way back. DeMar makes it back safely on the tank. Through it all, Bair continues to fire until his pinned-down men get out. Wounded four times and still cradling his machine gun, he finally takes cover behind some rocks until he can be moved back to an aid station.

That night, Lieutenant Colonel Woodhouse has grim news to report to Regiment. He tells Colonel Schneider that G Company had taken the hill, but that casualties were so great that they could not hold it. He reports that only about 75 men are left in G Company including some headquarters personnel. He points out that the hill is full of caves and tunneling and that they have lost three tanks and had to leave some Marine dead behind.

I am sure that this pullback message came as a great shock to Regiment and to Division Headquarters because on Guam I had already learned about General Shepherd's thinking regarding a Marine pull-back. At one point during the battle on Guam, when I had suggested to Colonel Schneider that our forward troops be pulled back 200 yards to take up a more defensible position than that which they had gained during the fighting that day, I was abruptly rebuked. The colonel informed me in no uncertain terms: "The general says a Marine can always hold any ground that he can take." So I'm sure that Division put intense pressure on Regiment when they learned that a Marine company had been able to take a small insignificant looking hill and yet been unable to hold it.

Division was only slowly discovering the full strength of the enemy they were facing. Captured enemy documents were beginning to reveal the names of such enemy forces as the 44th Independent Mixed Brigade, the 15th Independent Mixed Regiment, as well as antitank forces. It was later learned that after the failed Japanese offensive of May 4th, Colonel Yahara put into effect a plan of action that involved returning the 44th Independent Mixed Brigade and the 6th Special Regiment to Sugar Loaf to assist the 62d Division in defending the hill, and they would have the full support of the 32d Army Artillery Group. These combined forces were numbered in the thousands, perhaps eight thousand all together. Of course, they were stretched across a broad front on the Shuri/Sugar Loaf line, but the tunnels made it possible for the enemy to pour as many of these thousands as he needed into the caves and pits on Sugar Loaf. Against this massive enemy force, the Sixth Marine Division had unknowingly sent a company of less than 200 Marines. To Division, it still looked like a routine mission of conquering a stubborn little hill. It was not.

Chapter 27

The Chaos Continues

Despite Battalion's negative report to Regiment regarding G Company's valiant but failed attempt to hold Sugar Loaf on May 12, the Second Battalion was ordered to continue the attack on May 13. Again elements of the battalion succeeded in reaching the top of Sugar Loaf, but again, contrary to the General's combat premise that Marines never give up ground once gained – we were unable to hold the ground we had taken and were forced off the hill. This was to be repeated a dozen times before the General's premise was finally proven to be true and the ground was held.

As the attack continued, Lieutenant Joe Bystry's F Company platoon was the first to be hit by enemy mortars. With heavy casualties, he and his platoon sergeant gathered up their wounded and their weapons and beat a retreat off the hill. His commanding officer, Captain Mike Ahearn, was also wounded by a machine gun burst in the leg. When Lieutenant Colonel Woodhouse learned of the Captain's wounds, he called Lieutenant Pesely, the company executive officer, and told him to relieve Ahearn and take command of F Company.

According to Ed Pesely's account here's what happened on that hill after he took over F Company. "First", Ed told me, "I had to get Mike back to an aid station, but he wouldn't go. He just kept putting other wounded on stretchers that the corpsman would bring for him. Finally, the colonel stayed with us until Ahearn gave his command radio over to me.

"Since our regiment had already taken more than 800 casualties in the last three days of fighting, we were hoping for some kind of relief on the morning of May 14th," Ed continued.

"Instead," he said, "our regiment was ordered to resume the attack. So on that miserable rainy morning, Woodhouse assembled me and the other two company commanders, and gave us orders to continue the attack toward Naha. Unfortunately for us, those three small hills still stood in our way, including that tough nut in the middle that the colonel now named 'Sugar Loaf'. Still, none of us at Battalion, Regiment, or Division had any idea of the true strength and significance of those three little hills at that time," Ed emphasized.

The officers and men of the Twenty-Second were just little players in a Big Picture attack. The Big Picture plan was for the two corps of the Tenth Army to clear the western and eastern approaches to Shuri and envelope General Ushijima's flanks. Spearheading this grand plan were the depleted forces of our three Companies E, F, and G of the 2nd Battalion, 22d Marines, with the 29th and the 4th Marines in support.

As a sound tactical commander, Lieutenant Colonel Woodhouse intended to delay his attack until the 1st Marine Division came on line to protect the Twenty-Second's left flank. However, the colonel's tactical plan was quickly overruled by the Assistant Division Commander, Brigadier General William T. Clement, who arrived at the battalion command post with field orders obviously written by a Division Headquarters that just didn't understand the situation. The orders simply directed the battalion to move out immediately before the 1st Division came on line and pursue the attack *at all cost*. Those words *at all cost* were accepted and followed literally by the Second Battalion, resulting in one of the most horrendous and costly battles on Okinawa.

The new orders from the general disrupted Lieutenant Colonel Woodhouse's tactical plans and made a simultaneous direct assault against the three hills necessary. Unfortunately, as the senior company officer still on his feet, my friend First Lieutenant Ed Pesely was now in command of F Company, and F Company was designated by the colonel to lead the attack.

Ed was not only a good friend, but a good solid Marine who was never a glory seeker looking for medals, but who won them anyhow by being in the wrong place at the wrong time and just doing his job. This was certainly one of those times and one of those places.

"Ed," the colonel tells him and the other two company commanders, "here's the plan. F Company will lead the assault by sending one platoon against Hill 1 and one platoon against Hill 3. As soon as those hills are taken, the F Company platoon on Hill 1 will be relieved by E Company, and the F Company platoon on Hill 3 will be relieved by G Company. Then, Ed, you will move out with all three of your platoons and take Sugar Loaf. Any questions?"

"What kind of support do we get?" Pesely asks. "Do we get any tanks or smoke?"

"Yes," the colonel tells him. You'll have five tanks, and we'll cover your advance with artillery smoke shells."

When the colonel learns that there will be no smoke shells because the artillery has run out of them, he compensates by sending the tanks out five minutes ahead of the infantry. He hopes the troops will get concealment from the smoke and dust kicked up by the tanks and supporting high-explosive artillery fire. The 75 survivors of the G Company – now organized into one platoon – relieve the 1st platoon of Fox Company on Hill 3, while Easy Company relieves the 2d platoon Fox Company on Hill 1, and the full strength of Fox Company moves against the center hill, Sugar Loaf.

While the executive officer of Easy Company, Lieutenant Jack Fitzgerald, waits in support in the defilade provided by a railway channel, he is somewhat surprised to see the regimental chaplain, Father Kelly, come up to the front lines with the battalion executive officer, Major Henry A. Courtney.

As a devout Catholic, Courtney has brought the chaplain to the front lines to offer communion to the troops being prepared for what the major apparently thinks will be a suicide attack. Knowing that as senior officer at the front he will be leading the attack, the major gets down on his knees and accepts the host from the Father.

Major Courtney, a handsome twenty-eight-year-old officer, joined the 22d Marines after our Guam operations. Therefore, unlike many of the officers junior to him, he had never experienced combat with us prior to Okinawa. perhaps because of that he had been very quiet and unassertive in training preparations for the Okinawa campaign. However, on Okinawa after a couple of weeks in a combat environment, he blossomed as a very competent battalion executive officer with whom I was privileged to serve on our battalion headquarters staff. Of course, the image of a battalion headquarters as some kind of remote command base does not jibe with the reality of a Marine Corps battalion headquarters in combat.

When deployed in combat, a Marine battalion usually has two command posts – a conventional CP located with the reserve company behind the two forward companies, and a forward CP up front coordinating the operations of the two assault companies. In our battalion, it was standard operating procedure for the battalion executive officer, a lieutenant, a radioman, and a couple of runners to operate from the forward CP position near the assault companies.* So if it was a surprise to Lieutenant Fitzgerald to see Father Kelly giving the host to Major Courtney at the front lines, it was not a surprise for him to see the major preparing to coordinate the continuing attack on Sugar Loaf Hill.

Even for those who were there, the chronology of events for the fateful battle for Sugar Loaf is impossible to follow. So many things were happening in so many places to so many individuals on those three godforsaken hills, it would have taken a Steven Spielberg movie crew with a dozen cameras to catch the action. But here's the way Ed Pesely remembers it on Sugar Loaf on the night of 14/15 May 1945.

"The colonel keeps his promise and sends me five tanks to support our attack, but it only takes the enemy about 25 minutes to knock them out with what I think were 47mm armor-piercing projectiles. Anyhow we gain the base of the hill by dark, with Lieutenant Gaumnitz's platoon out front. Lieutenant Hutchings and the mortar section are on Hill 3 waiting to be relieved by Lieutenant Nealon of G Company when Major Courtney comes

---

* *On Okinawa I was the lieutenant at Major Courtney's side until I was injured and evacuated before the battle of Sugar Loaf. It is certain that only my earlier injury and evacuation allowed me to survive to write these memoirs.*

along and tells me he sees Marines on top of Sugar Loaf. He thinks it must be Lieutenant Gaumnitz's platoon. I tell him I don't think so, I think they are Japs. Even through Courtney has no visible weapon, he doesn't hesitate to wander around the base of the hill checking on our various positions. After awhile he comes back and says he is planning a night attack on the summit to relieve the Marines who are up there. It is plain that he expects us all to follow him, even though we keep insisting that those aren't Marines at the top but are the enemy.

"Of course when he leads off, we follow. We move in the dark in a single column along a narrow path, freezing ourselves motionless as we are caught in the intermittent glare of the flares from our star shells. We know that the enemy can see us coming, and soon all hell breaks loose. As our column moves on, the Japanese artillery and knee mortars are blasting all around us. Then a light flashes from the top of the hill. We quickly shoot at it, and it goes out. Courtney yells, 'Knock it off and let's get to the top of the hill and relieve our guys'. But we know they are Japs, not our guys.' Still we follow the major in single file up that narrow trail. Soon more Jap mortars and artillery shells are coming in at us. We radio the colonel and call for artillery. When we get to the top, the Jap grenades come smoking over the hill. We grab them and throw them back because we are running out of our own grenades. Courtney yells at me; 'Go back to Battalion and get all the grenades you can get'. Lieutenant Hutchins says it will take two for one of us to get through, so he joins me.

"On the way in the dark, we run into an amtrac picking up casualties. We try to commandeer it to go get the grenades as the major has ordered, but the wounded are pleading with us, 'Give us a break, Pese, we've been lying here in the mud all day. Let him take us back'

"So we hurriedly help gather a few wounded and take them back to the aid station, and then we go for the grenades. I see a confused Marine sitting on the edge of shell hole full of water, but when I go over to help him, he tumbles dead into the water.

"The CP and Aid Station are a few minutes apart. When I get to the CP, the colonel says he will give us all the men and grenades he has. So we load up the ammo and I divide the 27 replacements he gives me into two groups, and we head back to the hill.

"Now in the glare of bursting shells I can see people moving around on the top, And at the foot of the hill we are having a hard time finding the trail back up. When our tractor gets stuck in the mud and can't back up, Courtney yells at us to keep coming with the grenades. Finally, by midnight we are back on the top wrenching open the grenade cases with our K-Bar knives and bayonets. Then we have to show the green replacements how to throw a grenade. Many of them were civilians just weeks ago, and others are radiomen, cooks, and truck drivers, with no real infantry experience.

"By now, we can see the Japs getting ready on their side of the hill for another run at the top. So we walk and crawl along the top dropping grenades into every hole on their side. It is bedlam when our grenades start popping on their troops. Many of our grenades are white phosphorus which set fire immediately to anything organic, but especially to human flesh. And the phosphorus keeps burning and smoking until smothered by water or mud. Naturally, the Japanese are screaming in pain and misery.

"I go over to recover the carbine I had loaned to Courtney because he had no weapon when he launched the attack earlier. While we are all ducking Japanese shells, I'm caught by a burst of shrapnel in the chest and neck and my right arm. After we sprinkle some sulfa powder on the wounds, I learn that Courtney has been fatally wounded, making me senior officer on the hill – an honor I'm not looking for.

"Well, if things had been bad – and they had – now they got worse. I knew the Japs were preparing to take the top of the hill again. I was certain that, like us, they also had orders to hold that hill *at all cost*. But as the senior officer still standing on our side, now it was my job to try and hold that hill.

"To break up the expected Jap attack, I tell the colonel to put all the artillery he can direct to hit over the top about 100 yards onto the reverse slope where the Japs are gathering. He starts the artillery barrage, with me calling the target coordinates. First 100 yards away, then 50 yards. And the colonel asks me how close are the Japs anyhow. I tell him, if they were any closer they would be in my vest pocket. 'The fact is, Colonel,' I said, 'I now see Japs between our artillery bursts and our positions. We may be goosing them right into our foxholes.' While I'm calling the coordinates, I suddenly realize that hot metal from our artillery has just landed in my foxhole, and when I see the glow from a Japanese flare at my feet, I reach down and nervously light a cigarette on it."

"Well, Pese, what can I do for you?" the colonel asks.

"Send me more troops", I tell the colonel. "It sure as hell is getting lonely on our side, and the Japs sound like they're having a block party on the other side of the hill."

"I'm working on it," the colonel replies." "Just hold on, Pese, and believe me – I am working on it, but we don't have anybody left at Battalion."

"As I give the radio back to my radioman who is my foxhole partner, I hear some Japanese yelling 'To hell with Mrs. Roosevelt,' and 'You die, Marine.'

"With Courtney dead, chaos on the hill, and Battalion telling me they can't help, I just lay myself down quietly in my foxhole, bleeding a little and waiting for the nightmare to end. When my radioman raises up to urinate, a burst of machine gun fire slices off his pistol holster, and that's the last thing I remembered before passing out to sleep.

"The next thing I remember is waking up still in the nightmare and hearing my radioman tell the colonel that we are about to be overrun. I grab the radio, and Woodhouse tells me that help is on the way from the Third Battalion's K Company under the command of Lieutenant Reg Fincke, who I know to be a damn good officer.

"Of course, I don't know that the colonel has told Fincke that there are only eight men left on Sugar Loaf, and that if Fincke can't take over and hold the hill *at all cost*, all of my guys who have died trying will have died for nothing."

As Fincke's K Company moves toward the hill, his replacement troops see that the entire approach to the hill is littered with dead Marines – hundreds of dead Marines. Maybe scores of still dying Marines – but there is no way to stop the killing for compassion.

The new troops move up the slope, and somehow Lieutenant Fincke with four officers and 99 men make it up the hill without taking any casualties. They quickly fall into the existing foxholes, pushing the bodies of the dead former occupants aside. But K Company's luck is not to last. The Japs seem to be aware of their arrival. Soon mortar streaks are visible from behind Sugar Loaf, and the K Company machine gunners open up on the mortar positions with their tracers.

Pesely went on to tell me: "When the mortar shells start landing around K Company's machine gun emplacement, I yell 'Down! Down!' Then I see several shells explode near the gun, and there is a direct hit, knocking out the gun and the crew. After that the only noise I can hear comes from the wounded. Lieutenant Fincke has caught a blast that blew most of his legs away. They put him on a stretcher, but one of the stretcher-bearers slips and the lieutenant falls off, and rolls down the hill and dies. That's the way things went for us that night on the hill.

"The next thing I remember another lieutenant from K Company comes up to me looking for Fox Company. It's Lieutenant Reg Fincke's executive officer. He confirms that Fincke has died so he is taking command of K Company, which is now holding the top of the hill."

By dawn, there are only about 20 Marines, including the wounded, still hanging on to their positions on Sugar Loaf. With F Company and K Company both decimated, Colonel Woodhouse now turns to the 2d Battalion, 29th Marines to "mop up" what he thinks to be the Japanese remnants of the battle. No one yet realizes that the Japanese on that hill have an inexhaustible supply of troops available through a network of tunnels and interconnected caves.

"AT 0800," Pesely remembers, "I finally got the order from the colonel to bring my men back off the hill. There are only seven of us left of the 40 or 50 who had made the original attack with Courtney. Since I am leaving the hill, I turn my radio and command over to Lieutenant Roe of K Company with orders to hang on until D Company 29th Marines arrives.

"Finally, I am on my way out of that nightmare, but I rejoice too soon. As I hear the amtracs grinding toward my little group, suddenly the enemy gun ports at the base of Sugar Loaf open up with direct fire on our escape vehicles. Then our tractor bogs

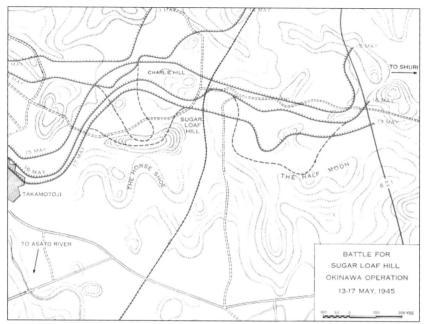

Battle lines were meaningless in the 10-day seesaw struggle for Sugar Loaf Hill. (Map from 6th Div Hqs)

down in the mud and the crew bails out and hides in a ditch.

"When I radio that to the Colonel, he swears that he will get a tractor to us if he has to drive it himself. The colonel is true to his word. The next crew are 'Gung Ho' Marines who shoot up the enemy ports with automatic fire while we load the tractor with our wounded. Still bleeding with my own wounds, I jump aboard the tractor on top of a stretcher case, and we are out of there. At last, my endless nightmare has really ended."

Once Ed was off that hill his war was over. After three years of living, training, and fighting on the jungle islands of the Pacific – from Samoa and Guadalcanal to the Marshalls, the Marianas, and the Ryukyus – Ed was ready to take his shrapnel-laden body and his exhaustive combat fatigue to the hospitals on Saipan, Hawaii, and finally back home.

Meanwhile, back on that stubborn little hill, the battle continues to rage. Company after company in the 22d, the 29th and the 4th Marines try over and over again to take that hill for one last time. But it was five more days of bloody frontal attacks and fierce enemy counter-attacks before the Marines succeed in proving their general right once again – "A Marine can always hold any ground he can take."

Yes, a Marine can do it, but there's a price to pay. In this case, the ten-day battle that ended with the capture of Sugar Loaf – that little 50-foot hill – cost the 6th Marine Division, 2,662 killed and wounded. Two Hundred and sixty-six casualties per day to gain a tiny hill is an obscene price to pay, but what makes a Marine different is that to accomplish his mission it's a price he's willing to pay.

In combat you have three options: fight, freeze, or flee. Fight often means to attack even when it's a fatally foolish option. Freeze often means to stay put even when fight or flee is clearly indicated. And flee often means to run even when fight or freeze would be wiser. We always call he who fights a hero, and often he who freezes, but we usually call he who runs a coward. The survivors of any diverse and extended combat experience are those who are quickest to learn when to exercise which of those three combat options. Of course, in the Marine Corps those three options are rarely left to the individual but are decided by the command as long as the command remains in control.

At the height of the battle on Sugar Loaf, as each command echelon from Division, to Regiment, to Battalion, to Company lost direct control of the field operations, it became every man for himself – each to choose his combat option. Few dared to run, most fought with uncommon bravery, and those who froze kept their fingers on the trigger and piled mounds of dead enemy bodies in front of their foxholes.

For his leadership in attacking Sugar Loaf Hill, Major Courtney was awarded the Medal of Honor posthumously, and a Marine Corps camp on Okinawa bears his name today. And for freezing in his foxhole for four days and refusing to retreat off that hill while dispatching 58 enemy soldiers, Corporal James Day earned the same high honor and lived to retire as a general many years later. For his part as senior officer holding that hill through that terrible night, Lieutenant Pesely declined a second Silver Star in order to receive a lesser medal he didn't already have – a Bronze Star with combat "V" for valor. Everyone who fought in

Sugar Loaf after the battle – the innocent little hill that destroyed my battalion and regiment. (USMC Photo)

any of the dozen battles for that hill deserved a medal, but the only individual medal that almost everyone did receive was the Purple Heart.

By the end of 21 June 1945, the battle for Okinawa had taken the blood of 8,227 men of the 6th Marine Division. That number of killed and wounded exceeded the original strength of the rifle platoons and companies that had landed on Easter Sunday morning just 82 days earlier. Including the replacements that were fed into the lines, the small assault units had suffered greater than 100% casualties.

"For extraordinary heroism in action against enemy Japanese forces during the assault and capture of Okinawa…" the Sixth Marine Division was awarded the nation's highest unit award, the Presidential Unit Citation.

Japanese antitank guns firing 47mm armor-piercing projectiles quickly broke up our coordinated tank-infantry attacks. (USMC Photo)

On the top of Sugar Loaf on 23 May 45 looking back on the battleground where hundreds had died a week before. (USMC Photo)

Snapshots of the Battle of Okinawa *(USMC Photos)*

*Okinawa – easiest landing;
toughest battle.*

*We advance quickly against
invisible enemy.*

Fireteam with light machine gun.

*Final four survivors of Jap unit
wave white flag.*

*Torrential rain and mud drowns
our ammo tractors.*

*Native Okinawans – the jetsam of
the battle.*

Chapter 28

Picking up the Pieces

While the battle had been raging on Okinawa, many of the severely wounded and injured were being continuously transported by hospital ship to the 5th Convalescent Hospital, APO 244, on Saipan where I was recuperating from my own injuries. When the doctors told me that my torn tendons would take at least six weeks to heal, I felt guilty, especially with the grim daily battle reports and the more serious casualties streaming in. It was the first time in three campaigns and thirty months in the combat zone that I was not with the battalion throughout the entire combat action. In none of the other campaigns had I been "lucky" enough to be hit and evacuated early. Now that my change of luck had put me in the hospital, I didn't like it. My heart was still with the battalion.

The difference between the life of the true combatants in a war and that of those servicemen assigned to supporting roles was revealed to me in striking fashion while I was in the hospital on Saipan. By chance I met a lieutenant in the Army who was a fellow patient in the hospital for some minor elective surgery. As he was being discharged he invited me to visit him at his quarters. Although I was still on crutches, I managed to get into his jeep, and he drove me to his residence. Since he was only a first lieutenant like me, I was surprised that he had a personal jeep and his own island cottage. It was situated on a hill with a magnificent view overlooking the ocean.

When I entered the cottage, I was further amazed to see that he had a personal POW "house boy" dressed in servant's white jacket. As I settled into a comfortable island-style wicker armchair opposite my Army friend, the house boy brought us each a bourbon and water.

"How do you rate all this?" I asked him. "What's your job?"

"Well, I'm the petroleum officer," he replied. I supervise the pipeline that carries the fuel from the beach up to the airstrip. In civilian life, I was a petroleum engineer, so this is where the Army put me." Then he explained that he had a crew of 30 or 40 Japanese POW's assigned to him as workers, so he scrounged a couple of white steward's jackets from the Navy for his house boy to wear. Getting up from the chair, he said: "Let me show you around." As we walked with drinks in hand through his little cottage, he disclosed a bedroom that was any bachelor's delight, with a closet full of women's clothes and shoes.

"Why do you have all this female stuff?" I asked.

"Well, it belongs to some of the nurses at the hospital," he told me. "You saw what a tough grind they have down there. When the hospital ships come in, they work around the clock. Maybe two or three days without a break. so when they get time off they need some place to rest. I offer them my place, and they love it. They come up here and forget the war and the bloody casualties – at least for a day or two. And I sure don't mind. Some of them are pretty cute."

"Yeah, I noticed," I told him; "but you and I have sure been fighting a whole different war." After that jolting visit, I returned to the hospital and the real world of hard-working nurses and bleeding casualties.

I was still in the hospital on Saipan when my best friend, Pesely, was evacuated off that damn little hill that had destroyed our regiment and killed so many of our comrades. But I didn't see Ed when he came through Saipan. The docs had immediately decided that after his three years overseas they would send him directly to Hawaii and San Francisco to nurse his flesh wounds and his severe combat fatigue.

But what about my other best friend, Heavy – Lieutenant Richard M. Pfuhl, the icon of the Second Battalion, Twenty-Second Marines? As always, Heavy was out front in the battle for those three stubborn little hills – spotting the Japs, directing tank fire, and helping with the wounded until he felt that searing sensation of a bullet passing through his thigh, testicles, and into his buttocks. But the real damage of that bullet was not to his flesh. It was to his psyche.

Finally, an enemy bullet had penetrated his invincible golden shield. It was the same golden shield we were all relying on. It was the one that would somehow get us through those impossible desperate situations when everyone around us fell while we stood there unscathed. But for Heavy and the rest of us who had already survived three years and three combat campaigns, the last nick in that shield at this point in the war was a sign that the gods had at last forsaken us. So as it happened to each of us, one by one, we felt like we had now been left to our own feeble resources. Such abandonment was intolerable to Heavy, so for the first time he began to take personal concern for his own safety. Sadly, it was noticed by the colonel; and Heavy was withdrawn from the front and given command of the Headquarters Company – an abject humiliation to a fighting icon. If Heavy hated his new assignment at Battalion, he loved the little colonel who gave him his orders. So it came as a great shock to him when his very close friend and fellow ball player, Lieutenant John Fitzgerald, called him from the front and told him the colonel had been shot in the head and was barely breathing.

By the time they got the wounded colonel back to the CP, it was too late. As Heavy remembered the little 135 pound Colonel Woodhouse, he was not only a great commander but "pound for pound the greatest Marine I ever saw." With the passing of the colonel, a new CO shows up and offers Heavy a nothing job. Heavy tries for a job in a rifle company in another battalion and is turned down. Then, after all the bloody fighting on those three little hills, the Japanese capitulation begins, and Naha, the capital city of Okinawa, falls easily to the Americans. Heavy's war is over. I am discharged from the hospital, and he and I come together at the Transient Center, Fleet Marine Force, Island of Guam.

Now, fifty-four years later as I write this book, I remember the last time I saw Heavy. it was July of 1945 and we were back on Guam. I was sitting in my tent reading my mail when I was shocked by the news from my mother that my father had died suddenly of a heart attack in February before our April landing on

Okinawa. She had kept the news from me afraid that I would be so upset that I might do something rash and get myself killed. But now I was upset because all through the Okinawa campaign, I was dreaming about the day the war would end and I would get home again and see my mother and father. I kept imagining what they were doing and what their daily lives were like while I was fighting in Okinawa. There were so many things I had wanted to tell my father. I wanted to go to some ball games with him again at Comiskey Park in Chicago. I wanted to enjoy a good homemade spaghetti dinner with him and our Italian relatives. I wanted him to have a chance to be proud of a son who had joined the greatest fighting force in the world and had survived to tell about it. Anyhow, now none of that was to be.

Now instead of picturing that homecoming, I pictured him wheezing and choking for breath as his heart closed down and he fell lifeless to the floor. One minute ago a vital former athlete not yet old at 60, and now lying cold and dead. Sudden death that I had learned to expect and accept in war, I now had to apply to my own family who I thought were safe back home in civilian life.

Although I was not a drinker and would usually give my liquor ration away to those who enjoyed it, I dragged out my fifth of bourbon and invited Heavy into my tent for a drink. I poured us each a cup of straight booze, and I swigged mine down in a couple of gulps. Heavy looked at me like I had lost my mind. Then I could see that he knew I had taken some kind of emotional hit.

"What's up, Jonesey?" he asked.

"My father died last February," I told him

"February," he repeated "why are you taking it so hard now?"

"I just found out," I said; "all the time we were on Okinawa, my mother kept it to herself, worried that I might do something stupid." Then I took another swig of the booze.

"Well, that's the way mothers are," he said.

"Yeah, I know," I answered, "but it's hard for me now to realize that for the past six months I've been thinking of my father at home alive. It was good knowing that the daily lives of our families at home went on, safe from the killing and dying over here. But now I find out that all that time since last February my father has been dead and gone, with my mother holding it all in so as not to upset me. Here have another drink, Heavy," I said filling his cup again.

"You better go easy on that stuff," he said. "You're not used to it. I don't think I ever saw you drink booze before, If you want to drink like us, you're going to have to train with me and Whiskey Don," he told me.

Heavy knew what he was talking about. It wasn't very long before I literally went ape. And I don't mean it figuratively; I mean it literally. The booze soon converted me into a chimpanzee. If you ever saw the old Tarzan movies – it wasn't long before I was the Tarzan chimp. I was soon romping around that tent on all fours, whisking myself up onto one cot and down onto another. I leaped across the room like a wild animal. I even made growling noises. I chattered, I screamed a chimpanzee scream. I was a wild animal letting out all the pent up emotion of the last three years and three combat campaigns in one wild rampage. I did something the Japanese enemy couldn't do – I scared hell out of Heavy.

The next morning came in with a terrific hangover, but after I went to the barbershop in a PX hut and got a haircut and shave I felt pretty good. I was happy to know that I was on the standby list for a flight back to the States. I also learned that I had passed the physical that said I was free from communicable diseases so it was safe to allow me to fly back and reenter the United States. (What would they have done with me if I hadn't passed that test?)

At any rate, they didn't fly me back. They stuck me on an escort aircraft carrier with a half-dozen other Marine transient officers and floated us back. Going back by any means would have suited me, including swimming, because I knew that our division's next amphibious assault would tragically trump all that had gone before. We were scheduled for a landing just north of Tokyo. Our rough estimates predicted total U.S. casualties at a million – with ten times as many on the Japanese side. Fortunately, the two atom bombs ended the war and resulted in fewer dead Japanese than the Okinawa campaign – which still seems like a dreadful price until you compare that price with our predicted estimates for a troop landing on the Japanese mainland.

We received the news of the atom bombs on Hiroshima and Nagasaki aboard ship when we were about half way back to the

United States. On our two-week voyage, we were at sea at the time the bombs were dropped and during the actual Japanese surrender. So on VJ Day, our aircraft carrier was standing 200 miles off San Francisco, and all the ship's crew and transient officers were eager to get ashore for once-in-a-lifetime celebration. But our black-shoe Navy Captain was of the old school, so he decided it wouldn't be good to turn his crew and some wild Marine transients loose on San Francisco after months and years of sex-starved sea and jungle living. Instead he kept us 200 miles at sea, just floating around and listening by radio to the madcap celebrations ashore.

When we finally got ashore the day after VJ Day we made a direct assault on the Mark Hopkins hotel. Conquering the bar at the Top of the Mark was out first Stateside objective. It was our new Sugar Loaf Hill. So we loaded up with ammo in the form of a fifth of booze each to make sure we wouldn't be caught empty handed as we tackled this strategic civilian enclave.

As we passed through the broken glass doors that led into the hotel lobby, it was clear to us that the first wave had already broken through this stronghold on VJ Day while we had languished helplessly out at sea. But the hotel elevators were still working fine, and we soon reached the top and clumsily reentered into this unreal civilian world.

Here we were, three Marine lieutenants in our mildewed green uniform pants, combat jackets, and island boondockers, each carrying his own fifth of booze in a brown paper bag. We sat down uneasily at a table not far from one occupied by three very good-looking young ladies. We each ordered a bourbon on ice in a tall glass and no water. When the drinks arrived we filled the glasses from the booze in our paper bags. The girls were watching, and I heard them snicker – not a mean snicker, just a friendly snicker. Then a couple of guys at the bar in expensive suits and fancy ties grinned quietly and quickly turned away when they saw us look up.

"Who the hell are these people, and why are they dressed so funny," I thought. "Don't they know about the war?" They looked to us like soft little aliens from some other planet. At that moment, I felt nothing at all in common with them. I quickly scanned the room thinking how much more comfortable it would be to sit down and have a drink and a conversation with my Japanese counterpart – someone else who would know what war was all about. But there were no enemy counterparts at the Top of the Mark, so the three of us just talked to each other and swigged down our booze.

Before we could recall and try any old pick-up lines, the girls broke the ice and invited us to join them. They seemed to be genuinely interested in who we were and what we had done; and the drunker we got, the more protective they were of us. We already had our orders endorsed by the Headquarters of the Department of the Pacific and had been given a 30-day delay to our next assignment. But we were all eager to get home to the Los Angeles area. The problem was transportation. We had no priority, and without it you couldn't get aboard a train. However, one of the girls worked for the railroad company so she arranged immediate passage for us on the midnight run to Los Angeles. During that drunken trip, I shared a two-bunk compartment with a buddy. Fortunately I had the upper bunk, so I was privileged to throw up on him rather than the obvious alternative, as we sped through the night to home and family.

Chapter 29

The Decompression Chamber

When a diver stays too deep or too long in the sea before resurfacing, he must reenter the atmosphere very slowly and very carefully or suffer severe shock. When I reentered my mother's Hollywood apartment and faced a gaggle of relatives gathered for my homecoming, the shock set in. First, this was not my home. I had enlisted in the Marine Corps from my original home in Chicago. I had never lived in Los Angeles, nor had I ever seen Hollywood before, except for a short visit as a small child. And although it was great to see my wonderful mother and the familiar faces of some aunts and cousins, the familiar face of my father was missing never to be seen again. Things had changed during my three-year absence. And, of course, I had changed most of all.

My young cousin, Billy, who was fourteen in high school when I left, was now editor of the Daily Bruin at UCLA. He quickly stuck his hand in my backpack and pulled out my Colt. 45, which fortunately did not have a loaded magazine.

"Did you kill any Japs with this?" he asked. As though the war was just that simple – as though the answer to that question was significantly relevant to what I had experienced in three years of combat.

"I don't know, Billy," I told him. "I fired it a few times, but a pistol isn't for hunting Japs. It's for protection when they come hunting you. It's still in my pack because I was sleeping with it under my pillow in the hospital on Saipan. When I left the hospital three weeks ago, a Japanese infiltrator had just sneaked into our hut and cut the throat of one of the patients. That's why I didn't turn it in at the hospital when I was discharged. It's been my Teddy Bear."

Well, despite how strange this whole civilian scene seemed to me, I was glad to be back in the States, but I didn't feel like I was back home yet. I knew I wouldn't feel like I was back home until I visited my hometown of Chicago.

Since I was still in uniform on leave, I managed to book transportation on the Super Chief to Chicago. Unlike the troop trains, this was first-class transportation across the United States. Now I was hobnobbing with fellow passengers Gary Cooper and Martha Raye. And Martha Raye, who did an outstanding job with the USO, was kind enough to invite all the servicemen traveling in uniform to her private party in the train's Club Car as we traveled through the prohibition "dry" state of Kansas.

I was on my way to Chicago, even though I now had few relatives left there. It seems that they had all migrated to California or elsewhere during the war, but I wanted to visit friends and the old neighborhood on Chicago's Southside. I especially wanted to look up some old girl friends. Oddly enough, one whom I had dreamed about several times overseas was a first-grade classmate. Her name was Beverly and she had sat in front of me in class, and one day – to my surprise – she had turned around and given me my first kiss at age six.

Of course, upon my arrival in Chicago, my first order of business was to see my father's relatives and visit his grave. His sister, who didn't speak much English, turned the chore of relating the circumstances of his death over to their Parish priest. And the young priest took me to my father's gravesite. As I stood there staring down at the plot with the simple headstone, I was strangely self-conscious as I sensed that the young Italian priest was waiting for some kind of outburst from me. I felt that he was expecting an emotional scene, but instead of emotion I felt a total numbness. I had let out all that emotion back in that tent on Guam the day I had received the news of my father's death and got drunk with Heavy.

Now it was just me, a young man, staring at the grave of an old man – a grave that contained an old dead body that was just one more body added to the thousands of young dead bodies I had seen in the war. And I had long ago ceased to think of any dead body as the person it had once been. Of course I wished my father were alive and that we could pick up where we had left off, just as I had wished that for the many comrades I had lost in the war; but war teaches reality, and reality teaches the folly of denial.

"Your father lived a good life," the priest told me. "He is one of the few men I have known who told me that he had no regrets about his life, and that if he had it to do over again, he would do it pretty much the same way." I thanked the priest, said goodbye to my Italian relatives, and then did what I couldn't do in front of the priest at the grave or in that tent on Guam. I cried when I was alone.

It was now time to start looking for some other threads of the life I had left in Chicago. Although I did manage to locate Beverly, the six-year-old girlfriend of my dreams, something had changed since that first-grade kiss of twenty years ago. Beverly was now an attractive and successful businesswoman and still single and presumably available for a relationship, but now we were separated by a war that had changed me profoundly but had not touched her at all. Her life had stood still. She still lived with her parents, and at the young age of twenty-five was dressing and acting like a prematurely aged spinster. After just one dinner, it was clear there were never really any threads outside of my dreams for me and Beverly to pick up.

I went to the old neighborhood to look up Veronica, who I remembered as a beautiful young Irish Catholic girl during our high school days. Well, the war had significantly affected her. While working as a nurse she had met a young Irish Catholic sergeant in the U.S. Army and they had married and now had two lovely young children. So much for a possible romance with Veronica. Or course, you can never go home again, so I headed back to my mother's new home in Hollywood.

After the expiration of my thirty-day delay, I reported for duty at the United States Marine Corps Recruit Depot, San Diego, California. Even though the fighting was now over, the Marine Corps still needed recruits. In fact my 6th Marine Division had been very busy since I left them in early August of 1945. A significant contingent of the division had been organized into a special landing force under Brigadier General William T. Clement for a landing on Honshu, the main island of Japan. Since the

Japanese had already surrendered, it was to be a peaceful landing and occupation, but the Marines were slow to believe it. Their skeptical apprehension was intensified on August 16 when a Japanese torpedo was observed to cross the bow of the *USS Ozark* that was carrying General Clement and his landing team staff to join the third Fleet in the waters off Honshu on their way to the occupation of Japan.

Therefore over the next two weeks as the Marines landed one group after another at various points in Sagami Bay and Tokyo Bay they went ashore battle-ready and prepared to meet resistance. However, now the Japanese complied meekly with the orders for surrender, which ended, of course, with the famous formal surrender by the Japanese Commanders to General Douglas MacArthur aboard the *USS Missouri* in Tokyo Bay on September 2, 1945.

Our 6th Marine Division's solemn contribution to the United States Victory in the Pacific was 8,227 Marines killed and wounded in the 82 days of fighting on Okinawa, approximately a 50% casualty rate for the division, but a greater than a 90% casualty rate for the three infantry regiments. It was for their sacrificial determination to win on Okinawa that the Marines of the 6th Division were awarded the Presidential Unit Citation.

By now my "foxhole" had shifted to the Bachelor Officers Quarters in the Marine Recruit Depot, San Diego, with responsibility for supervising the training of new recruits in the skills of hand-to-hand combat including bayonet training and knife fighting. But I was now free every night to chase the girls in San Diego.

I hooked up with a handsome Navy dentist, the ex-husband of movie actress Eleanor Parker, who I felt would boost my success rate in the dating game, and I was right. We soon fell in with a bevy of five young schoolteachers who lived together in a large house on Mission Beach. We met them one night at the Hotel Coronado in the same large dining room where we were told Edward the Prince of Wales had met Wally Simpson.

It seems like I should have been satisfied with my new duty station, but after a few weeks Stateside at the Marine Base, I began to realize I was not cut out to be a career Marine. I didn't care for governmental bureaucracy, which had never affected my career in the jungles overseas but which now loomed large and troublesome in the political and spit-and-polish culture of the Service in the States. Anyhow, I declined a regular commission and applied for separation and a return to the Inactive Reserve which was granted in November of 1945.

It so happened that at the time I was released from active duty in San Diego, my old friend, Lieutenant Pesely was being transferred from Camp Pendleton, located a few miles from my San Diego station, to the Marine Corps Schools at Quantico, Virginia. With more years in the service than I had, he decided to make a career in the Corps.

When I learned that Pesely was driving his car back to the East Coast, I agreed to ride along with him. I had never seen New York, and I had no fixed goals. So after the two of us spent a weekend with the girls of Mission Beach, we took off one Saturday night and started driving to the East Coast, with two of the girls following us in their car as far as the Arizona border. At about midnight, we kissed them goodbye, turned them around and sent them home. At that moment I felt totally free, completely unhinged from the Marine Corps and totally devoid of all commitments, with nothing but a blank slate upon which to write my future.

We didn't stop to sleep until we got to El Paso. When we awoke about noon on Sunday, we headed across the border to Juarez for the afternoon bullfights. Neither of us had ever seen a bullfight, so we weren't sure what to expect. But as this unique ceremony unfolded, the emotional impact of the dramatic music and the colorful pageantry forced us to focus our attention on this morality play. This was the first true life-and-death situation we had experienced since we'd left the battlefield. When we realized that either the bull or the matador would truly die, and there would be no artificial intervention, we began to relate to this honest spectacle of reality.

In the combat world that we had just left, there was no fairness. There was no heavenly intervention. Brave souls were pitted against each other and flesh against metal, in the most unfair circumstances imaginable. The young and the innocent on both sides died indiscriminately with the evil sinners. Now here in this sand arena on a sunny Sunday afternoon, the angry black bull is cast in the role of evil determined to kill the brave and virtuous matador. And the virtuous matador must defend himself with honor and dignity, disdainful of fear in the face of death. To us at that time in our lives, it seemed like a magnificent metaphor to a Marine in combat, except that the Marine's odds were not nearly as good as those of the matador. Anyhow, it was the only blood game in town, and our eyes were glued to the action.

After a day with me in New York, Pesely headed back to Quantico to his new assignment, and I roamed around 42d and Broadway, thinking that maybe I should have stayed in the Corps. After all, it was a home, and I no longer had any other. But who was I kidding? The San Diego Base never felt like home. The Marine Corps I missed was in Samoa, on Guadalcanal, Guam, and yes even on Okinawa. Oh, I didn't miss the combat – the fighting and the fear of landing on hot beaches – but I sure missed the camaraderie that I shared with some of the bravest souls the world is ever likely to know.

I stayed a few more days in New York, met a girl named Miriam, shared a couple of coffee dates with her talking about her Stanislavsky acting classes, and then I quietly stole back into civilian life and put the war games behind me.

Epilogue

W ars end for the non-participants, but they never end for the true combatants. As I write this book it is over a half century since VJ Day of 1945,but I still weep over many of the recollections that I have put on these pages. I weep for the brave men I served with, living and dead, many whose deeds were often performed under conditions of chaos and terror against seemingly insurmountable odds. Yet they prevailed.

I am satisfied that the Marines have an answer to that age-old conundrum: "What happens when an irresistible force meets an immovable object?" If that irresistible force is a Marine, the immovable object moves! And every Marine is trained to have unquestioning faith in that proposition. In battle he must prove it to be true or die trying. I know of no other fighting force in the world with an Esprit to match that of the United States Marines, and there is no greater honor than to have been one of them on the field of battle.

Still, I deplore war and war game heroics. I have no respect for those politicians who lead their countries into wars for any less purpose than to defend one's country and its vital interests – or to ally itself with world forces of good in the vital interest of humanity when fighting against such clear and obvious world forces of evil as fascism. Unfortunately for the common Japanese soldiers in our enemy's ranks, circumstances required them to fight and die for an evil fascist government. That is not to say there were no evil men among those common soldiers. There were many evil men among them all the way up to their top commanders. The Japanese forces that we encountered in the field often committed atrocities against our POW's, against innocent civilians in the local native populations, and even against their own subjects on the island of Okinawa.

But as a military officer it has been my experience that when common soldiers commit atrocities, the fault lies with their commanders. Only the most incompetent lax commander would allow his troops the freedom to commit wanton acts of violence at any time because to do so is to relinquish the command and control of his troops. And any commander who authorizes or tolerates such violence is not only an evil person, but he is also a fool who is allowing his troops to divert their energies away from their true military objectives. With that in mind, I am ending this book with a letter from an enemy soldier who, I think you will agree, does not appear to be evil.

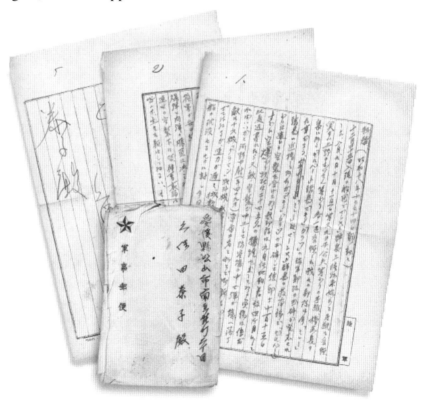

A Japanese soldier's last letter home, taken from his body on Kwajalein in February 1944.

The reader will remember that when I went ashore on Kawjalein Island in February 1944, as I stepped over and walked among the four thousand dead Japanese bodies, I reached down and took a letter from the pocket of one of the dead soldiers. It was written in Japanese, of course, so I couldn't read it. Since we had been pounding this little island with our dive-bombers and large naval guns for many days. I assumed this might be a soldier's last letter home, and that it would reveal the feelings of a soldier who knew he was about to die. And since the last page of this neat five-page letter ended in a hasty scrawl, I assumed that he had finished the letter while in the heat of our attack.

When I returned from the war that letter rested in my footlocker for fifty years until I found the right person to translate it. What follows is a translation by my good friend, Junko Matsumoto, whose father, General Kenji Matsumoto, was stripped of his rank as the last military member of a 500-year-old Samurai family line when he stood against the Tojo Cabinet's plans to launch a war against the United States.

December 24, 1943

Dear Yasuko:

I received the first mail from you, Moyoko, Kimio and others since our force landed in the Marshall Islands. Those letters were dated August, September, October and November 1943 which were delivered by the transport ship entered in the Marshall Islands on December 23, 1943.

Our force is now in Miray Island (Kwajalein). I would think that you have heard the news that our Navy forces in Makin and Tarawa of the Gilbert Islands have died in honorable defeat. Miray island is located in the southernmost end of the Marshall Islands, and it is very close to Makin and Tarawa.

After those two forces were defeated, we have enemy air raids almost every day since November 15th. Since our force landed in Miray in September, twenty-five have been killed, and wounded are double that in just four months.

Now, I must stop writing… here comes enemy attack again...

Lt. Kono (49 years old), two soldiers on duty and myself are in the shelter, and we pray to God "please do not hit us".

I must tell you that in this air battle, there are sixteen Grumman fighters, and our side has only nine fighting planes. Even though our pilots have been well trained, our fighting planes are not speedy. A large transport ship which entered in the port of this island yesterday has already been attacked and sunk. The next target is our barracks. Enemy's bullets are coming down like hail. The bullets are about the size of my third finger.

Americans are proud of themselves; proud they are No.1 in the world. It is true. In the materialistic world, Japan is like a child compared with America. Our fighters cannot go near their base in the daytime because they have brought in some super antiaircraft guns at their base.

Though they are our enemy, they are just splendid. Well, I should not admire them too much because that won't buy me anything if I lose my life in their attack. During a 15-minute air battle, the enemy pilots completed their mission. Then they turned around and headed to their base at high speed, waving their handkerchiefs at us. Our fighters tried to chase them as fast as they could, but our fighter plane's speed is limited. It just looks like a child in an adult game.

In our poor defense front, the last thing we can prepare is the human bullet. HUMAN BULLET!! DIE WITH HONOR!! What a tragic battle plan!! From island to island, if each of our forces dies in honorable defeat, one after another, what will happen to Japan!!

We requested that our headquarters send us more planes, antiaircraft guns, cement, etc. These requests that we have made are our only hope to cope with what we are facing here every day in this tragic situation.

The issue of the battle between the enemy's bombs and our "human bullets" is clear. How can human flesh be tough enough? Those two things are totally different substances.

Each one of us is on the verge of a nervous breakdown, and what's more, many of our men suffer with dysentery; so they don't look like live men and their faces are blue.

Once in a while I get some sake to drink, and I have some savings for you. The total amount is 210 Yen. I will advise you when I can mail this deposit book to you. When I came here, I hoped to do some fishing, but, if I try, I might be the fish caught by the enemy's bullet!

It seems that the enemy has a regular schedule for his air raids, usually around 8AM, 10AM and noon. In the afternoon, I would think that the enemy-san might be tired and need some rest. However, once in a while we have a surprise attack in the afternoon, and this unexpected air raid usually causes more serious casualties than the others. Many of our men's hands, legs, heads, etc are blown off from their bodies and those pieces are scattered all over the ground. Every time we see these tragic and hell-like scenes, we all get angry at our Headquarters. Why can't they do anything for us! Why can't they send more planes, antiaircraft guns, etc. to the front! We really wish that we could bring top commanders to the front who are stationed in Tokyo or Osaka to let them see this tragic situation with their own eyes. We are now facing another of the enemy's dreadful attacks! It's 11:45 AM and we are all deadly exhausted.

Today, its December 24th and New Year's day is coming very soon. Good day or bad, we will probably have a great gift of enemy bombing. I just hope I can survive until the end of this year.

I am so happy to hear from you about the growth of Chizuko.

I will prepare a package to send you with soap, shoes, handkerchiefs, towels and so on. I will ask someone who is returning to Japan shortly to take these things with him.

A Happy New Year to you all!

Kumataro Kubota

At Miray Island(Kwajalein) the Marshall Islands
On January 1st, 1944

Although this Japanese soldier got his wish and lived to the end of the year, he didn't live long enough to mail the letter and send his family the package he had promised them. Now that we know the contents of the letter, we are trying, with the help of Ms. Matsumoto, to locate his children. We want to send them his letter to let them know that — like most soldiers of every country — his last thoughts were not for some abstract political cause. They were for his family. ☐

1995 photo of author standing by the plaque from the Old Marine Barracks that his battalion recovered from the trash heap on Guam in 1944.

Index

Note: All names, persons and rank are real except the following:
* Real person and real last name according to my best recollection.
** Pseudonym used to protect privacy of a real person.

Bibliography

• *History of the Sixth Marine Division*, by Major General Lemuel C. Shepherd, Jr. USMC and staff, edited by 1st Lt. Bevan G. Cass, 1948 by Infantry Journal Press.
• *The U.S. Marine Corps Story*, by J. Robert Moskin, Third Edition 1992, Little Brown and Company.
• *Tennozan*, by George Feifer, Ticknor & Fields 1992.
• *Killing Ground on Okinawa*, by James H. Hallas, Praeger Publishers 1996.
• *Chasing the Sun*, by Richard M. Pfuhl, Ten Square Books/Harlo Press 1979.
• *War in the Pacific*, by Edwin P. Hoyt, Avon Books/Hearst Corporation 1980.
• *World War II*, by David G. McCullough, editor; American Heritage 1966.
• *Okinawa*, by Lt. Col. A. J. Barker, Galahad Books/Bison Books Ltd. 1981.
• *The Battle for Okinawa*, by Colonel Hiromichi Yahara, John Wiley & Sons 1995.
• *The Pacific War*, by Saburo Ienaga, Pantheon Books/Random House 1978.
• *First to Fight*, Lt. Gen. Victor H. Krulak, USMC, Naval Institute Press 1984.
• *Okinawa 1945*, Recorded Interviews & Statements, by 6th Division Marines.
• *The Second World War*, by John Keegan, Penguin Books 1990.